E-Commerce, Competition & ASEAN Economic Integration

The **ISEAS – Yusof Ishak Institute** (formerly Institute of Southeast Asian Studies) is an autonomous organization established in 1968. It is a regional centre dedicated to the study of socio-political, security, and economic trends and developments in Southeast Asia and its wider geostrategic and economic environment. The Institute's research programmes are grouped under Regional Economic Studies (RES), Regional Strategic and Political Studies (RSPS), and Regional Social and Cultural Studies (RSCS). The Institute is also home to the ASEAN Studies Centre (ASC), the Temasek History Research Centre (THRC), and the Singapore APEC Study Centre.

ISEAS Publishing, an established academic press, has issued more than 2,000 books and journals. It is the largest scholarly publisher of research about Southeast Asia from within the region. ISEAS Publishing works with many other academic and trade publishers and distributors to disseminate important research and analyses from and about Southeast Asia to the rest of the world.

E-Commerce, Competition & ASEAN Economic Integration

EDITED BY

CASSEY LEE • EILEEN LEE

CC**CS** COMPETITION
& CONSUMER
COMMISSION
SINGAPORE

ISEAS YUSOF ISHAK
INSTITUTE

First published in Singapore in 2020 by
ISEAS Publishing
30 Heng Mui Keng Terrace
Singapore 119614

E-mail: publish@iseas.edu.sg
Website: <http://bookshop.iseas.edu.sg>

ISEAS Library Cataloguing-in-Publication Data

Names: Lee, Cassey, editor. | Lee, Eileen, editor.
Title: E-Commerce, Competition & ASEAN Economic Integration / edited by Cassey Lee and Eileen Lee.
Description: Singapore : ISEAS – Yusof Ishak Institute, 2020. | Includes index.
Identifiers: ISBN 978-981-4762-16-8 (paperback) | ISBN 978-981-4762-17-5 (pdf)
Subjects: LCSH: Electronic commerce--Southeast Asia. | Competition--Southeast Asia. | Southeast Asia--Economic integration.
Classification: LCC HF5548.325 A9E19

Typeset by International Typesetters Pte Ltd

CONTENTS

PART IV

ACKNOWLEDGEMENTS

This book is an outcome of a research collaboration between the Competition and Consumer Commission of Singapore (CCCS) and ISEAS – Yusof Ishak Institute (ISEAS). We are grateful for the support of Mr Toh Han Li (Chief Executive of CCCS), Ms Ng Ee Kia (Assistant Chief Executive of CCCS), Mr Choi Shing Kwok (Director of ISEAS), and Mr Tan Chin Tiong (Senior Advisor, ISEAS and former Director, ISEAS). We also thank Mr Poh Lip Hang (formerly CCCS) who was one of the key drivers during the early stages of the book project. Finally, we would like to thank our copy editor, Ms Sheryl Sin Bing Peng.

ABOUT THE CONTRIBUTORS

Yot Amornkitvikai, Lecturer, College of Population Studies, Chulalongkorn University

Kala Anandarajah, Head, Competition & Antitrust and Trade Lead Partner, Corporate Governance

Kathleen Azali, Founder of C2O library & collabtive, Surabaya

Sanchita Basu Das, Economist, Asian Development Bank (ADB)

Yose Rizal Damuri, Head of the Department of Economics, Center for Strategic and International Studies

Cassey Lee, Senior Fellow, ISEAS – Yusof Ishak Institute, Singapore

Eileen Lee, staff member, Policy and Markets Division, Competition and Consumer Commission of Singapore (CCCS), 2016–18

Siwage Dharma Negara, Senior Fellow, ISEAS – Yusof Ishak Institute, Singapore

Nguyen Thi Hong Van, Lecturer, Electronic Commerce Department, Foreign Trade University, Hanoi, Vietnam

Nguyen Van Thoan, Associate Professor, Electronic Commerce Department, Foreign Trade University, Hanoi, Vietnam

Lip Hang Poh, staff member, Policy and Markets Division, Competition and Consumer Commission of Singapore (CCCS), 2016–17

Shanti Aubren T. Prado, Policy Research Officer IV, Philippine Competition Commission

Meg L. Reganon, Senior Technical Assistant, Philippine Competition Commission

Tanya Tang, Partner (Chief Economic and Policy Advisor), Rajah & Tann Singapore LLP

Jiraporn Tangpoolcharoen, Specialist, Office of Strategy, Electronic Transactions Development Agency (Public Organization) (ETDA)

Tham Siew Yean, Senior Fellow, ISEAS – Yusof Ishak Institute, Singapore

Zheng Xi, Associate, Rajah & Tann Asia Singapore LLP

1

INTRODUCTION

Cassey Lee and Eileen Lee[1]

E-commerce markets have grown significantly within ASEAN in recent years. According to a report by AT Kearney in 2015, retail e-commerce has a total market size of US$7 billion in the six largest economies within ASEAN[2] (AT Kearney and CIMB ASEAN Research Institute 2015). Currently, Singapore, Malaysia, Thailand, Indonesia, Vietnam and the Philippines all generate less than 4 per cent of their retail sales online (UNCTAD 2015). This is low in comparison with other e-commerce markets such as the Republic of Korea (16 per cent) and China (7 per cent), which suggests that there is room for further growth in e-commerce (CCCS 2017). In a more recent report, Google and Temasek (2018) estimated that the Southeast Asian internet economy reached $72 billion in gross merchandise value in 2018. Growth potential in e-commerce and internet-based operations in ASEAN is tremendous, given that the number of internet users in the six largest economies in ASEAN has risen from 244 million in 2015 to 283 million in 2017. The number of internet users in the region is projected to continue to grow at an annual rate of 17.7 per cent until 2020 (CCCS 2017).

The rapid growth of e-commerce markets in the region has brought about significant benefits to both consumers and businesses. From the perspective of consumers, they benefit from an increased access to a greater variety of goods and services via e-commerce platforms. From the perspective of businesses, they benefit from access to new markets, reduced barriers to entry, and operational cost savings (CCCS 2017).

Despite the growth and benefits of e-commerce, there are challenges that could hinder the growth of e-commerce in ASEAN. In order to realize the full potential of the e-commerce market in ASEAN, improvements are required in terms of technological infrastructure, and in the regulatory and legal environment in which e-commerce firms operate across ASEAN.

In terms of the technological infrastructure development in ASEAN, many ASEAN member states still lag behind in global rankings in terms of the speed, efficiency and reliability of their internet services despite significant investment in their technology infrastructure (International Telecommunication Union 2016). Broadband access also remains expensive in some ASEAN member states in comparison with other developed countries, thereby inhibiting access to e-commerce markets for consumers and businesses (UNESCAP 2013). Other issues that businesses and consumers face in making purchases online include the poor logistics and delivery systems and the weak payment infrastructure in some ASEAN member states, amongst others.

The regulatory and legal environment in which e-commerce firms operate across ASEAN may also hinder the growth of e-commerce in the region if proper regulations and legal framework are not in place in each ASEAN member state. Notably, cybersecurity issues are a key concern for consumers in making purchases online, given that four of the top five worldwide riskiest countries for cyber-attacks are in ASEAN (Sophos 2013). In order to build trust among consumers, further work would be needed to address cybersecurity issues.

Anti-competitive behaviour by firms in e-commerce markets may also hinder the growth of e-commerce in the region. For instance, the anti-competitive conduct of large incumbent firms may restrict entry by new players to a particular market when they are able to exercise market power and thereby exclude or marginalize competitors. Competition authorities therefore have a role to play in ensuring a level "e-playing field" in order to promote the growth of e-commerce in the region. Given that e-commerce is a new emerging sector in ASEAN, it is therefore necessary for competition authorities to look into whether the legal framework provided by existing competition policy and law would be sufficient to deal with all competition challenges brought about by e-commerce.

From the regional perspective, cross-border e-commerce is particularly challenging in the ASEAN region due to different national rules and regulations in each ASEAN member state. Currently, consumers and businesses are discouraged from purchasing goods and services from overseas firms due to uncertainty of the customs and tax rules in each ASEAN member state. This is because there are differences in the import duties and taxes payable when purchasing goods from different ASEAN member states.

There are also differences in the approaches to the application of competition policy and law in each ASEAN member state. This could pose challenges to firms looking to operate internationally across ASEAN, given that firms may not be fully aware of the differences in the application of competition policy and law in each member state. To address these concerns, ASEAN is intensifying cooperation in the e-commerce sector to facilitate cross border e-commerce transactions in ASEAN as part of the ASEAN Economic Blueprint 2025 (ASEAN 2015).

This book consists of four parts. The first part—Chapter 2—discusses the role played by e-commerce in ASEAN economic integration as well as the challenges in growing e-commerce in ASEAN. The second part—Chapter 3—discusses how e-commerce activities impact competition assessment, focusing on two fundamental steps of competition assessment: (i) market definition; and (ii) market power. The third part—Chapter 4—discusses the role of e-commerce and trade policy. The fourth part—Chapters 5 to 10—discusses the current status of e-commerce development in ASEAN member countries, including Thailand, Indonesia, Malaysia, Singapore, the Philippines and Vietnam. Each of these chapters discusses the key impediments to growth of e-commerce in the country and proposes policy recommendations to (i) grow the e-commerce sector in the country; and (ii) achieve economic integration among ASEAN countries through the e-commerce sector.

NOTES

1. Eileen Lee was a staff member of the Policy and Markets Division at Competition and Consumer Commission of Singapore. While this chapter was contributed by a former staff member of the Competition and Consumer

Commission of Singapore, the views expressed in the chapter are personal
and do not represent the official position of the Competition and Consumer
Commission of Singapore.
2. The six largest economies within ASEAN include Indonesia, Malaysia, the
    Philippines, Singapore, Thailand and Vietnam.

REFERENCES

ASEAN Secretariat. *ASEAN Economic Community Blueprint 2025*. Jakarta: ASEAN
    Secretariat, 2015. https://www.asean.org/storage/2016/03/AECBP_2025r_
    FINAL.pdf.
AT Kearney and CIMB ASEAN Research Institute. "Lifting the Barriers to
    E-commerce in ASEAN". 2015.
CCCS (Competition and Consumer Commission of Singapore). *Handbook on
    E-commerce and Competition in ASEAN*. Singapore: Competition and Consumer
    Commission of Singapore, 2017.
Google and Temasek. *e-Conomy SEA 2018 - Southeast Asia's Internet Economy
    Hits an Inflection Point*. Singapore: Google and Temasek, 2008.
International Telecommunication Union. "ICT Development Index". 2016. Internet
    World Stats, http://internetworldstats.com/stats.htm.
Sophos. *Security Threat Report 2013: New Platforms and Changing Threats*. 2013.
UNCTAD (United Nations Conference on Trade and Development). *Information
    Economy Report: Unlocking the Potential of E-commerce for Developing
    Countries*. New York and Geneva: United Nations Conference on Trade
    and Development, 2015.
UNESCAP (United Nations Economic and Social Commission for Asia and the
    Pacific). *An In-Depth Study of Broadband Infrastructure in the ASEAN Region*.
    Bangkok, Thailand: United Nations Economic and Social Commission for
    Asia and the Pacific, 2013.

PART I

2

E-COMMERCE AND ASEAN ECONOMIC INTEGRATION

Cassey Lee and Sanchita Basu Das

1. Introduction

The ASEAN region is fast emerging as a growing market in the global e-commerce landscape. With a total population of 650 million, a rising middle class and a newly established economic community in 2015, the region is often considered as the next gold rush for e-commerce and internet-based operations. Despite the hype about the potential of the region, many challenges remain before e-commerce can truly flourish in each ASEAN member country. Cross-border e-commerce is challenging in the ASEAN region due to different national rules and regulations as well as quality of infrastructure. It is with these developments in mind that e-commerce has become an increasingly important area of focus in ASEAN economic cooperation.

This chapter examines the role played by e-commerce in ASEAN economic integration by focusing on a number of issues. We begin by discussing some of the basic concepts and definitions related to e-commerce in Section 2. This will then lead to an examination of the state of e-commerce in the ASEAN region in Section 3. Section 4 discusses the framework for ASEAN cooperation in the development of e-commerce and some of the challenges that lies ahead. Section 5 concludes.

2. Definition, Concepts and Framework

Defining E-commerce

OECD provides a comprehensive definition of e-commerce:[1]

> An e-commerce transaction is the sale or purchase of goods or services, conducted over computer networks by methods specifically designed for the purpose of receiving or placing of orders. The goods or services are ordered by those methods, but the payment and the ultimate delivery of the goods or services do not have to be conducted online. An e-commerce transaction can be between enterprises, households, individuals, governments, and other public or private organisations. To be included are orders made over the web, extranet or electronic data interchange. The type is defined by the method of placing the order. To be excluded are orders made by telephone calls, facsimile or manually typed e-mail.

The key emphasis in the above definition is on transactions carried out over computer networks which today mostly involve the internet. The definition also suggests that the delivery of goods and services does not have to be conducted online. This implies that such goods and services may or may not include digital goods (e.g. e-books) and services (e.g. cloud storage). Furthermore, the definition also excludes digital payment. An e-commerce may involve an order that is placed online but paid on the basis of cash on delivery (COD). Though e-payment is not a necessary element of e-commerce, it is an important facilitator of e-commerce. There are other related services that facilitate e-commerce, for example, logistics. These elements are part of what is known as the e-commerce ecosystem.

The E-commerce Ecosystem

The term "ecosystem" is often appended to e-commerce to describe a set of interlinked activities that enables e-commerce transactions. To understand the nature of the e-commerce ecosystem, it is first useful to describe the key processes in a typical e-commerce transaction (see Figure 2.1). These processes are placement of order, payment and delivery.

There are a number of activities or services that usually take place to support these processes (see Figure 2.2). Prior to placing an order,

FIGURE 2.1
Processes in an E-commerce Transaction

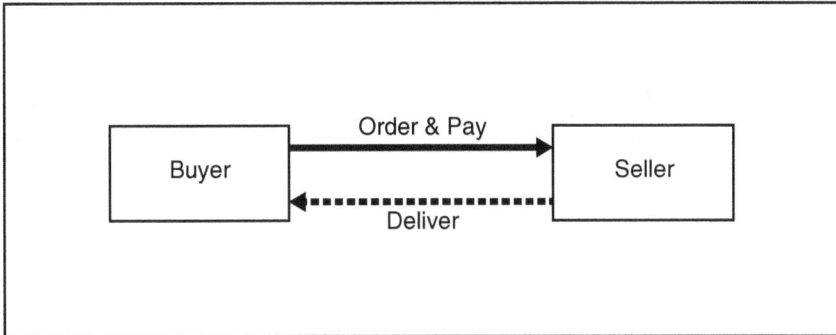

Source: Authors.

FIGURE 2.2
Activity Chain in E-commerce

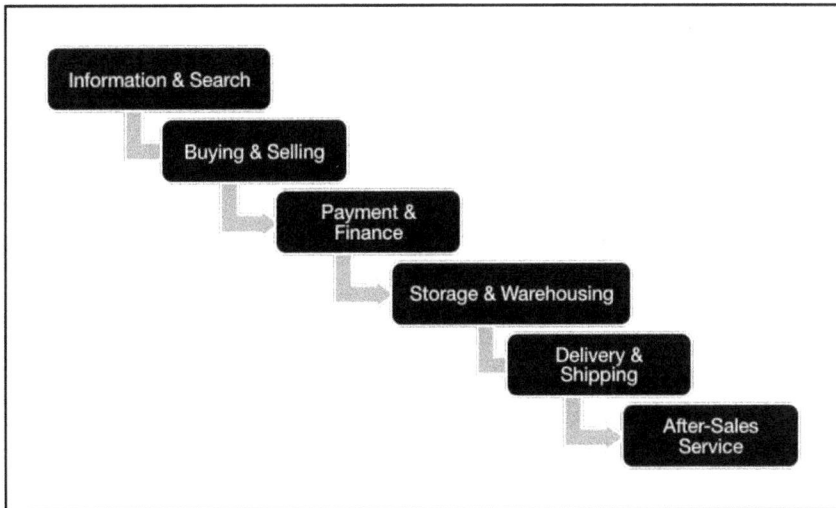

Source: Authors.

the buyer usually searches the internet for the best deal. The internet search activity should not be taken for granted as search engines (e.g. Google, Explorer) and the placement of advertisement (sponsored placement) at websites (e.g. Facebook) can be manipulated in ways that may affect buyers' access to information and hence his/her final decision. The payment system is another important element of the e-commerce ecosystem that facilitates transactions. Payment could have a financing element particularly when it is deferred (e.g. interest-free instalment). From the seller's side, physical goods may need to be stored in a warehouse before it is shipped and delivered to the buyer. Storage may also be needed for digital goods e.g. cloud though the space requirement is more modest. Finally, an important element of the e-commerce ecosystem is the after-sales services.

From an organizational perspective, some of the activities in the ecosystem can be delivered by firms owned by the seller. A highly vertically integrated seller may own its own payment system, warehouse, and delivery system. Comparing the e-commerce markets in the United States and China, the degree of vertical integration depends on several factors such as the level of development of infrastructure and payment systems as well as government regulations. Alibaba, an e-commerce firm in China, is highly integrated with its own payment system (Ant Financial, or formerly known as Alipay) and logistics (Cainiao). Amazon, which emerged in a market with relatively mature logistics and e-payment markets, was initially less vertically integrated. However, in its quest for greater efficiency and returns, plans are underway to be more integrated in the future.

Measuring E-commerce

Given the precise definition of e-commerce, measuring the volume of e-commerce transactions or sales is theoretically a relatively straightforward exercise. These transactions can be classified into different types of e-commerce depending on the participants involved, namely consumers, businesses and government. The four basic types of e-commerce transactions include: (i) Consumer to Consumer (C2C), (ii) Business to Consumer (B2C), (iii) Business to Business (B2B), and (iv) Business to Government (B2G). Other variations include extended versions such as B2B2C which involves businesses (B) selling on platforms (B) to consumers (C).

Even though the definition of e-commerce is relatively easy, publicly available data on e-commerce is scarce. Much of the data on e-commerce is fragmented and in private domain. The next section reviews some of the available data to assess the state of e-commerce in ASEAN member countries.

3. The State of E-commerce in ASEAN Countries

Evaluating the size of e-commerce market in Southeast Asia is a challenging task. Data availability for public use and analysis is a huge problem. Although the income value from e-commerce transaction is captured in the countries' national accounts statistics, it is not reported as a separate category. Almost all data are available in the private domain of e-commerce players, such as Alibaba, Amazon, EBay, JD.com and Lazada, or financial services providers like Visa, Amex and Mastercard. Information on cross-border e-commerce is even more scarce (UNCTAD 2016). Estimates often do not make a distinction between domestic and international transactions. In this scenario, the most plausible options are the enterprise surveys (to capture B2C and B2B) or consumer surveys (to capture B2C and C2C). Some of the well-publicized survey estimates for Southeast Asian markets are obtained from AT Kearney, Google and Temasek, and a few others. These are summarized in Table 2.1. Estimates of market size differ across the different sources due to different methodologies. Whilst country rankings across the sources, the top four country markets can be identified. They are, in no particular order, Indonesia, Malaysia, Singapore and Thailand.

The size of an e-commerce market is determined by a number of inter-related factors such as population size, demography profile (age profile), income per capita (purchasing power), internet penetration/utilization, internet usage and infrastructure quality, transport and logistics infrastructure quality.

Population Size and Age Profile

The total population of ASEAN countries is around 640 million in 2016 (see Figure 2.3). This is a fairly large figure—ASEAN's share of the global population is around 8.6 per cent. The distribution of population across ASEAN countries is very uneven. Indonesia is the biggest country as it accounts for 40.9 per cent of the ASEAN population. Other ASEAN countries with a fairly large population include the Philippines, Vietnam and Thailand.

The age profile of the population is another important factor. Countries with a younger population may have greater tendency to engage in e-commerce. ASEAN countries as a whole has a relatively young population. About 35 to 60 per cent of its population are below the age of 35 (see Figure 2.4). Two countries that have a larger proportion

TABLE 2.1
Estimates of E-commerce Market Size in ASEAN Countries (USD billion)

	E-commerce Retail Sales, 2013	Online Sales, 2014	E-commerce Retail Sales, 2015	E-commerce Market, 2015	E-commerce Sales, 2016	E-commerce Potential, 2020	E-commerce Market, 2025
Brunei							
Cambodia							
Indonesia	0.1	1.1	1.3	1.7	5.29	25–30	46
Lao PDR							
Malaysia	0.2	0.496	1.3	1.0	1.97	10–15	8.2
Myanmar							
Philippines	0.1		1	0.5	0.05	8–12	9.7
Singapore	0.3	0.86	1.7	1.0	2.13	7–10	5.4
Thailand	0.19	1.1	0.9	0.9	2.89	12–15	11.1
Vietnam	0.08		0.8	0.4	1.71	5–7	7.5
Sources	UBS	Euromonitor	AT Kearney	Google-Temasek	Statistica	AT Kearney	Google-Temasek

FIGURE 2.3
Population Size of ASEAN Countries (million)

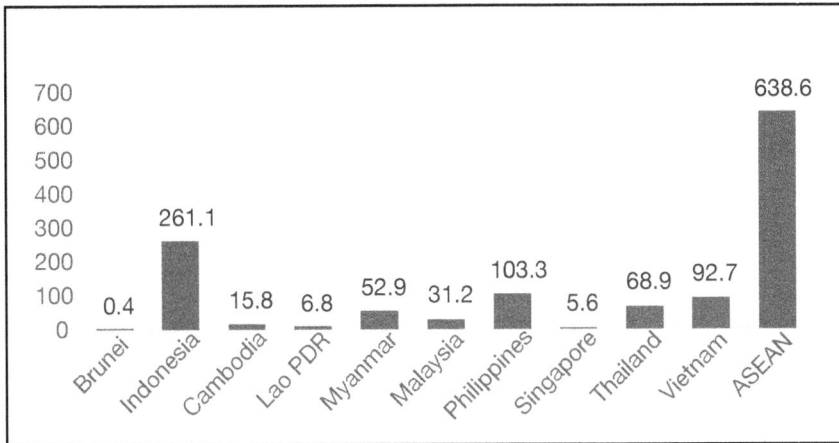

Source: World Bank.

FIGURE 2.4
Age Profile of Population in ASEAN Countries

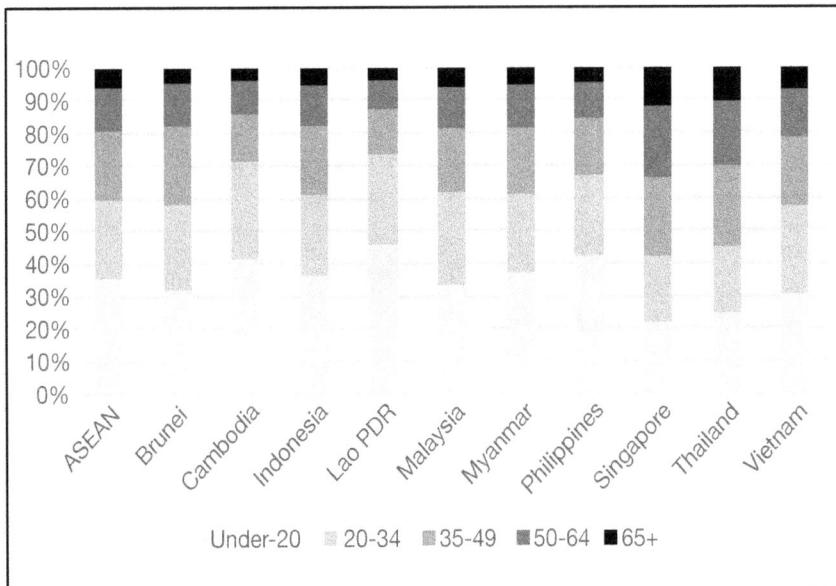

Source: United Nations.

of older population are Singapore and Thailand where more than 30 per cent of their population are 50 years old and above.

Even though a country may be large, its e-commerce potential may be negated by low income per capita. There is a significant income per capita gap between high-income countries such as Brunei and Singapore and other ASEAN members (see Figure 2.5). The two upper middle-income countries in the region are Malaysia and Thailand.

FIGURE 2.5
GNI Per Capita of ASEAN Countries

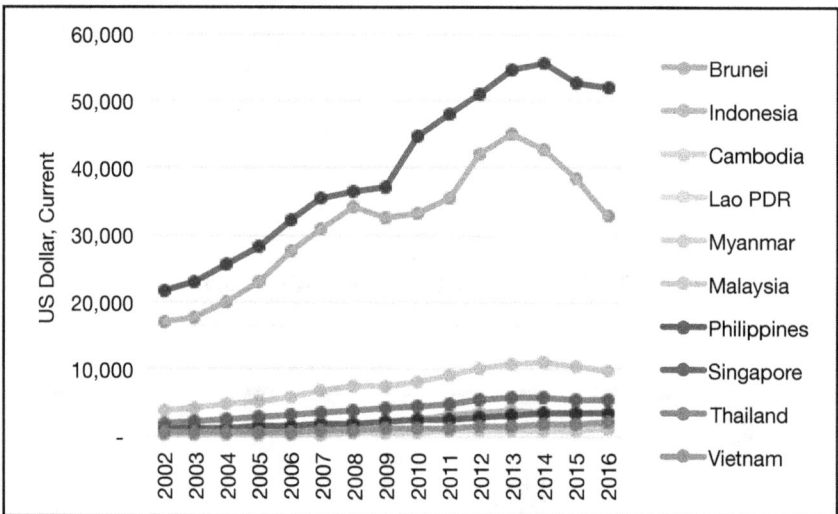

Source: World Bank.

ICT Infrastructure and Usage

There are also significant disparities in ICT usage and infrastructure amongst ASEAN countries. Mobile broadband penetration is fairly high in these countries with the exception of Lao PDR and Myanmar (see Table 2.2). However, there are significant differences in the percentage of individuals using the internet. ASEAN countries with less than 30 per cent of individuals using the internet include Cambodia, Indonesia, Lao PDR and Myanmar. Not only is the internet speed in many of these countries slow, the cost of using mobile broadband is also relatively high.

TABLE 2.2
ICT Usage and Infrastructure, 2016

Country	Mobile Cellular Subscriptions per 100 Persons	% of Individuals Using Internet	International Internet Bandwidth per Internet User (kbits/s)	Mobile Broadband Prices 1GB (% GNI pc)
Brunei	121	75.0	76.2	0.6
Cambodia	125	25.6	23.6	2.2
Indonesia	149	25.4	24.9	2.0
Lao PDR	55	21.9	17.5	4.2
Malaysia	141	78.8	42.6	1.4
Myanmar	89	25.1	6.4	5.7
Philippines	109	55.5	43.4	2.1
Singapore	147	81.0	982.9	0.3
Thailand	172	47.5	49.2	1.2
Vietnam	128	46.5	91.3	3.2

Sources: ITU; World Bank.

Payment and Financial Systems

E-commerce transactions are greatly facilitated by the presence of electronic payment systems. This often requires a fair participation of buyers and sellers in the financial system. Available data from the World Bank shows that a high proportion of the population in many ASEAN countries still do not have accounts with financial institutions (see Figure 2.6). Less than a third of the individuals surveyed in these countries had an account with a financial institution in 2014. This would hamper the use of the financial system as a means to settle e-commerce transactions. This can be seen from the low percentage of online shoppers that use online payments for their transactions (see Figure 2.7). As a result, cash-on-delivery (though not an ideal solution) has been adopted by e-commerce companies such as Lazada in Indonesia, Malaysia, Philippines, Thailand and Vietnam. One possible approach that can overcome this problem is to use mobile payment systems which have become increasingly popular in retail e-commerce.[2] The growth in mobile payment systems has been

FIGURE 2.6
Percentage of Individuals with Account at Financial Institutions, 2014

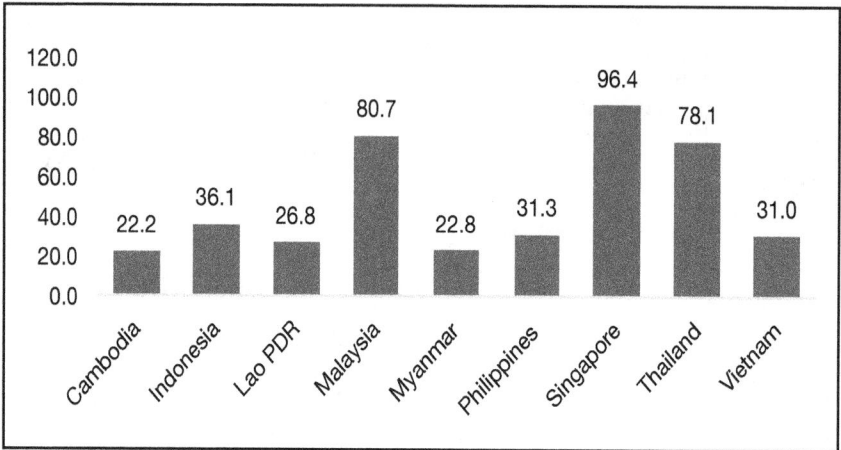

Source: World Bank.

FIGURE 2.7
Online Shoppers Using Online Payments, 2013

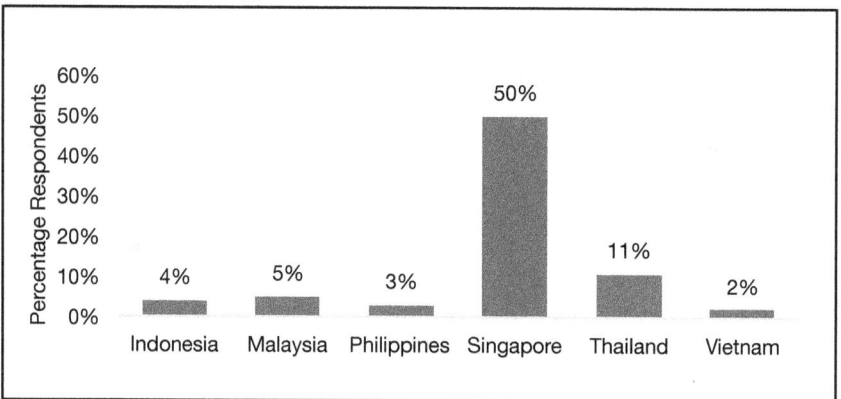

Source: AT Kearney.

driven by banks, e-commerce companies (e.g. Alipay) as well as ride-sharing companies (GoPay and GrabPay). Mobile payment is still at a relatively nascent stage in ASEAN countries today compared to

China, for example. Competition is heating up in the mobile payment markets in many of these countries, especially with the entry of new players such as Alipay and Grab. Mobile payment systems are likely to play an increasingly important role in Southeast Asian e-commerce in the future.

Transport and Logistics

Finally, a key component of the e-commerce ecosystem is transport and logistics. The delivery of physical goods (as opposed to digital goods) transacted through the internet requires an efficient transport and logistics system. This is an important "last-mile" component of the e-commerce ecosystem. An inefficient transport and logistics system may increase the transaction cost of e-commerce. Overall, the quality of transport and logistics infrastructure in most ASEAN countries are still deficient (see Figures 2.8 and 2.9). Singapore and to a lesser extent, Malaysia, are exceptions. The values of the ratings in the Logistics Performance Index for the ASEAN countries do indicate that there are country-level differences in terms of the various performance components (see Figure 2.9). For some countries, customs issues are more problematic than logistics (e.g. Brunei) while for others, it is the reverse (Indonesia). Regardless of the challenges posed, large e-commerce companies such as Lazada are investing and building up their transport and logistics networks.

Overall Assessment

E-commerce has great potential in ASEAN countries. There are significant factors that can hamper e-commerce growth but technological changes and private sector investments are likely to overcome some of these problems. Amongst the ASEAN countries, the UNCTAD's B2C E-Commerce Index suggests that Singapore and Malaysia are the two leading markets in this region even though these countries have smaller population than other ASEAN members such as Indonesia and Thailand (see Figure 2.10). However, the faster economic growth and improvements in infrastructure in the countries with larger population are likely to accelerate e-commerce development going forward. Whether ASEAN-level cooperation in e-commerce can provide further impetus to regional economic integration is examined next.

FIGURE 2.8
Quality of Infrastructure

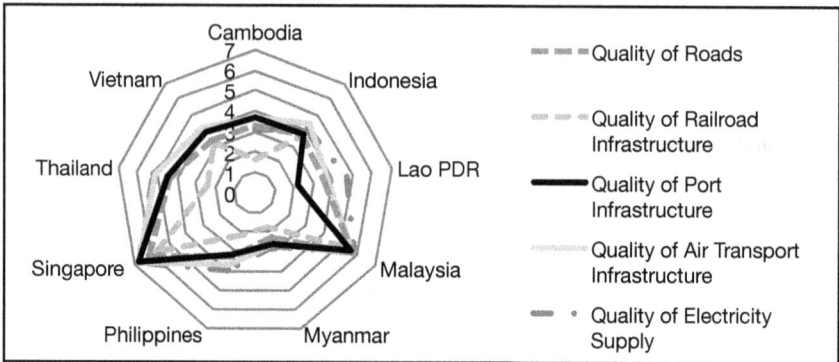

Notes: Index 1 (extremely underdeveloped) to 7 (extensive and efficient) for the Quality of Roads, Quality of Railroad Infrastructure, Quality of Port Infrastructure and Quality of Air Transport Infrastructure. Index 1 (extremely unreliable) to 7 (extremely reliable) for the Quality of Electricity Supply. Data for Brunei is not available; railroad infrastructure data is not available for Laos.
Source: *The Global Competitiveness Report 2015–2016*, World Economic Forum.

FIGURE 2.9
Logistics Performance Index, 2016

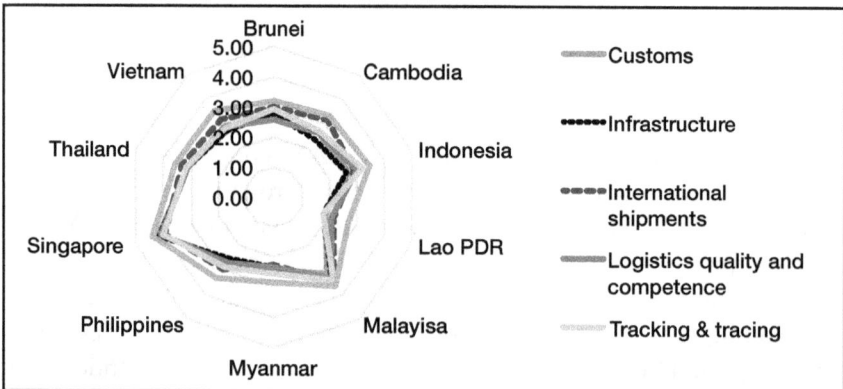

Notes: The efficiency of customs and border management clearance rated from very low (1) to very high (5) in the survey question. The quality of trade and transport infrastructure rated from very low (1) to very high (5) in the survey question. The ease of arranging competitively priced shipments rated from very difficult (1) to very easy (5) in the survey question. The competence and quality of logistics services rated from very low (1) to very high (5) in the survey question. The ability to track and trace consignments rated from very low (1) to very high (5) in the survey question. The frequency with which shipments reach consignees within scheduled or expected delivery times rated from hardly ever (1) to nearly always (5) in the survey question.
Source: World Bank.

FIGURE 2.10
UNCTAD's B2C E-commerce Index

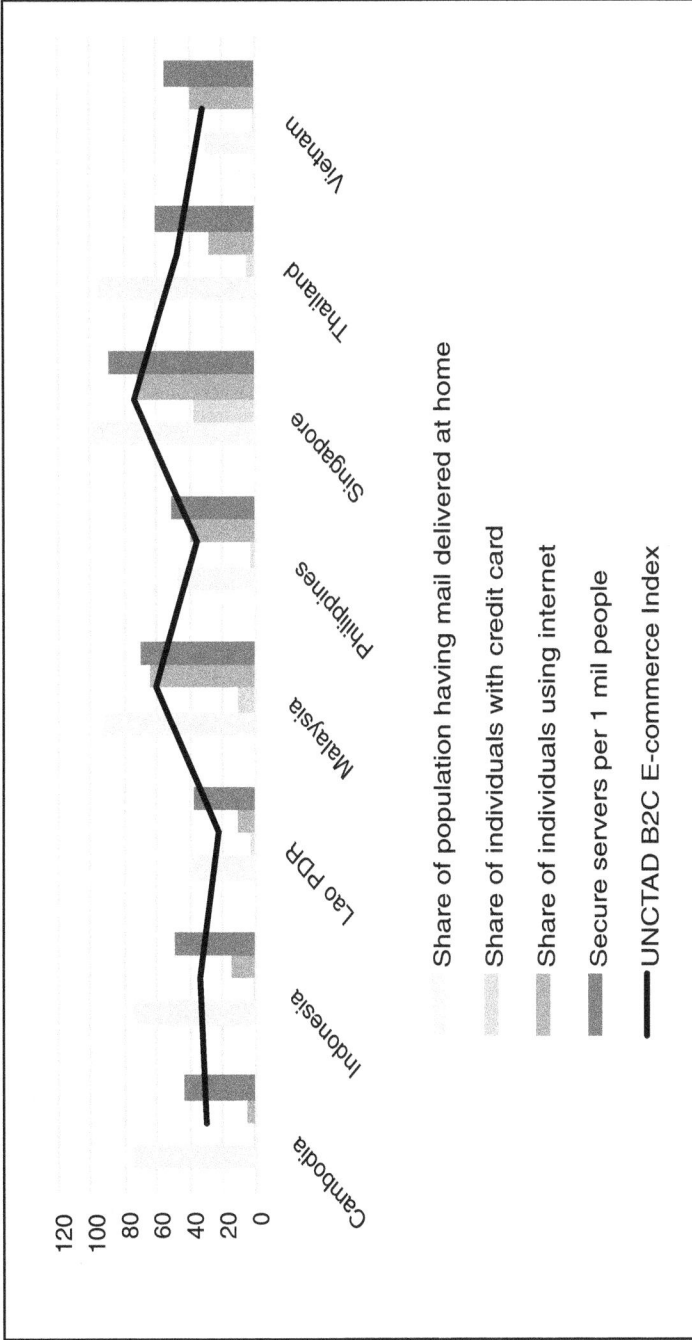

Share of population having mail delivered at home

Share of individuals with credit card

Share of individuals using internet

Secure servers per 1 mil people

UNCTAD B2C E-commerce Index

Source: UNCTAD.

4. E-commerce and ASEAN Economic Integration

Economic integration in the ASEAN context has two dimensions. The first dimension is greater intra-regional investment and trade. The second dimension relates to the concept of open regionalism in which ASEAN member countries are also engaged in integration with the global economy. E-commerce facilitates ASEAN economic integration in both these dimensions. It enhances cross-border trade and facilitates the participation of firms in the global production network.

At the firm-level, e-commerce improves information flows and market access. It also assists firms in making better use of their existing capacities as well as enable them to undertake informed decision to optimize inventories which improves the supply chain management process. This translates into firm-level productivity improvements. For example, according to the World Bank, Vietnamese firms using e-commerce have managed to increase their total factor productivity (TFP) by an average of 3.6 percentage point *vis-à-vis* the firms that are not using it (World Bank 2016). E-commerce also increases consumer welfare by improving information about products, range of products and purchasing options. With these benefits in mind, ASEAN member countries have sought to deepen cooperation in e-commerce with the view to accelerate regional economic integration.

ASEAN cooperation in e-commerce is covered in three policy documents, namely:

– e-ASEAN Framework Agreement
– AEC Blueprints 2015 and 2025
– ASEAN ICT Masterplans 2015 and 2020

e-ASEAN Framework Agreement

The e-ASEAN framework document provides the common wish list of activities that member countries need to undertake to build an e-commerce platform in their economies and subsequently in the region. The AEC plans contain commitments in terms of stipulated action lines related to drafting policies and legal infrastructure for cross-border e-commerce transactions. The ICT master plans provide guidelines on the development of the telecommunications network and trade in ICT goods and services among the ASEAN economies.

The e-ASEAN Framework Agreement, the master document stating the countries' intent-of-action related to ICT development and e-commerce, was signed by ASEAN leaders in 2000. The agreement covered six focus areas, one of which was "growth of electronic commerce".[3] Under the electronic commerce, countries had agreed to work on seven issues: (i) e-commerce legal framework, (ii) consumer protection, (iii) regional electronic payment system, (iv) intellectual property rights, (v) cybercrime legislation and prevention, (vi) developing authentication and security policies and (vii) taxation issues (ASEAN Secretariat 2000).

AEC Blueprints 2015 and 2025

E-commerce was featured prominently under the "Competitive Economic Region" pillar of the AEC 2015 Blueprint.[4] Giving reference to the master document, it categorically stated the objective was "to lay the policy and legal infrastructure for electronic commerce and enable on-line trade in goods (e-commerce) within ASEAN through the implementation of the e-ASEAN Framework Agreement and based on common reference frameworks" (ASEAN Secretariat 2008, p. 23). The Blueprint further provided a strategic schedule for 2008–15, describing the actions to be undertaken by member states over the eight-year period (see Table 2.3) (ASEAN Secretariat 2008).

At the end of the 2015 timeframe, as one looks at the implementation performance of AEC commitments, it is observed that the pillar of "Competitive Economic Region" is one of the laggards (see Figure 2.11). The ASEAN member countries managed to implement only 90 per cent of their total commitments under the pillar. More particularly, about the e-commerce actions, while the earlier AEC progress reports, namely the AEC Scorecards, reported implementation of one measure (see Table 2.4), the final report on implementation progress, published by the ASEAN Secretariat, reported that "the elements of taxation and electronic commerce are beyond the scope of this analysis" (ASEAN Secretariat, 2015a, p. 59).

Following the establishment of the AEC 2015, the AEC 2025 sought to attain five inter-related goals:

i.   A highly integrated and cohesive economy;
ii. A competitive, innovative, and dynamic ASEAN;
iii. Enhanced connectivity and sectoral cooperation;
iv. A resilient, inclusive, people-oriented, and people-centred ASEAN; and
v.   A global ASEAN.

TABLE 2.3
Strategic Schedule of Commitments under E-commerce in AEC 2015

2008–9	2010–11	2012–13	2014–15
Member countries to enact their e-commerce laws; Implement harmonized guidelines and principles for electronic contracting and online dispute resolution services; Adopt regional framework and strategy for mutual recognition of digital signatures; Continued capacity building and information sharing for member countries on e-commerce legal infrastructure activities (e.g. Public Key Infrastructure, institutional strengthening for Certification Authority, etc.).	Update and/or amend relevant legislations in line with regional best practices and regulations in e-commerce activities; Adopt the best practices/ guidelines on other cyber-law issues to support regional e-commerce activities; Advancing cross-border electronic transactions, through pilot implementation of mutual recognition of foreign digital signatures.		A harmonized legal infrastructure for e-commerce fully in place in ASEAN.

Source: ASEAN Secretariat (2008).

FIGURE 2.11

Implementation of AEC Scorecard Measures by AEC Pillar, 2015 (%)

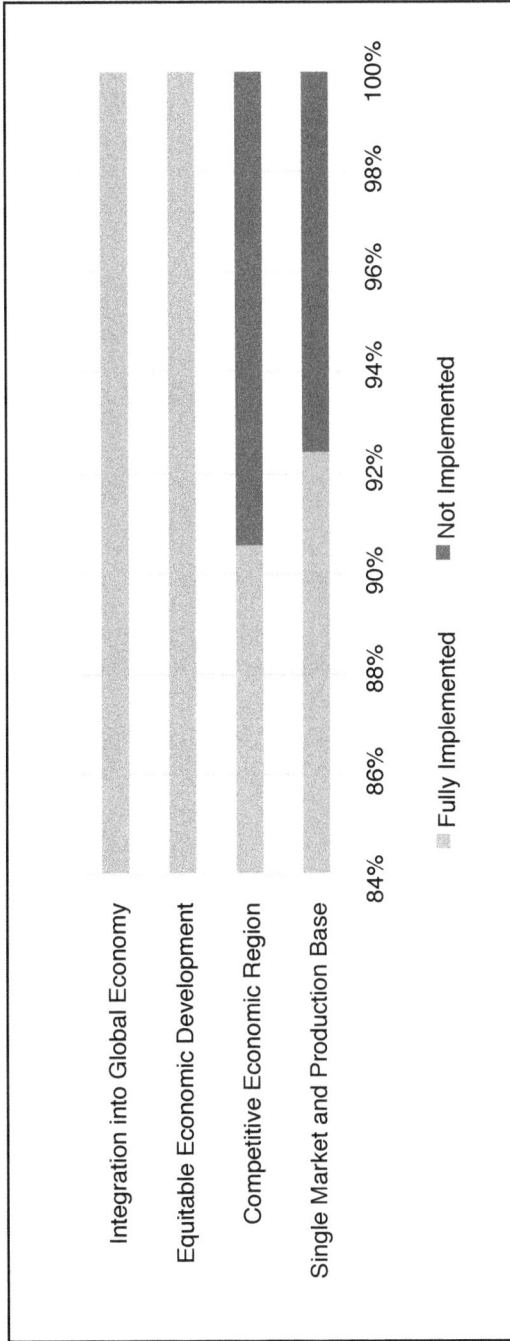

Source: ASEAN Secretariat (2015a).

TABLE 2.4
Progress of E-commerce Measures under AEC Scorecard I and II

Phase I (2008–9)		Phase II (2010–11)	
Fully Implemented	Not Fully Implemented	Fully Implemented	Not Fully Implemented
–	–	1	–

Source: ASEAN Secretariat (2012).

Situating itself under the goal of "Enhanced Connectivity and Sectoral Cooperation", ASEAN countries have promised to

> intensify cooperation on e-Commerce building upon Article 5 of e-ASEAN Framework Agreement adopted by ASEAN Leaders in November 2000, with a view to develop an ASEAN Agreement on e-Commerce to facilitate cross-border e-Commerce transactions in ASEAN (ASEAN Secretariat 2015*b*, p. 24)

It should be noted that Article 5 of e-commerce framework agreement covers member countries' desire to facilitate the growth of e-commerce sector by adopting appropriate regulatory and legislative frameworks in the national economies. ASEAN further provided the Consolidated Strategic Action Plan for the AEC 2025 measures covering the period from 2016 to 2025 (see Table 2.5). The actions to be undertaken in the next ten years are mainly in the areas of consumer protection, dispute settlement mechanism, authentication of digital signature, cyber security and data protection (ASEAN Secretariat 2017).

ASEAN ICT Masterplans 2015 and 2020

The issues of hard infrastructure to build ICT networks were addressed in the ASEAN ICT Masterplans 2015 and 2020. The ASEAN ICT Masterplan 2015 focused on trade and investment in ICT-related goods and services to enable building telecommunications infrastructure, thereby narrowing the digital divide and building a competitive ASEAN. While the document discussed the establishment of the ASEAN Broadband Corridor and ASEAN Internet Exchange Network, it also listed actions to develop a common framework

TABLE 2.5
AEC 2025: Consolidated Strategic Action Plan

Strategic Measures	Key Action Lines	Timeline
Harmonized consumer rights and protection laws	Integrate e-commerce considerations into the ASEAN High-level Consumer Protection Principles; Develop guidelines/code of good online business practices based on self-regulation best practices; Conduct regular consumer rights awareness training for consumers and consumer associations.	2016–25
Harmonized legal framework for online dispute resolution, taking into account available international standards	Establish Alternative Dispute Resolution (ADR) mechanisms, including online dispute resolution systems, to facilitate the resolution of claims over e-commerce transactions.	2016–25
Inter-operable, mutually recognized, secure, reliable and user-friendly e-identification and authorization (electronic signature) schemes	Study suitable mechanisms for authentication of electronic signatures and trade documents, based on internationally recognized practices; Establish an international coordination mechanism amongst cyber security agencies in responding to cyber security incidents.	2016–25
Coherent and comprehensive framework for personal data protection	Develop Regional Data Protection and Privacy Principles (Rules System); Identify the responsibilities of businesses in personal data protection.	2016–25

Source: ASEAN Secretariat (2017).

for network and information securities and sharing Public-Private-Partnership (PPP) models with each other. The document further promised to undertake studies to lower intra-ASEAN roaming charges and identify gaps in e-service delivery in ASEAN countries. Regarding the ASEAN ICT Masterplan 2020, the focus shifted to wide-ranging issues. In addition to building ICT infrastructure and increasing trade and investment in IT-related products, the plan documented disruptive developments in ASEAN economies (such as new media, content security and cyber threats) and encouraged all sectors to adopt ICT in their activities so as to lower business cost and foster economy-wide growth and innovation.

The ASEAN countries have reported notable progress under the ASEAN ICT Masterplan 2015. In order to create a conducive environment for businesses, ASEAN has developed a framework to facilitate transparent and harmonized ICT regulations. The countries have shared best PPP practices for ICT projects. They have also encouraged the use of e-services across the region so as to provide better accessibility to people at a lower cost. The member countries have worked out a list of fifteen common e-Government services that are beneficial for their citizens. Efforts for greater awareness among people with regard to laws and regulations for cyber security are said to be raising confidence among people for the use of ICT in their daily lives.

The ASEAN countries are encouraging creativity and innovation among entrepreneurs. They have introduced platforms like ASEAN ICT Awards that are meant to encourage innovation across firms and ASEAN CIO Forum to exchange best practices among ICT players. With regard to infrastructure development, though this has been far from being adequate, ASEAN countries take immense pride in the number of people with access to ICT services such as the internet and mobile cellular services. The member countries have also been working on information and network security infrastructure projects. Other than these, the ASEAN countries have been active in imparting ICT skills development for people and undertaking activities like ASEAN Cyberkids Camp (to raise ICT awareness among kids), Training Program of ICT and IT for the Elderly and People with Disabilities and Free Open Source Software Adoption in Secondary

Schools to bridge the digital divide in ASEAN (ASEAN Secretariat 2015c).

In addition to ASEAN countries' own integration initiatives under e-commerce, the countries also intend to expand it to other trade and investment partners. To start with, ASEAN–Australia–New Zealand trade agreement has included e-commerce as a key area of cooperation. This is mainly to assist small- and medium-scale enterprises (SMEs) and encourage information flow across participating members. The agreement includes commitments of cooperation under e-commerce and addresses issues of transparency, domestic regulatory framework in line with international convention, consumer protection, data protection and paperless trading. The Regional Comprehensive Economic Partnership (RCEP), a sixteen-party trade initiative led by ASEAN, that is currently getting negotiated is also said to include e-commerce as one of its chapters.

5. Conclusions

The potential of e-commerce in ASEAN countries is without doubt immense. However, several challenges have to be addressed before e-commerce can fully flourish in these countries. One key challenge is the relatively inadequate ICT infrastructure in many ASEAN countries. Whilst broadband mobile is available in all ASEAN countries—the quality (speed and reliability) and user cost of such services vary significantly across these countries. The same problem is encountered in transport and logistics. Another problem that has received some attention in ASEAN cooperation is the harmonization of laws that are relevant for e-commerce. This is important to support cross-border e-commerce transactions. Whilst some progress has been achieved in this area, a number of issues need to be tackled, notably, the lack of capacity-building and intra as well as inter-country coordination in legal implementation and enforcement (UNCTAD 2013). Overall, the momentum on the implementation of policies and legislations to support e-commerce has picked up in recent years. More recently, the digital economy has become a key area of focus for ASEAN countries—as witnessed by Singapore's emphasis on this area as the ASEAN country chair for 2018. This bodes well for e-commerce growth and development in ASEAN countries.

NOTES

1. Source: https://stats.oecd.org/glossary/detail.asp?ID=4721 (accessed 25 January 2018).
2. "Mobile Payments Sideswipe Credit Cards in Southeast Asia", *Nikkei Asian Review*, 23 January 2018.
3. The other areas are—the establishment of ASEAN information infrastructure, liberalization of trade in ICT products and services and of investments, facilitation of trade in ICT products and services, capacity building and e-society and e-government.
4. The other pillars of AEC 2015 were Single Market and Production Base, Equitable Economic Development and Integration into the Global Economy.

REFERENCES

ASEAN Secretariat. "2000 e-ASEAN Framework Agreement". Jakarta: ASEAN Secretariat, 2000. https://cil.nus.edu.sg/wp-content/uploads/formidable/18/2000-e-ASEAN-Framework-Agreement.pdf.
———. *ASEAN Economic Community Blueprint.* Jakarta: ASEAN Secretariat, 2008. http://asean.org/wp-content/uploads/archive/5187-10.pdf.
———. *ASEAN Economic Community Scorecard: Charting Progress Toward Regional Economic Integration, Phase I (2008–2009) and Phase II (2010–2011).* Jakarta: ASEAN Secretariat, 2012.
———. *ASEAN Economic Community 2015: Progress and Key Achievements.* Jakarta: ASEAN Secretariat, 2015a.
———. *ASEAN Economic Community Blueprint 2025: Progress and Key Achievements.* Jakarta: ASEAN Secretariat, 2015b.
———. *ASEAN ICT Masterplan 2015 – Completion Report.* Jakarta: ASEAN Secretariat, 2015c.
———. "ASEAN Economic Community 2025 Consolidated Strategic Action Plan". Jakarta: ASEAN Secretariat, 2017. http://asean.org/storage/2017/02/Consolidated-Strategic-Action-Plan.pdf.
AT Kearney and CIMB ASEAN Research Institute. "Lifting the Barriers to E-commerce in ASEAN". 2015. https://www.atkearney.co.uk/documents/10192/5540871/Lifting+the+Barriers+to+E-Commerce+in+ASEAN.pdf/d977df60-3a86-42a6-8d19-1efd92010d52 (assessed 1 December 2017).
UBS. "ASEAN eCommerce: Is ASEAN at an Inflection Point for eCommerce?" 13 June 2014.
UNCTAD (United Nations Conference on Trade and Development). *Review of E-commerce Legislation Harmonization in the Association of Southeast Asian*

Nations. Geneva: United Nations Conference on Trade and Development, 2013.

————. "In Search of Cross-border E-commerce Trade Data". UNCTAD Technical Note No. 6, April 2016. http://unctad.org/en/PublicationsLibrary/tn_unctad_ict4d06_en.pdf.

World Bank. *Digital Dividends*. Washington, D.C.: World Development Report, The World Bank Group, 2016.

PART II

3

E-COMMERCE AND COMPETITION LAW
How Does Competition Assessment Change With E-Commerce?

Eileen Lee and Lip Hang Poh[1]

1. Introduction

E-commerce has garnered considerable attention from competition authorities, given that there are a growing number of competition cases related to digital commerce in recent years. For instance, the US Department of Justice prosecuted David Topkins, an art seller on Amazon Marketplace, for price fixing. Topkins conspired with other sellers to fix the prices of posters using customized algorithms between September 2013 and January 2014 (United States Department of Justice 2015). Most Favoured Nation (MFN) clauses have also been the subject of investigations by the European Union DG Competition (EU DG COMP) and national competition authorities in EU member states.

Given that competition authorities are in the business of regulating business behaviour, how does e-commerce activities impact competition assessment? In this chapter, we consider the impact of e-commerce on two fundamental steps of competition assessment:

a.   Market definition; and
b.   Market power.

Market definition is typically the first step of competition assessment as it provides a framework for analysis through identifying the competitive constraints acting on a seller of a product or service. It can be thought of as a "quick and dirty" tool to determine if a seller is likely to have market power.

Competition law essentially "regulate" business behaviour that hampers market competition. It is primarily concerned about whether the exercise of market power by business entities leads to any adverse impact on competition. In an abuse of dominance case, it is clear that the abuse of market power by a dominant undertaking perpetuates its market position in ways unrelated to competitive merits. Competitors acting in concert e.g. in price-fixing or production control cartels create and abuse market power. Merger control, on the other hand, is concerned from the ex-ante perspective, i.e., whether the merged entity has the market power to increase prices unilaterally, leading to non-coordinated effects in a horizontal merger situation, or foreclosure of competitors in the supply chain in a vertical merger situation.

Drawing from the findings on consumer and business behaviour from the EU DG COMP's preliminary e-commerce sector study report and the Competition Commission of Singapore's (CCS) commissioned report on *E-commerce and its Impact on Competition Policy and Law in Singapore*, we study how these findings impact these two fundamental steps of competition assessment.

2.   E-commerce Activities: Consumer and Seller Behaviour

This section documents findings from reports published by the EU DG COMP and CCS on how e-commerce changes the behaviour of businesses and consumers.

The EU DG COMP's preliminary report on the e-commerce sector inquiry was published in September 2016. It was aimed at,

...obtaining an overview of the prevailing market trends, gathering evidence on potential barriers to competition linked to the growth of e-commerce and understanding the prevalence of certain, potentially restrictive, business practices and the underlying rationale for their use.

The study was carried out on the basis of responses to questionnaires sent to companies that are active in e-commerce in EU (EU DG Comp 2016).

CCS[2] commissioned DotEcon Ltd. to conduct a research report to understand the development and characteristics of e-commerce, the specific competition issues that e-commerce activities can give rise to, as well as the implications for competition policy and law in Singapore. The overall objective is to identify whether changes brought about by e-commerce, like new business models, may require specific attention when conducting competition assessments and whether the competition law framework in Singapore can effectively deal with competition issues that might arise in an e-commerce context. The report, which was published in December 2015, was based on a number of case studies involving interviews with e-commerce industry players in Singapore, review of the extant literature on e-commerce and competition law, overseas competition law investigations and published survey data.

Sellers

From the perspective of sellers, the rise of e-commerce activities changes the nature of commerce in a variety of ways. It lowers the distribution cost and reshapes supply chains of companies. It also supports the provision of a larger variety of products available to buyers, including niche products that are not supplied by traditional brick-and-mortar stores. Some have gone as far as to claim that e-commerce is the "death knell" of traditional brick-and-mortar stores. The following paragraphs summaries the impact of e-commerce on sellers.

E-commerce Changes Business Models

Business models have significantly evolved because of the proliferation of e-commerce. Traditional brick-and-mortar retailers, in order to keep up with the times, have changed their business models to "click-and-mortar", offering their wares for sale in both online and offline platforms, a strategy often referred to as "omni-channel retailing".

Interestingly, "pure play" firms (i.e., a firm that conducts business only online and not through traditional offline channels), have also started to move towards establishing physical retail presences, be it through pop-up stores or permanent stores (EU DG Comp 2016; DotEcon 2015). Brynjolfsson et al. (2013) predicted that retailers will converge towards an omni-retail channel strategies, where consumers trade and interact with sellers through online and offline channels (Brynjolfsson et al. 2013, pp. 23–29).

The EU DG COMP report noted that 70 per cent of retailers offer an equivalent choice of brands and models in both offline and online platforms. Approximately 20 per cent of retailers offer a greater choice online and 10 per cent of retailers offer a greater choice offline (EU DG Comp 2016). Six out of 10 of retailers surveyed adopt a multi-channel approach retailing both online and offline (EU DG Comp 2016).

Traditional intermediaries are also displaced by new intermediaries. The travel sector is a clear example of how e-commerce radically affects business models and markets. While traditional travel agents continue to play a role in the travel industry, this role is much diminished in Singapore. As more consumers turn to the internet (e.g., online travel websites and airline websites) to make travel bookings, the scope for travel agents to value-add shrinks if they are unable to differentiate themselves (DotEcon 2015).

E-commerce Generates Cost Savings for Businesses

For instance, in the supply of physical products, the improved communication and coordination between manufacturers, wholesalers and retailers in an e-commerce environment can substantially reduce distribution costs, for example, through practices such as "drop-shipping" (Office of Fair Trading 2000). Drop-shipping refers to a distribution model where a retailer does not itself keep products in stock, but rather passes the customer order on to wholesalers who will then fulfil the order. Some companies which have used the drop-shipping distribution model include Blogshop Singapore and Cleocat-fashion (Office of Fair Trading 2000).

In some instances, the cost structure for a product may even be affected by e-commerce and the resultant cost structure could be one whereby the fixed costs are high relative to marginal costs. This is particularly true for digital content, where the internet is the means of delivery as well as transaction. This would include products such as media news, information and data services.

E-commerce Allows Businesses Access to a Wider Geographic Pool of Customers

Businesses are no longer constrained by the geographic limitations of physical stores as they can sell their products to more customers locally as well as overseas through e-commerce channels.

However, geographic expansion of markets may be limited by business practices and trade barriers. For example, manufacturers may place restrictions on distributors/retailers such that they are unable to sell beyond a pre-determined geographic area. The EU report noted that almost half of the surveyed manufacturers make use of territorial exclusive distribution agreements. A larger majority of manufacturers use selective distribution to exclude pure play retailers for at least a part of their products. Half of the surveyed retailers report to be affected by at least one contractual restriction to sell/advertise online (EU DG Comp 2016).

The CCS report also noted that traditional barriers to cross-border trade e.g., differences in applicable law which may create contractual risks, costs associated with cross-border payments, currency exchange risks and import duties may similarly limit geographic expansion of markets (EU DG Comp 2016).

E-commerce Technologies Afford Businesses the Means to Price Discriminate

Firms may discriminate on the basis of geographic location or by charging lower prices to registered users. For example, Agoda.com offers "insider deals" i.e., cheap tickets or room rates for registered users.

The EU report noted that a wide range of information is collected through e-commerce transactions: location, product, price, purchase and browsing history, frequency of visits, device and payment methods used, and personal information. Detailed user information may similarly increase the scope for price discrimination and enable narrowly defined customer groups to be targeted directly (EU DG Comp 2016).

E-commerce Markets Exhibit Network Effects and May Favour Larger Firms

Online platforms, e.g., Business to Consumer (B2C) marketplaces, act as intermediaries and connect a number of different users to facilitate transactions. These are known as "multi-sided platforms". The platform can be "two-sided", if it serves two distinct customer groups or it can be "multi-sided" with a number of different customer groups using the platform. Examples of e-commerce platforms include online job portals, hotel websites and online restaurant booking services.

One underlying characteristic of online platforms is the existence of direct and indirect network effects. The term "network effect" refers to cases where the value of certain products and services to an individual user depends on the number of its other users. Network effects may be direct[3] or indirect.[4]

The CCS's commissioned report revealed that e-commerce platforms may bring about competition issues related to concentrated market structures, as sellers benefit from an increase in the number of potential customers, and buyers benefit from the increase in the range of sellers (DotEcon 2015). Markets may tip in favour of a small number of firms, or even a single dominant market.

Buyers

With regard to the impact of e-commerce on buyers, it should be noted that spending via e-commerce channels are "uneven" i.e. they differ across sectors. E-commerce activities are not "created equal", spending via e-commerce channels are higher in some sectors. According to the Singapore Department of Statistics, travel (air-tickets, hotel bookings and package tours) and clothing account for the largest share of household expenditure online (Singapore Department of Statistics 2015). Other survey findings confirm that fashion and travel are the top two online retail categories in Singapore.

There are a few reasons for this phenomenon. First, buyers may have a strong preference for shopping in store for some types of items. Euromonitor reports suggest that consumers in Singapore tend to prefer shopping in store for big ticket items (Euromonitor 2014). Concerns over payment security, product compatibility (e.g. electronics), product quality (e.g. fresh produce), and shipment times, are other possible reasons (DotEcon 2015).

It is also observed that apart from shopping both in store and online, buyers also "multi-home" when it comes to shopping online i.e. buyers frequently use a number of different B2C online platforms. B2C marketplace industry players interviewed as part of the CCS commissioned report, reflected that multi-homing is common for buyers and also sellers (DotEcon 2015).

3. What Does E-commerce Mean for Market Definition?

Market definition is the key step to providing the framework for competition analysis through identifying the competitive constraints acting on a seller of a given product. For example, are online marketplaces competitors to brick-and-mortar stores? It will identify quickly, cases where business conduct or agreements do not have appreciable adverse effects on competition or where businesses do not possess market power.

The hypothetical monopolist test (HMT) is a conceptual approach used to define markets. A market definition normally contains two dimensions: the product and the geographic market (DotEcon 2015).

Hypothetical Monopolist Test

The HMT identifies all the products that buyers regard as reasonably substitutable for the focal product (i.e. demand-side substitutability) (CCCS 2007). Once those substitute products are identified, all those firms that could potentially supply the focal product and substitutes can be identified (supply-side substitutability). The test also involves asking whether a hypothetical monopolist controlling a group of focal products can raise prices that are small but significantly above competitive levels. In general, an increase of about 10 per cent above the competitive price is used for the test, although the actual percentage increase used may vary depending on the particular facts of each case.

The general application of the HMT and the assessment of demand and supply-side substitutability remains relevant in the context of an e-commerce environment. For example, the HMT is generic enough to consider whether firms with different business models are in the same relevant market. If online retailers providing a particular range of products cannot "profitably increase prices above the competitive level" because customers migrate to purchasing offline, or offline sellers would commence online sales, then offline and online channels are part of the same market. On the other hand, if online retailers are able to do so, then online and offline sales would constitute separate markets.

However, in the short term, the application of the HMT may be complicated by the lack of reliable sales and price data and by the speed of change in e-commerce markets (Office of Fair Trading 2000). In particular, the degree to which online retailers and traditional retailers compete depends on the rate at which buyers and sellers change their purchasing behaviour in response to the availability of products and services online. This in turns affects the appropriate delineation of the product market.

Product Market

The standard considerations of the assessment of the product dimension of a relevant market continue to apply in the e-commerce environment. It involves the understanding of the extent to which buyers will switch away from purchasing the focal product; and the extent to which suppliers will switch to supplying the product in response to the exercise of market power.

The growth of e-commerce, however, is likely to raise a number of interesting questions for the definition of the product market:

(i)   Does e-commerce create new markets?
(ii) How would price discrimination in an e-commerce environment affect market definition?
(iii) How would the resultant changes in cost structures due to e-commerce affect market definition?

Does E-commerce Create New Markets?

When goods and services are available through both online and offline channels, it raises the question on whether both channels are part of the same product market. As discussed earlier, the standard considerations of the assessment of the product dimension of a relevant market helps to determine the extent to which online and offline channels are substitutable and compete with each other.

In some instances, e-commerce simply creates an additional sales channel, which competes with the offline channels (Office of Fair Trading

2000). E-commerce may also support a greater variety of products and allow suppliers to create new services that may plug gaps in the chain of substitution, resulting in a wider product market definition. As an example, Laundry Box's services and price range may place the offer somewhere in the middle of self-service laundrettes and premium laundry services. Whilst users of self-service laundrettes might not consider premium laundry services as a sufficiently close substitute to give rise to a competitive constraint (and vice versa), there might be a sufficient number of customers in either segment that consider Laundry Box's services as a substitute. This new service may then connect the formerly separate markets (DotEcon 2015).

In other instances, e-commerce appears to create entirely new products and services, and thus new economic markets (Office of Fair Trading 2000). For example, comparison-shopping search engines and many electronic marketplaces offer a service which was previously unavailable, and would have been deemed as a new economic market (Office of Fair Trading 2000).

Another possibility would be a "converged" retail market where the line between online and offline is blurred such that the need for a well-delineated online versus offline market definition is unnecessary.

How Would Price Discrimination in an E-commerce Environment Affect Market Definition?

The extent to which price discrimination is present in an e-commerce environment may have the effect of segmenting markets. With price discrimination, the presence of a sufficiently large group of customers who would be prepared to switch to another product is no longer effective in protecting infra-marginal customers from facing increases in prices. In addition, the notion of a single "market price" on the basis of which a market definition exercise would be undertaken may no longer be appropriate (DotEcon 2015).

With the reduction of transaction costs due to e-commerce activities, it is possible for buyers who have been offered less favourable prices to seek products and services from alternative suppliers. Actual prices may then converge a single "market price". However, price discrimination may still occur with geo-blocking[5] and other geographical restrictions. Such restrictions would undermine the ability of shoppers to seek alternative products and services offered by overseas suppliers, and result in a narrower product market definition.

How would the Resultant Changes in Cost Structure due to E-commerce Affect Market Definition?

If cost structure is one whereby the fixed costs are high relative to the marginal costs, companies may enjoy cost savings from increasing its production and/or producing two or more distinct goods. In other words, the cost structure is said to be characterized of economics of scale and scope (DotEcon 2015). This may in turn lead to a wider product market definition for the following reasons:

a. First, as there are economies of scope for suppliers to enter new market segments at low costs, it would facilitate supply side-substitutability. This would in turn, support a wider product market definition.

b. Second, for a given price elasticity, the lower the marginal costs, the lower the profits arising from a price increase by a hypothetical monopolist. This is because monopolist will tend to lose a larger margin on each unit of sales volume lost. Thus, if the hypothetical monopolist test was applied strictly in this instance, the lower marginal costs would support a larger set of focal product and its substitutes, and may result in a wider product market definition.

Geographic Market

The standard considerations of the assessment of the geographical dimension of a relevant market would also continue to apply in the e-commerce environment. The geographical market refers to the area over which substitution takes place. If buyers will travel further afield to buy products when their local prices are increased, then the geographical spread of the market is wide and vice versa. If sellers from afar will now supply to local markets because the local price has risen, then the geographic market is also wider than the situation where only local sellers are willing to supply.

The adoption of e-commerce has the potential to expand the geographic scope of a market, given that the cost for consumers to visit a website is independent of its geographic location (DotEcon 2015). This widening of the geographical market is a game changer for B2C transactions, where buyers are relatively small and unsophisticated and might have previously bought products and services only from their local providers. Many Business to Business (B2B) markets, by contrast, will already have a relatively wide geographical market, as a result of buyers making larger purchases and being better informed about the available suppliers (Office of Fair Trading 2000).

In the context of online shopping, the key issue of geography/ distance is not about the need to travel to the seller, but potential concerns that consumers may have from purchasing from a remote online seller. For example, there may be concerns about shipping costs, delays in delivery fulfilment, payment security or lack of warranties when buying from distant sellers. In these circumstances, an increase in value might have the opposite effect, i.e., consumers may be more concerned about purchasing high-value items from distant online sellers and may prefer trusted and reputable online sellers (DotEcon 2015).

In essence, the following factors would typically be considered in determining whether online channels are an effective substitute for offline channels:

a. The availability of logistic services to allow products to be imported;

b. The attitude of customers towards the potential risks associated with cross-border transactions;

c. The presence of other barriers to trade (e.g. selective distribution agreements, cross border payments, import duties); and

d. The extent to which suppliers engage in geographic price discrimination (e.g., geo-blocking).

Multi-sided Markets

Because of network effects, multi-sided platforms pose distinct issues for market definition, which is often complicated further by the fact that many of the most widely used online services (e.g., email, search, video and music streaming) offer their services to one customer group for free, while charging another customer group a fee.

The nature of multi-sided platforms poses interesting questions which would need to be addressed when defining relevant markets:

a. Whether separate and distinct markets should be defined for the different services offered by platforms to the different user groups, or whether there is a single market for the services provided by the platform; and

b. How standard approaches such as the Hypothetical Monopolist Test might be applied to platforms.

Generally, when a single market is to be defined, the relevant price for the application of the Hypothetical Monopolist Test would be the sum of charges to all users. For example, if a platform charges both buyers and sellers a fee for transacting, the relevant price would be the sum of these charges. Otherwise, the Hypothetical Monopolist Test can be performed separately for each market, using the fee charged to the respective customer group.

Where separate but interrelated markets are defined, the impact of a price increase by the hypothetical monopolist will have to take into account the network effects that are characteristic for multi-sided platforms. For instance, the profitability of an increase in the price to the sellers group will have to be assessed taking into account that any immediate reduction in revenue might lead to a loss of business from the buyers group, which then triggers a reduction in revenue and so on. It may well be the case that a price increase by a hypothetical monopolist that would be profitable without these network effects will become unprofitable once the network effects are taken into consideration.

In the case of an interrelated multi-sided markets, it would be inappropriate to apply a one-sided Hypothetical Monopolist Test to define markets. However, the logic of the Hypothetical Monopolist Test could be extended to account for the indirect network effects between both sides of the market when judging the profitability of a price increase. In particular, one should check the profitability of a rise in price on each side of the market to ascertain the impact of the price increase (Filistrucchi et al. 2014).

Relevance of Past Market Definitions

The dynamic changes in the e-commerce market limit the relevance of using past data when analysing current (or future) market definitions. This also limits the degree to which market participants and competition authorities can rely on precedent cases when assessing relevant markets (Filistrucchi et al. 2014). For example, the rate of internet penetration and advent of mobile commerce render past market definitions irrelevant today. However, over the longer term, this may be less of an issue as it would be possible for competition authorities to collect reliable sales and price data to define markets (Filistrucchi et al. 2014).

Lastly, while parallels can be drawn between sectors when defining markets, the proliferation of e-commerce activities can differ greatly between sectors e.g. grocery retail versus travel sector, limiting the inference that one can draw when relying on past market definitions to inform current competition assessments.

4. What Does E-commerce Mean for Market Power Assessment?

Market power arises when a business does not face sufficiently strong competitive pressure. In competition law economics, market power is often defined as the ability to profitably sustain prices above competitive levels or to restrict output or quality below competitive levels. Competition authorities typically measure or determine the extent of market power using:

a. Market share;
b. Barriers to entry and expansion; and
c. Buyers' power.

Market Share

Market share measures the extent of existing competition that a business faces in the market.

Traditional measures of market share. The traditional measures of market share tend to be sales revenue, volume and sometimes capacity to supply when there are homogenous goods.

These measures may not be adequate when assessing multi-sided markets, particularly, where services are typically provided for free to certain groups of users and where capacity is not an important feature of the market. Where it is not appropriate or possible to measure market share on the basis of sales or capacity (e.g., because a service is offered for free to consumers), alternative measures of market share for online activities may be considered. For example, the number of users within each user group on each side of the platform would be helpful. In the case of a two-sided platform, it might be useful to collect data on the total number of buyers and the total number of sellers that connect to the platform. It may also be relevant to obtain the revenue derived from the different user group for each side of the platform.

Interpreting market share. It is often argued that the history of market share is more informative than considering market share at a single point in time as it reveals the dynamic nature of the market.

However, as noted in our earlier discussion on the relevance of past market definitions, the changes in e-commerce market limit the relevance of past data when analysing current (or future) market definitions. Such changes similarly limit the inference that one can draw from historic market share figures of e-commerce platforms as market power may be transitory.

It is widely accepted that the magnitude of market share, by itself, is not necessarily a reliable guide to measuring market power. The same can be said when applied in e-commerce market. For example, a high market share does not necessarily indicate that competition in the market is not effective. It may indicate that an innovative incumbent is reaping the benefits of its innovations over time.

On the other hand, relative market share may also be an important measure. For example, persistently high market share vis-à-vis other competitors with very low market share may be more indicative of market power of an online platform having an entrenched market position because of its network effects.

Volatile historic market share may also reflect that businesses are constantly innovating to stay ahead of each other and that no player in the market has market power.

Barriers to Entry and Expansion

While market share measures the extent of existing competition, barriers to entry and expansion measure the extent of potential competition that a business faces in the market. The lower the entry/ expansion barriers, the more likely it will be for potential competitors to restrain the market power that a business has.

Cost of entry. The effect of e-commerce on the cost of entry is ambiguous. While conventional wisdom suggests that entry costs into markets via online channels (e.g., websites/B2C marketplaces) are considerably lower than setting up a brick-and-mortar store, a "pure play" retailer may still face significant costs when investing in advertising, end-to-end logistics networks, and warehousing in the course of setting up its operations. Online marketplaces may, however, mitigate advertising costs for "pure play" retailers as they provide ready reach to buyers using the marketplace.

Network effects. An often-cited barrier to entry and expansion is network effects. The existence of strong network effects, such as the market "tips" in favour of an incumbent, may mean that competition becomes for the market. This makes it difficult or even impossible for new entrants to compete against the incumbent as the new entrants would have to establish a critical mass of users themselves. The high market share of Facebook amongst social media platforms and Google amongst internet search engines are examples of "highly-concentrated" market structures.

That said, it was observed in the CCS report that the existence of network effects may not necessarily lead to enduring market power in the case of online real estate agents, online travel intermediaries or dating websites. This is attributed to other reasons e.g., differentiated offerings by suppliers, and heterogeneity of consumer preference (DotEcon 2015).

Differences in assessing barriers to entry and expansion. While the analysis of the barriers to entry and expansion are closely related, they are likely to differ in the context of e-commerce markets. For example, the barriers to entry are low because the cost associated with setting up a new online marketplace is low. However, the barriers to expansion may be high due to the existence of network effects.

Customer data is another example on why barriers to entry and expansion differ. New entrants may find it difficult to replicate the vast customer data that incumbents have in order to compete effectively against them.

To become an effective competitive constraint, an entrant must be able to attain enough scale to constrain the market power of an incumbent. It is therefore important to assess these barriers together.

Buyers' Power

Buyers can constrain the market power that a business has through various means e.g., negotiating for better terms, switching to alternatives, intensifying competition amongst sellers or "sponsor" new entry.

Multi-homing and switching. Where customers (in cases of B2C marketplaces, both sellers listed on and buyers using the online platform are customers) are able to multi-home, there is greater scope for entrants to enter the market. That said, online platforms may introduce barriers to switching (e.g., migrating user data from one platform to another, offering loyalty discounts and rebates) such that customers are disincentivized to multi-home. Customers may also be ill-informed about alternatives. The same arguments apply for switching.

5. Conclusion

On the whole, while e-commerce changes the behaviour of businesses and consumers, it does not give rise to new issues that cannot be dealt with under the existing competition law framework. The fundamental steps in market definition and market power assessment are applicable under the e-commerce environment.

However, e-commerce is likely to affect the focus of investigations and present practical challenges to competition assessments by relevant authorities. In particular, it is highlighted in this chapter that the detailed application of the steps for market definition and market power assessment may require some minor adjustments. Empirical research based on actual competition cases are possible extensions to the study on e-commerce and competition law and may yield useful findings for competition assessments.

NOTES

1. Eileen Lee and Lip Hang Poh are staff members of the Policy and Markets Division at Competition and Consumer Commission of Singapore (CCCS) during 2016–17. While this chapter is contributed by staff members of CCCS, the views expressed are personal and do not represent the official position of CCCS.
2. Prior to 1 April 2018, the Competition and Consumer Commission of Singapore (CCCS) was known as the Competition Commission of Singapore (CCS).
3. The more users are connected to a network, the greater its value to others. Telecommunications networks are a prime example as the value of joining a particular telecoms network increases with the number of subscribers because the user can communicate with more parties.

4. The larger the number of sellers active on an online platform, the higher the utility of the buyers and vice versa.
5. Geo-blocking is an online practice that prevents shoppers in some countries from being able to buy products and services for cheaper prices overseas, through internet service provider (ISP) restrictions.

REFERENCES

Brynjolfsson, Erik, Yu Jeffrey Hu, and Mohammad S. Rahman. "Competing in the Age of Omnichannel Retailing". *MIT Sloan Management Review* (2013): 23–29.

CCCS (Competition and Consumer Commission of Singapore). *CCCS Guidelines on Market Definition.* Singapore: Competition and Consumer Commission of Singapore, 2007.

DotEcon. *E-commerce and its Impact on Competition Policy and Law in Singapore.* Singapore: DotEcon, 2015.

EU DG COMP. *e-Commerce Sector Inquiry Report.* EU DG COMP, 2016.

Euromonitor. *Retailing in Singapore.* Euromonitor, 2014.

Filistrucchi, Lapo, Damien Geradin, Eric van Damme, and Pauline Affeldt. "Market Definition in Two-sided Markets: Theory and Practice". *Journal of Competition Law & Economics* (2014): 293–339.

Office of Fair Trading. *E-commerce and its Implications for Competition Policy, Discussion Paper 1.* Office of Fair Trading, 2000.

Singapore Department of Statistics. "Household Expenditure Survey 2012/2013: Observations on Prevalence of Online Purchases". Singapore: Department of Statistics of Singapore, 2015.

United States Department of Justice. "United States Department of Justice", April 2015. Retrieved from United States of America v David Topkins. https://www.justice.gov/atr/case-document/file/513586/download.

PART III

4

E-COMMERCE AND TRADE POLICY

Cassey Lee

1. Introduction

Electronic commerce, or e-commerce, has become increasingly important globally. Based on UNCTAD's (2017) estimates, the value of global e-commerce was estimated to have reached US$25 trillion in 2015. Of this, US$7 billion are cross-border Business to Consumer (B2C) e-commerce. Using trade data from the World Bank, cross-border B2C accounts for only 0.04 per cent of total global exports. If we assume that the volume of Business to Business (B2B) e-commerce is nine times larger than that of B2C, e-commerce's share of global trade was 0.4 per cent in 2015. Though cross-border e-commerce is still a small portion of global trade, its share is likely to increase significantly in the future. Aliresearch (2016) estimates that global cross-border e-commerce will increase at an annual rate of 27.3 per cent during 2014–20.

The rising importance of e-commerce in global trade is also reflected not only in the inclusion of e-commerce related provisions in trade agreements but the increasingly more detailed coverage of such provisions. Of the 275 regional trade agreements (RTAs) in force and notified to the World Trade Organization (WTO) as of May 2017,

75 RTAs (27.3 per cent) explicitly addressed e-commerce (Monteiro and Teh 2017). More than 60 per cent of the RTAs that have entered into force between 2014 and 2016 contained e-commerce provisions (ibid.). The evolution of e-commerce provisions is also related to the evolution in e-commerce itself. Technological changes have been major drivers of this. Finally, e-commerce provisions in trade agreements also have important implications for domestic policies such as competition policy.

This chapter aims to examine the nature and evolution of e-commerce related provisions in trade agreements. The outline of the chapter is as follows. Section 2 discusses how e-commerce is contextualized within trade policy. Section 3 examines how e-commerce chapters in trade agreement have evolved and the factors driving these changes. Section 4 discusses some of the implications of these provisions for competition. Finally, Section 5 concludes.

2.   Contextualizing E-commerce in Trade Policy

The starting point for placing e-commerce within the context of trade policy is the definition of e-commerce. What is e-commerce and how is it related to cross-border trade in goods and services? The WTO defines e-commerce as "the production, distribution, marketing, sale or delivery of goods and services by electronic means".[1] Based on this definition, it is obvious that cross-border trade can involve e-commerce in which goods and services are ordered and paid through electronic means. Goods can be delivered either physically (software in compact disc) or electronically (software download).

In the early discussions on e-commerce and trade policy, all cross-border trade involving e-commerce in which physical goods are delivered are considered to be under the purview of the General Agreement on Tariffs and Trade (GATT) (Mattoo and Schuknecht 2000; Panagariya 2000). There was, however, some initial uncertainty on how to treat digital goods that are transmitted electronically. Should such trade of goods come under GATT or should they be considered as services which are under the jurisdiction of General Agreement on Trade in Services (GATS)? Based on the provisions in RTAs, there appears to be no consensus on the matter of goods that are delivered via electronic means or transmission (Monteiro and Teh 2017, p. 19).

The applicability of GATS's jurisdiction is clearer when e-commerce involves the delivery of services through electronic means. The most important type of commercial services in world trade in 2010 was business and ICT (48 per cent) followed by distribution (18 per cent) (Francois and Hoekman 2010). More recent data from the WTO (2018, Table A24) shows that the category "other business services" account for about half of world trade in commercial services.

In such a case, a RTA will explicitly specify that the supply of such services falls within the scope of obligations in provisions on trade in services. This applies to all four modes of services delivery:

> The electronic delivery of services falls within the scope of the GATS, since the Agreement applies to all services regardless of the means by which they are delivered, and electronic delivery can take place under any of the four modes of supply. Measures affecting the electronic delivery of services are measures affecting trade in services and would therefore be covered by GATS obligations.[2]

Overall, there is increasing interest and effort, as evidence by RTA provisions, to include e-commerce under the purview of trade agreements though the approaches and terms used might differ from one RTA to another. This is examined in greater detail in the next section.

3. E-commerce Chapters in Trade Agreements

The term e-commerce can appear in many types of provisions in RTAs. It can appear as part of a non-specific article to e-commerce such as a joint statement, a letter or an annex. There could also be a dedicated chapter to e-commerce (Monteiro and Teh 2017). E-commerce chapters in trade agreements have evolved over time. Weber (2015) suggests that there have been four distinct periods in the evolution of e-commerce chapters in trade agreements:

- 2000–2: Paperless trading
- 2003: The birth of e-commerce chapters
- 2004–11: A mixed picture
- 2014 and beyond: New generation of liberalized Preferential Trade Areas (PTAs)

Though the subsequent discussions do not use this periodization, it is still a useful framework to examine the evolution of e-commerce chapters in selected trade agreements.

The early provisions that are related to e-commerce in trade agreements focused on the promotion of trade facilitation using paperless trading. This is evidenced by the New Zealand–Singapore Closer Economic Partnership Agreement (2000). The paragraph on e-commerce was designated under "Part 4: Customs Procedures". It reads:

> With a view to implementing the APEC Blueprint for Action on Electronic Commerce, in particular the Paperless Trading Initiative, the Customs administrations of both Parties shall have in place by the date of entry into force of this Agreement an electronic environment that supports electronic business applications between each Customs administration and its trading community.

Though the above provision relates to trade facilitation, it is considered to be part of a strategy to promote e-commerce development. Reference is made to the APEC Blueprint for Action on Electronic Commerce (APEC-BAEC), which is a programme approved by APEC ministers in 1998. It is aimed at promoting e-commerce development.

Subsequently, the implementation of paperless trading is further encouraged by a stronger emphasis on the implementation and monitoring of paperless trading. This can be found in the agreement between Japan and Singapore for a New-Age Economic Partnership signed in 2002 which contained a whole chapter (five) with the heading "Paperless Trading". There are five articles in the chapter. These articles focus on cooperation to promote and realize paperless trading. A review mechanism is put in place to ensure timely implementation of paperless trading.

The United States–Singapore Free Trade Agreement (USSFTA) signed in 2003 marked a shift towards more detailed provisions on e-commerce. Article 14.2 of the e-commerce chapter (Chapter 14) ensures that the supply of services via electronic means fall within the scope of the other chapters of trade in services, financial services and investment. Article 14.3, which deals with digital product, contains several important provisions, namely:

- Zero customs duties, fees or charges on import or export of digital products by electronic transmission.

- Determination of the customs value of an imported carrier medium based on cost alone and not the value of the digital product stored.
- Non-discriminatory treatment of digital products and the authors, performers, producers, developers, or distributors of the products.

The e-commerce chapter in the USSFTA is a significant turning point as the status of cross-border e-commerce trade has become more formalized along the lines of the traditional provisions on trade in goods and services in trade agreements. The zero tariff on digital products transmitted electronically also provides a very clear and explicit provision on how such products should be treated within the trade regime.

By the late 2000s, though not all FTAs contained chapters on e-commerce, some of the FTAs signed during this time contained significantly more detailed treatment of e-commerce (Weber 2015). One example is the ASEAN–Australia–New Zealand Free Trade Agreement (AANZFTA) signed in 2009. Chapter 10 on e-commerce had the following objectives: (a) promote electronic commerce among the Parties; (b) enhance cooperation among the Parties regarding development of electronic commerce; and (c) promote the wider use of electronic commerce globally. The chapter contained provisions on the adoption of domestic regulatory framework for e-commerce (based on the UNCITRAL Model Law on Electronic Commerce), electronic authentication systems and digital certificates, online consumer protection, online data protection and paperless trading (customs). These provisions clearly indicate a trend towards more specific and micro-level cooperation aimed at building institutions (law and regulations) that facilitate e-commerce transactions.

More recently, an important development in e-commerce chapters in FTAs is the signing of the Comprehensive and Progressive Agreement for Trans-Pacific Partnership (CPTPP). Following the withdrawal of the United States from the Trans-Pacific Partnership (TPP) in early 2017, the renegotiation that resulted in the CPTPP involved the suspension of twenty-two items in the TPP. The chapter on e-commerce (Chapter 14 in TPP) was not affected. The e-commerce chapter in CPTPP contains many of the provisions found in earlier FTAs. These include a moratorium on duties on electronically transmitted goods, non-discriminatory treatment of digital products, electronic authentication systems and digital certificates, online consumer protection, online data protection and paperless trading. Newer-type provisions include:

i.   Location of computing facilities
ii. Source code

Many of these have implications for market access. This is discussed in greater detail in the next section.

4. Implications for Competition

Most recent FTAs have provisions on competition policy. E-commerce, in comparison, is a relatively new subject in trade agreements. Even though competition policy is already covered in FTAs, often as a distinct chapter, the e-commerce provisions do have implications on competition in domestic markets. The CPTPP, for example, is used to discuss this.

The moratorium on customs duties on electronic transmissions (Item 1 in Article 14.3 in TPP agreement) does imply that digital goods that are transmitted electronically have advantage compared to imported physical goods that are subject to custom duties. The idea behind the moratorium which dates back to WTO discussions in the late 1990s was aimed at encouraging the development of e-commerce. Whilst there is a provision (Item 2) that allows for imposition of internal taxes, fees or other charges on content transmitted electronically, it does not address direct imports via cross-border electronic transmissions.

Article 14.13 (Location of Computing Facilities) in the TPP states that a country cannot compel investors to use or locate computing facilities in that country as a condition for conducting business there. This clearly applies to multinational e-commerce companies that are interested to operate in the countries but maintain their data centres elsewhere. A government can impose such rules to achieve an objective such as security but this action must not be "arbitrary or unjustifiable discrimination or a disguised restriction on trade" (Item 3(a)). This type of provision links market access to related investments in vertical aspects of firms' operations.

Another provision that affects competition is that on source code (Article 14.17 in TPP). The provision applies to mass-market software or products containing such software. It states that:

> No Party shall require the transfer of, or access to, source code of software owned by a person of another Party, as a condition for the import, distribution, sale or use of such software, or of products containing such software, in its territory.

This provision clearly states that market access should not be conditional upon the transfer of source code. It separates market access from the protection of intellectual property rights (source code in this case).

The three examples from the e-commerce chapter in the CPTPP/ TPP clearly indicate that e-commerce provisions in trade agreements can have competition-related implications in areas such as level-playing field and market access. They can also link competition to other issues such as vertical investments and property rights.

5. Conclusions

Overall, e-commerce has become an increasingly important feature in trade agreements. E-commerce related provisions have evolved since the early 2000s. Early provisions focused on trade facilitation via paperless trading. Whilst this continues to be important in subsequent FTAs, new provisions that focused on moratorium of duties on electronic transmissions and non-discriminatory treatment of digital goods were added. Some of the provisions dealt with agreements to implement institutions that support the development of e-commerce. These included electronic authentication systems and digital certificates, regulations and laws on consumer protection and data protection. For some of the recent FTAs, the scope of the e-commerce chapter has grown cumulatively by including provisions in other preceding FTAs and incorporating new ones. New FTAs, such as the CPTPP, include important new provisions that affect competition in terms of level playing field and market access. Market access can also be tied to issues related to vertical investments and property rights. The e-commerce provisions in trade agreements are likely to evolve further in the future as e-commerce becomes more important and as technological changes bring about new challenges.

NOTES

1. World Trade Organization, "Electronic Commerce", n.d., https://www.wto.org/english/thewto_e/minist_e/mc11_e/briefing_notes_e/bfecom_e.htm.
2. World Trade Organization, "The Challenges Ahead", n.d., https://www.wto.org/english/tratop_e/serv_e/cbt_course_e/c6s5p2_e.htm.

REFERENCES

Aliresearch. "Global Cross Border B2C e-Commerce Market 2020: Report Highlights and Methodology Sharing", April 2016. https://unctad.org/meetings/en/Presentation/dtl_eweek2016_AlibabaResearch_en.pdf.

Francois, Joseph and Bernard Hoekman. "Services Trade and Policy". *Journal of Economic Literature* 48, no. 3 (2010): 642–92.

Mattoo, Aaditya and Ludger Schuknecht. "Trade Policies for Electronic Commerce". Policy Research Working Paper No. 2380. World Bank, 2000.

Monteiro, Jose-Antonio and Robert Teh. "Provisions on Electronic Commerce in Regional Trade Agreements". WTO Working Paper ERSD-2017-11, 2017.

OECD (Organisation for Economic Co-operation and Development). *Economic Outlook for Southeast Asia, China and India 2018 – Update*. Paris: Organisation for Economic Co-operation and Development, 2018.

Panagariya, Arvind. "E-commerce, WTO and Developing Countries". *World Economy* 23, no. 8 (2000): 959–78.

UNCTAD (United Nations Conference on Trade and Development). "In Search of Cross-Border E-commerce Trade Data". Technical Note No. 6, TN/UNCTAD/ICT4D/06, 2016.

———. *Information Economy Report 2017*. Geneva: United Nations Conference on Trade and Development, 2017.

Weber, Rolf. "Digital Trade and E-commerce: Challenges and Opportunities of the Asia-Pacific Regionalism". *Asian Journal of WTO & International Health Law and Policy* 10, no. 2 (2015): 321–48.

World Bank. *World Development Report 2016*. Washington, D.C.: World Bank, 2016.

WTO (World Trade Organization). *World Trade Statistical Review 2018*. Geneva: World Trade Organization, 2018.

PART IV

5

E-COMMERCE AND ITS DEVELOPMENT IN THAILAND

Yot Amornkitvikai and Jiraporn Tangpoolcharoen

1. Introduction

Information and communication technology (ICT) development since the late 1990s has enhanced the activities of entrepreneurs and enterprises by improving their access to digital networks. In addition, electronic commerce (e-commerce) has been a major engine in the development of global trade. This has been achieved by enhancing international value chains, market access, internal and market efficiency, and reducing transaction costs (UNCTAD 2015).

However, the use of e-commerce has been mainly restricted to large enterprises in developed countries (UNCTAD 2010). This implies that there might be barriers to e-commerce existing in developing countries, especially for small and medium sized enterprises. According to Kshetri (2007), barriers to e-commerce can be classified into the following: (i) economic barriers which refer to unreliable and costly power supply, inadequate ICT infrastructure and use, limited use of credit cards, lack of purchasing power, and weak financial systems, (ii) sociopolitical barriers which refer to weak legal and regulatory frameworks, cultural preferences for face-to-face interaction and reliance on cash in society, and (iii) cognitive barriers which may involve poor ICT literacy, awareness and knowledge related to e-commerce among both consumers and enterprises.

The objectives of this study are as follows: (1) to provide an overview of Thailand's e-commerce; (2) to discuss factors influencing the scope of e-commerce as suggested by the UNCTAD, such as internet access, payment systems for online purchases, and delivery systems; (3) to provide empirically based policy implications and recommendations in order to enhance the e-commerce performance of Thai entrepreneurs.

In this study, the survey of Thailand's e-commerce conducted by the Electronic Transactions Development Agency (Public Organization) (ETDA) in 2015 is used to investigate the factors influencing the performance of e-commerce enterprises as well as their e-commerce engagement (B2C, B2B, and B2G). This is the first study to examine Thailand's e-commerce using firm-level data from the survey.

2.   An Overview of Thailand's E-commerce

The OECD (2011, p. 72) has defined e-commerce as follows:

> The sale or purchase of goods or services, conducted over computer networks by methods specially designed for the purpose of receiving or placing of orders. The goods or services are ordered by those methods, but the payment and the ultimate delivery of the goods or services do not have to be conducted online. An e-commerce transaction can be between enterprises, households, individuals, governments, and other public or private organizations. To be included are orders made over the web, extranet or electronic data interchange. The type is defined by the method of placing the order. To be excluded are orders made by telephone calls, facsimile or manually typed e-mail.

The definition of e-commerce adopted by the ETDA is based on OECD's narrow definition of e-commerce transactions:[1]

> An internet transaction is the sale or purchase of goods or services, whether between businesses, households, individuals, governments, and other public or private organizations, conducted over the Internet. The goods and services are ordered over the Internet, but the payment and the ultimate delivery of the goods or services may be conducted on or off-line. To be included are orders received or placed on any Internet application used in automated transactions such as web pages, Extranets and other applications that run over the Internet, such as

EDI over the Internet, Minitel over the Internet, or over any other web enabled application regardless of how the web is accessed (e.g. through a mobile or a TV set, etc.). To be excluded are orders received or placed by telephone, facsimile, or conventional e-mail (OECD 2011, p. 72).

E-commerce has increasingly played an important role in boosting Thailand's economy and its competitiveness, since it helps expand the marketing channels to strengthen upstream and downstream enterprises in the supply chain, and also promotes the cooperation between enterprises (Chen and Zhang 2015). In addition, e-commerce is likely to boost international flows of many services significantly (OECD 2011). It has also offered considerable opportunities for enterprises in Thailand, especially Thai SMEs to grow and rationalize their businesses.

According to the ETDA (2016b), as shown in Figure 5.1, the value of the e-commerce[2] trading, including e-auction[3] in Thailand, increased from US$62.6 billion in 2014 to US$71.505 billion in 2016. This implies that e-commerce has increasingly become important for the country's economy, accounting for 43.47 per cent of the country's total sales value of goods and services and 16.59 per cent of GDP in 2015. According to the ETDA (2016b), the number of e-commerce entrepreneurs also increased from 502,676 establishments in 2014 to 526,324 establishments in 2015, implying a significant shift in consumer behaviour in the digital age. In response to these trends, the Thai government aims to promote the country's digital economy and enhance its competitiveness in the ASEAN Economic Community.

Business to Business (B2B) transactions is the most important type of e-commerce in the country in terms of the value of transactions (see Figure 5.2). This is followed by Business to Consumer (B2C) and Business to Government (B2G) transactions. From Figure 5.2 the e-commerce value of B2B was US$39.14 billion in 2016, accounting for 54.74 per cent of total e-commerce value in 2016. The importance of B2B e-commerce in Thailand could be due to upstream supply chain activities involving sub components or raw materials. Whilst the volume of B2B transactions has remained relatively stable in recent years, B2C transactions has increased rapidly from US$12.7 billion in 2014 to US$20.7 billion in 2016. As a result, B2C's share of total e-commerce value increased from 20.25 per cent in 2014 to 28.89 per cent in 2016.

FIGURE 5.1
Thailand's E-commerce Value, 2014–16

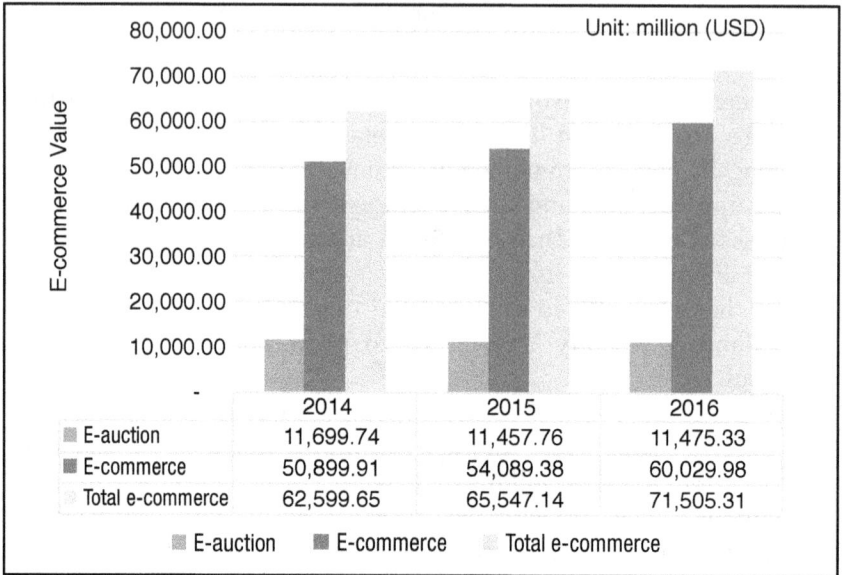

	2014	2015	2016
E-auction	11,699.74	11,457.76	11,475.33
E-commerce	50,899.91	54,089.38	60,029.98
Total e-commerce	62,599.65	65,547.14	71,505.31

Source: ETDA (2016*b*).

FIGURE 5.2
Thailand's E-commerce Value, Classified by
E-commerce Engagement, 2014–16

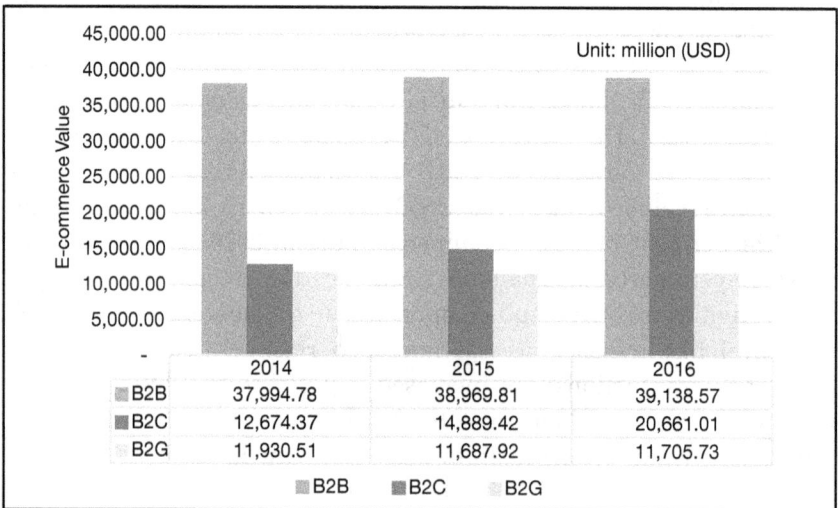

	2014	2015	2016
B2B	37,994.78	38,969.81	39,138.57
B2C	12,674.37	14,889.42	20,661.01
B2G	11,930.51	11,687.92	11,705.73

Source: ETDA (2016*b*).

In terms of the types of economic sectors, accommodation was the most important industry for Thailand's e-commerce (see Figure 5.3). Its share of total e-commerce was 30.21 per cent and 30.35 per cent in 2014 and 2015, respectively. This is followed by retail and wholesale trade, information and communication, transportation and storage, art, entertainment and recreation, insurance, and other services. However, by 2016, the retail and wholesale industry's share of total e-commerce value at 34.54 per cent was the largest.

FIGURE 5.3
E-commerce Value Classified by Industrial Sectors

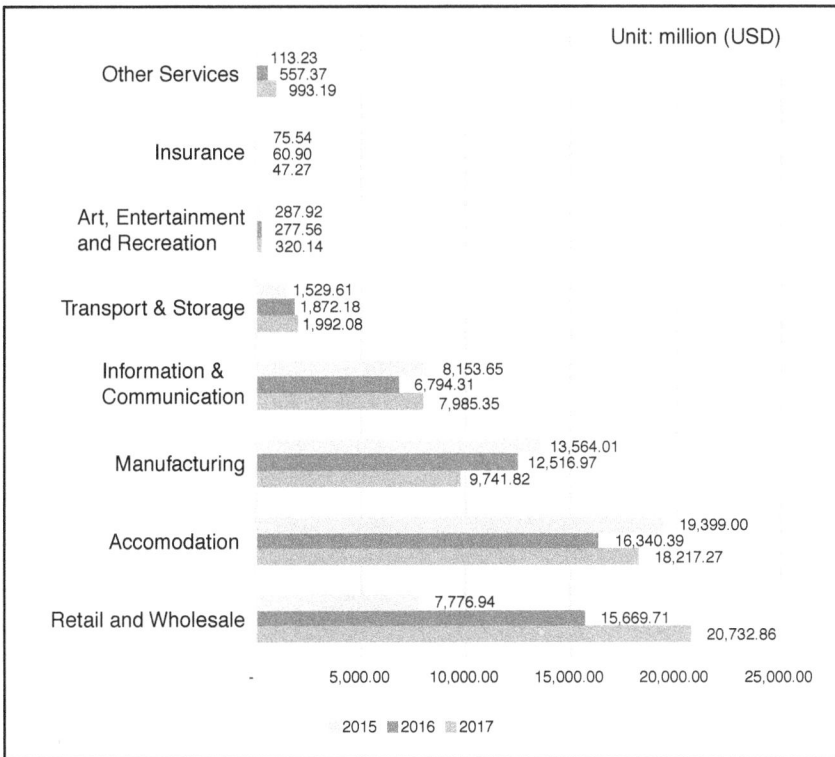

Source: ETDA (2016*b*).

Analysing the value of the different types of e-commerce in each industry, B2B is the predominant type of e-commerce in the manufacturing sector, accounting for 99.65 per cent of the total value of e-commerce value in the industry in 2016 (see Figure 5.4). However, B2C plays a predominant role in the art, entertainment, and recreation industry (91.94 per cent of its total e-commerce value). Finally, B2G does not seem to be an important type of e-commerce in any industrial sector.

According to the ETDA (2016b) as indicated in Figure 5.5, large enterprises still dominate the e-commerce market. Large enterprises' e-commerce value was US$27,559.04 million in 2016, accounting for 65.99 per cent of total e-commerce value in 2016. However, the e-commerce value of small and medium sized enterprises was US$14,206.39 billion in 2016, accounting for 34.01 per cent of total e-commerce value in 2016. These figures could imply that there is generally a lack of awareness of the full range of SME potential in adopting ICT for a variety of commercial and production-related purposes (OECD 2001). In contrast, large firms such as Lazada (Thailand) has significantly advanced over its domestic e-commerce competitors (ECOMMERCEIQ 2017).

FIGURE 5.4
E-commerce Value of Each Industry, Classified by
Types of E-commerce, 2016

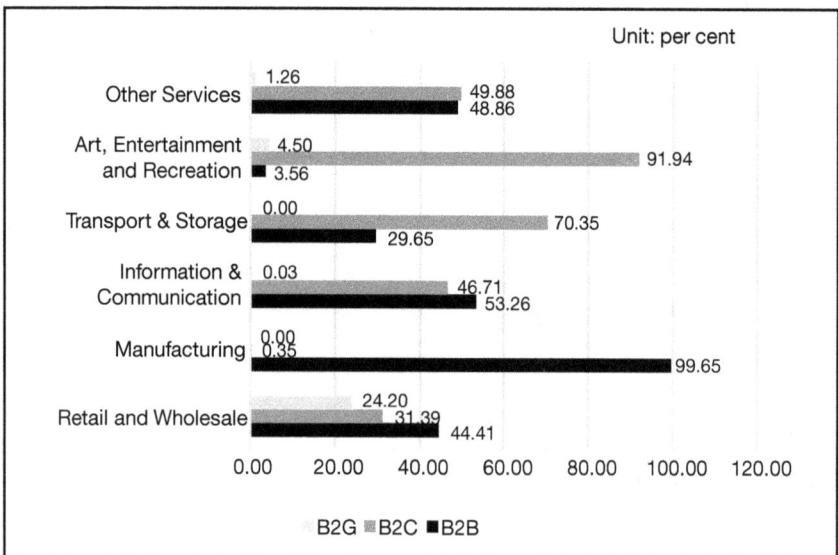

Source: ETDA (2016b).

FIGURE 5.5
E-commerce Value of Large Enterprises and SMEs

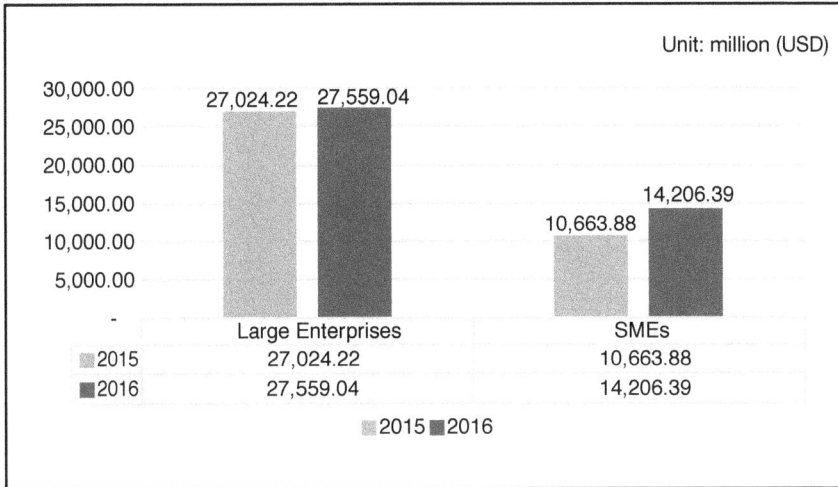

Unit: million (USD)

	Large Enterprises	SMEs
2015	27,024.22	10,663.88
2016	27,559.04	14,206.39

2015 ■2016

Source: ETDA (2016*b*).

Comparing Thailand's e-commerce size with other countries as indicated in Figure 5.6, it is found that Thailand's B2C e-commerce value per capita has increased from US$172.76 in 2014 to US$230.89 in 2015. Despite such rapid growth, Thailand is still far behind other countries such as the United States, Japan, South Korea, Singapore, China, and Malaysia. In the ASEAN region, Thailand's B2C e-commerce value per capita is still higher than Vietnam, the Philippines, and Indonesia.

Given the growing importance of Thailand's e-commerce, the Thai government has set out its policy to support Thailand's ICT infrastructure development, which emphasizes on using the ICT as a tool to promote the country's economy. As a result, various government agencies such as the Ministry of Digital Economy and Society and the National Electronics and Computer Technology Center also play an important role to strengthen the efficiency of Thailand's industrial sectors. In addition, the Department of Business Development under the supervision of the Ministry of Commerce supports the establishment of e-commerce businesses in Thailand (Panuspatthna 2013).

FIGURE 5.6
B2C E-commerce Value Per Capita for Selected Countries

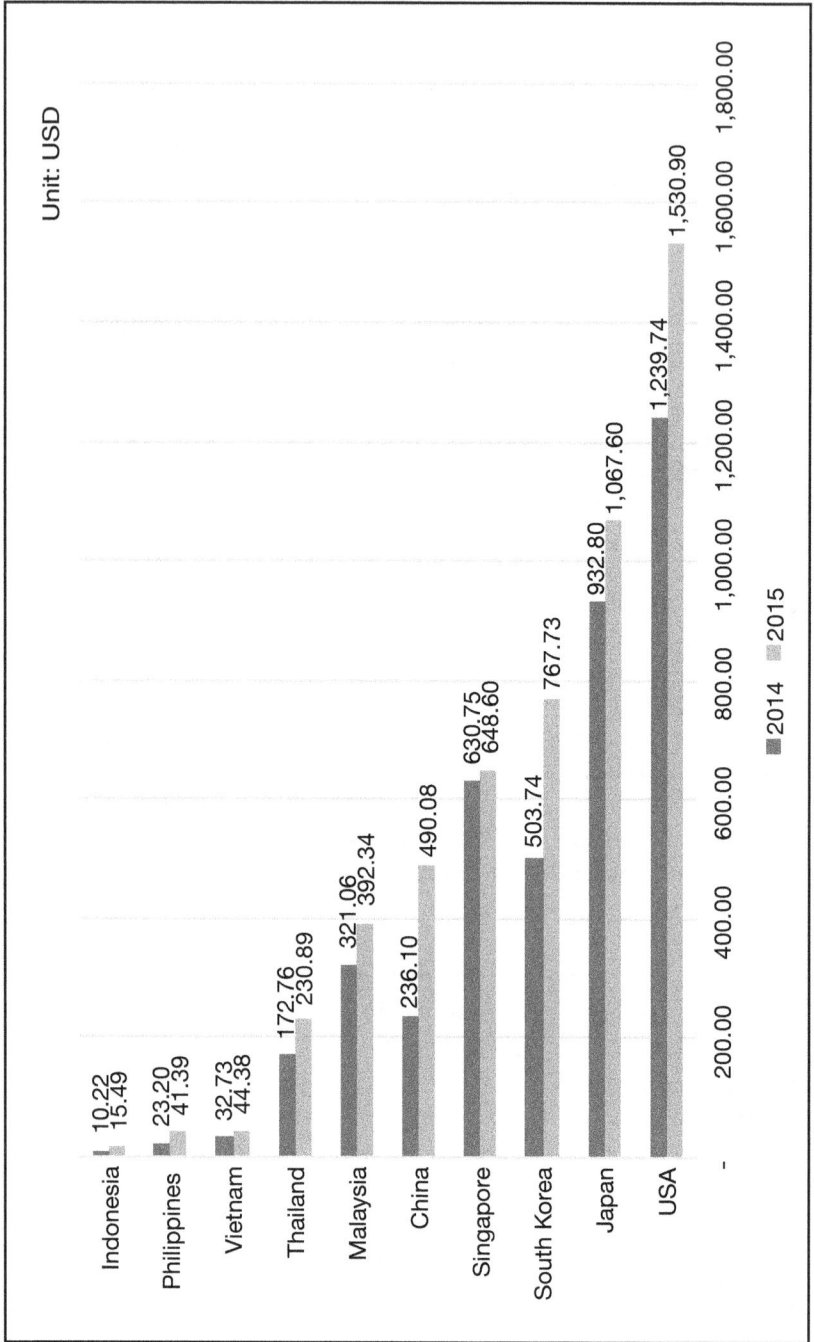

Unit: USD

Country	2014	2015
Indonesia	10.22	15.49
Philippines	23.20	41.39
Vietnam	32.73	44.38
Thailand	172.76	230.89
Malaysia	321.06	392.34
China	236.10	490.08
Singapore	630.75	648.60
South Korea	503.74	767.73
Japan	932.80	1,067.60
USA	1,239.74	1,530.90

Source: ETDA (2016b).

3.   Factors Influencing the Scope of E-commerce

According to UNCTAD (2015), to access a country's e-commerce potential, it is necessary to consider a number of factors influencing the scope for its e-commerce engagement, such as affordable internet access, mechanisms for paying for goods and services ordered online, effective solutions for their delivery (electronically or physically), and the legal and regulatory framework. These are discussed in detail as follows:

Internet Access

Internet access for both buyers and sellers is vital in conducting e-commerce businesses in the country. UNCTAD (2015) suggested that internet access is found to be positively related to firm size. This implies that larger firms tend to use internet more to conduct their online businesses than small firms (UNCTAD 2015). According to the ETDA (2015), internet usage has become increasingly important in Thailand due to changes in internet usage behaviour in many dimensions as follows: (i) increasing duration of usage, (ii) increasing usage site, (iii) cheap devices used to access the internet, (iv) activities carried out online, and (v) problems encountered in internet usage and its duration. According to Thai internet users' behaviour survey conducted by the ETDA in 2016, the average number of hours spent on the internet per week for Thai internet users vary across several attributes such as gender, generation, residence, educational attainment, and household income.

Comparing among age groups as indicated in Figure 5.7, Thais born during 1991–2000 (Generation Y) spent on average the longest hours on the internet, at 54.2 hours per week, followed by Thais from the Generations X, Z, and baby boomers.[4] This finding also implies that Generation Y are really interested in information technology (IT) and online communication, since the internet and social media are very popular while they are growing up. However, Thais from the baby boom generation are not really interested in using the interest and social media, resulting in the lowest hours on the internet, at 32.5 hours per week on average. In terms of geographical differences, internet users who reside in Bangkok metropolitan region spent on average the longest hours on the internet, at 53.8 hours per week, followed by those who reside outside municipal areas in other provinces (47.7 hours per week) and those who reside inside municipal areas in other provinces (44.4 hours per week), respectively.

FIGURE 5.7
Average Number of Hours Spent on the Internet Per Week, Classified by Internet User's General Attributes

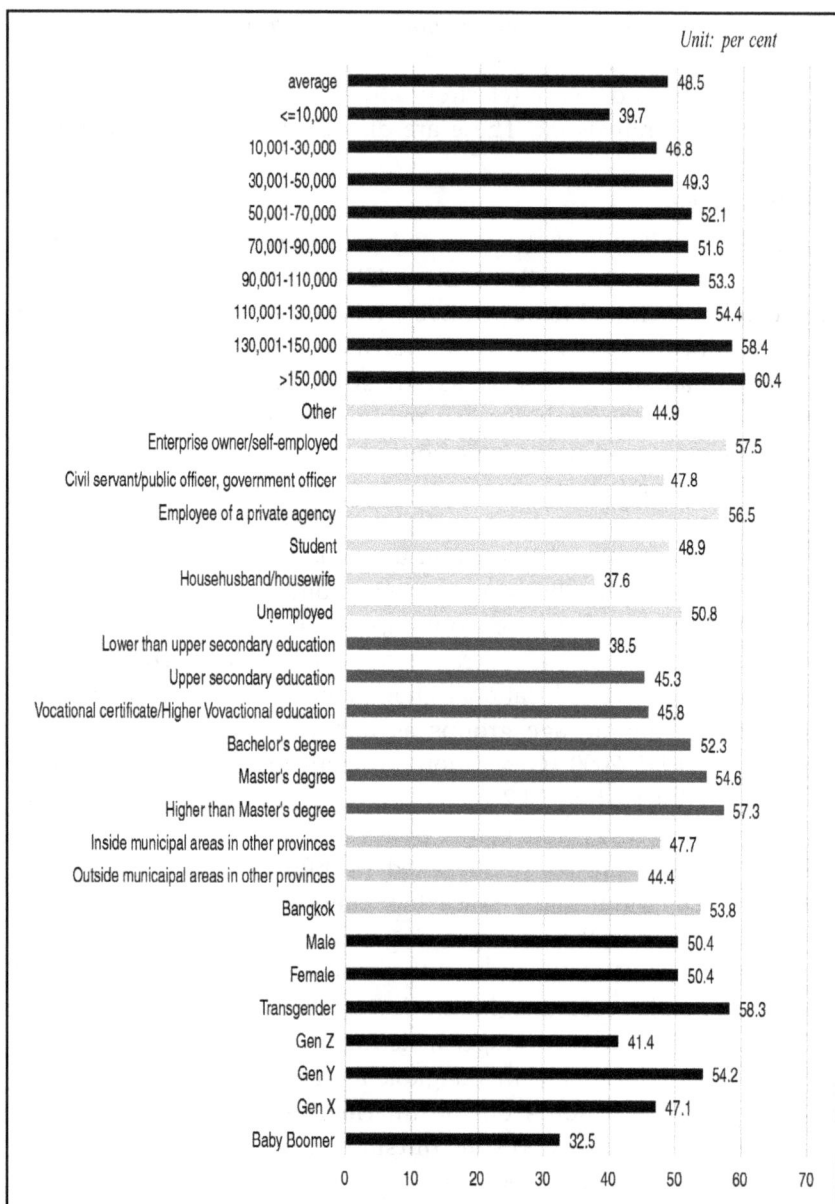

Unit: per cent

average	48.5
<=10,000	39.7
10,001-30,000	46.8
30,001-50,000	49.3
50,001-70,000	52.1
70,001-90,000	51.6
90,001-110,000	53.3
110,001-130,000	54.4
130,001-150,000	58.4
>150,000	60.4
Other	44.9
Enterprise owner/self-employed	57.5
Civil servant/public officer, government officer	47.8
Employee of a private agency	56.5
Student	48.9
Househusband/housewife	37.6
Unemployed	50.8
Lower than upper secondary education	38.5
Upper secondary education	45.3
Vocational certificate/Higher Vovactional education	45.8
Bachelor's degree	52.3
Master's degree	54.6
Higher than Master's degree	57.3
Inside municipal areas in other provinces	47.7
Outside municaipal areas in other provinces	44.4
Bangkok	53.8
Male	50.4
Female	50.4
Transgender	58.3
Gen Z	41.4
Gen Y	54.2
Gen X	47.1
Baby Boomer	32.5

Source: ETDA (2015*a*).

This suggests that the IT infrastructure in Bangkok metropolitan region is more readily available than that in other provinces (ETDA 2015*a*). In addition, education attainment and household income are positively related to the number of hours spent on the internet. Internet users with education attainment higher than master's degree spent on average the longest hours on the internet, at 57.3 hours per week, followed by internet users with master's degree (54.6 hours per week) and those with bachelor's degree (52.3 hours per week). Internet users whose yearly average household income is higher than 150,000 baht spent the longest hours on average at 60.4 hours per week. However, it is found that the number of hours spent on the internet decrease when their average household incomes reduce.

With respect to the employment status, it is found that internet users who are enterprise owners or self-employed are likely to spend on average the longest hours on the internet, at 57.5 hours per week, followed by employees of private agencies (56.5 hours per week), unemployed (50.8 hours per week), students (48.9 hours per week), civil servants (47.8 hours per week), and housewives (37.6 hours per week).

From Figure 5.8 it is found that 88.8 per cent of internet users mostly access the internet at home (accommodation), followed by at the workplace (43.2 per cent), travelling places (26.0 per cent), educational institutions (19.8 per cent), public places (13.2 per cent), internet café (3.1 per cent), and other internet usage sites (1.2 per cent). This implies that most internet users prefer to surf the net when they are at home or at the workplace, since they might find that these places are more secured for their online activities.

Comparing internet users by gender and generation group as indicated in Figure 5.9, it is found that internet users across all gender and generation groups mostly prefer to surf the net at home (accommodation). Comparing the use of internet at the workplace in all generation groups and gender, it is found that Generation Z internet users are likely to prefer surfing the net at home (accommodation), followed by internet users in Generations Y, X, and baby boomers, respectively. Most transgender internet users tend to surf the net at home (accommodation), followed by female internet users and male users, respectively. This descending order of gender groups is also

FIGURE 5.8
Internet Usage Sites for Internet Users, 2015

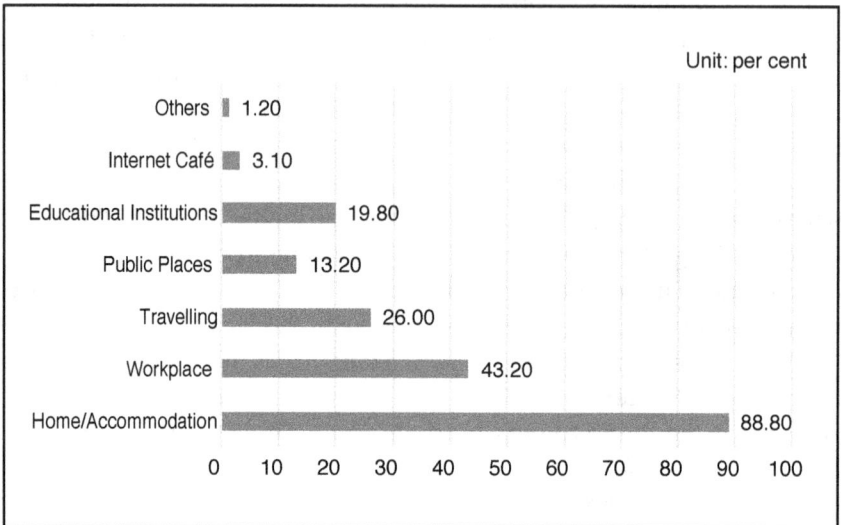

Source: ETDA (2015*a*).

applied for the case of travelling places. However, male internet users are likely to surf the net at their workplace, followed by female internet users and transgender users as indicated in Figure 5.9.

For e-commerce enterprises it is crucial to consider social media sites which internet users regularly use, since this would help understand consumer behaviours leading to an increase in e-commerce enterprises' revenues through these social media sites. Figure 5.10 shows that Facebook is the most popular site for internet users, since 92.1 per cent of internet users prefer to use Facebook as their first choice of internet sites, followed by Line app (85.1 per cent), Google+ (67.0 per cent), Instagram (43.9 per cent), Twitter (21.0 per cent), and WhatsApp (2.8 per cent), respectively.

When genders and generation groups are taken into consideration as indicated in Figure 5.11, it is found that Facebook is the most popular social media site for all generation groups. About 94.9 per cent of Generation Y internet users prefer to use Facebook as their

FIGURE 5.9

Internet Users Classified by Gender, Generation and Internet Usage Site

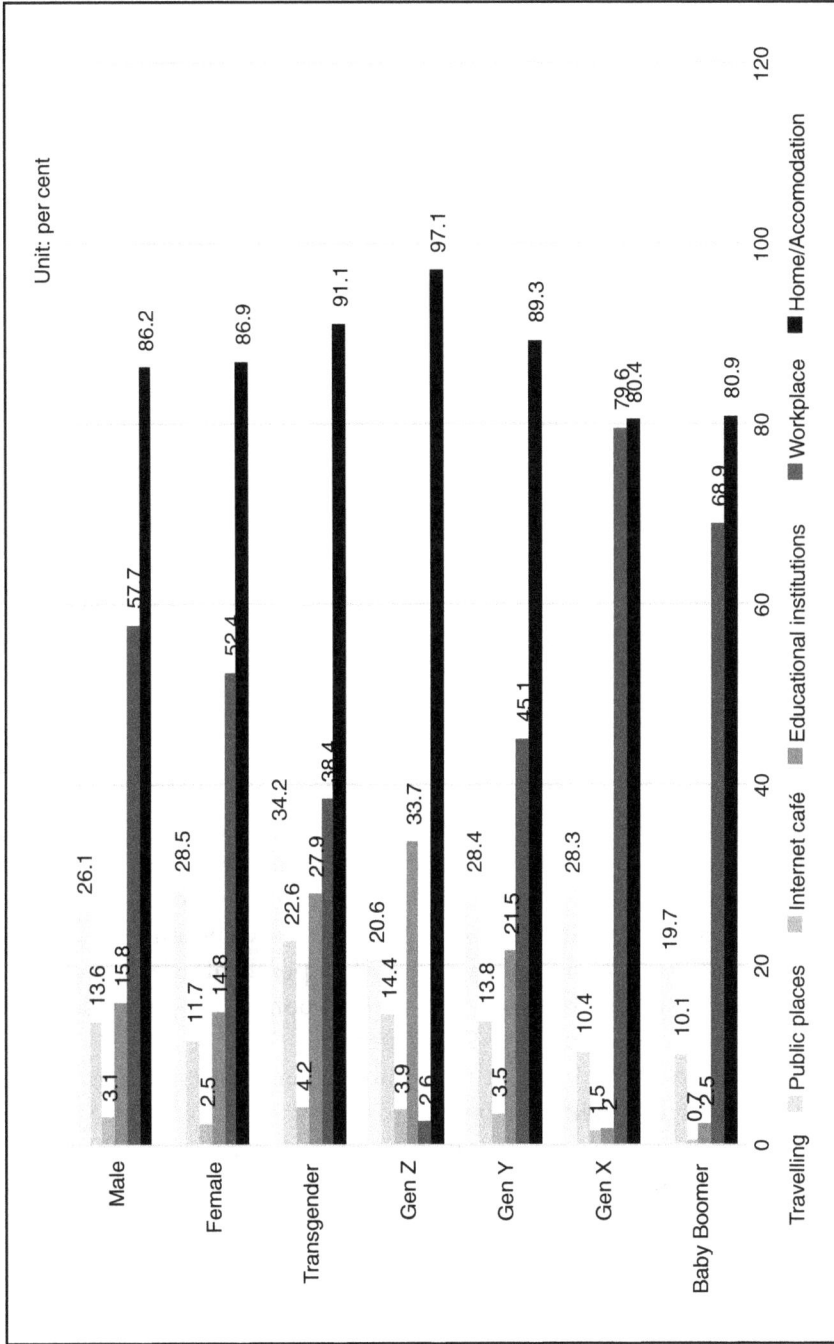

Unit: per cent

Source: ETDA (2015a).

FIGURE 5.10
Internet Users' Regularly Used Social Media Sites

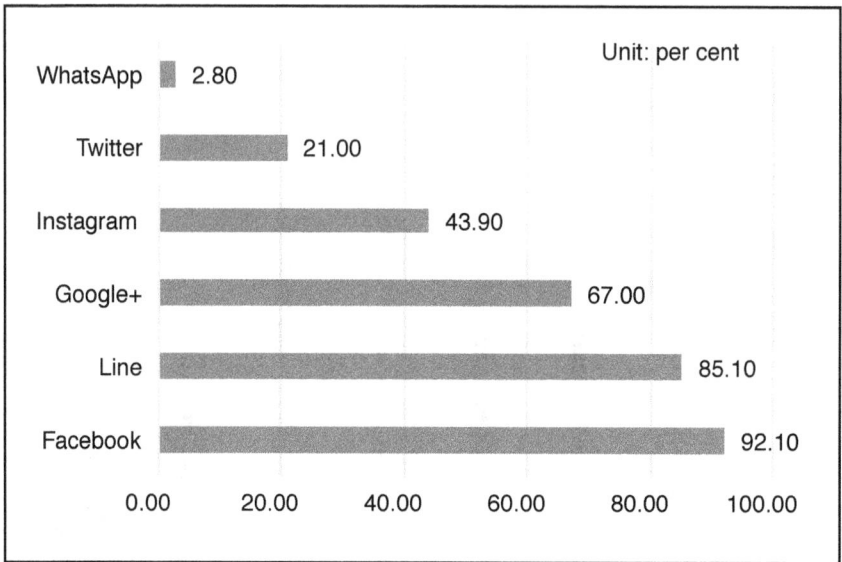

Source: ETDA (2015a).

first choice of social media site, followed by 91.5 per cent of Generation Z internet users, 90.5 per cent of Generation X internet users, and 75.6 per cent of baby boomer internet users. The private messaging app Line is ranked the second choice for all generation groups. More specifically, 92.5 per cent of Generation X internet users use Line app, followed by 88.3 per cent of Generation Y internet users, 81.6 per cent of baby boomer internet users, and 71.9 per cent of Generation Z internet users.

In addition, 75.7 per cent of baby boomer internet users prefer to use Google+, followed by 70.9 per cent of Generation X internet users, 66.0 per cent of Generation Z internet users, and 64.9 per cent of Generation Y internet users. For Instagram and WhatsApp applications, Generation Z internet users prefer to use these applications

FIGURE 5.11

Internet Users' Regularly Used Social Media Sites, Classified by Gender and Generation

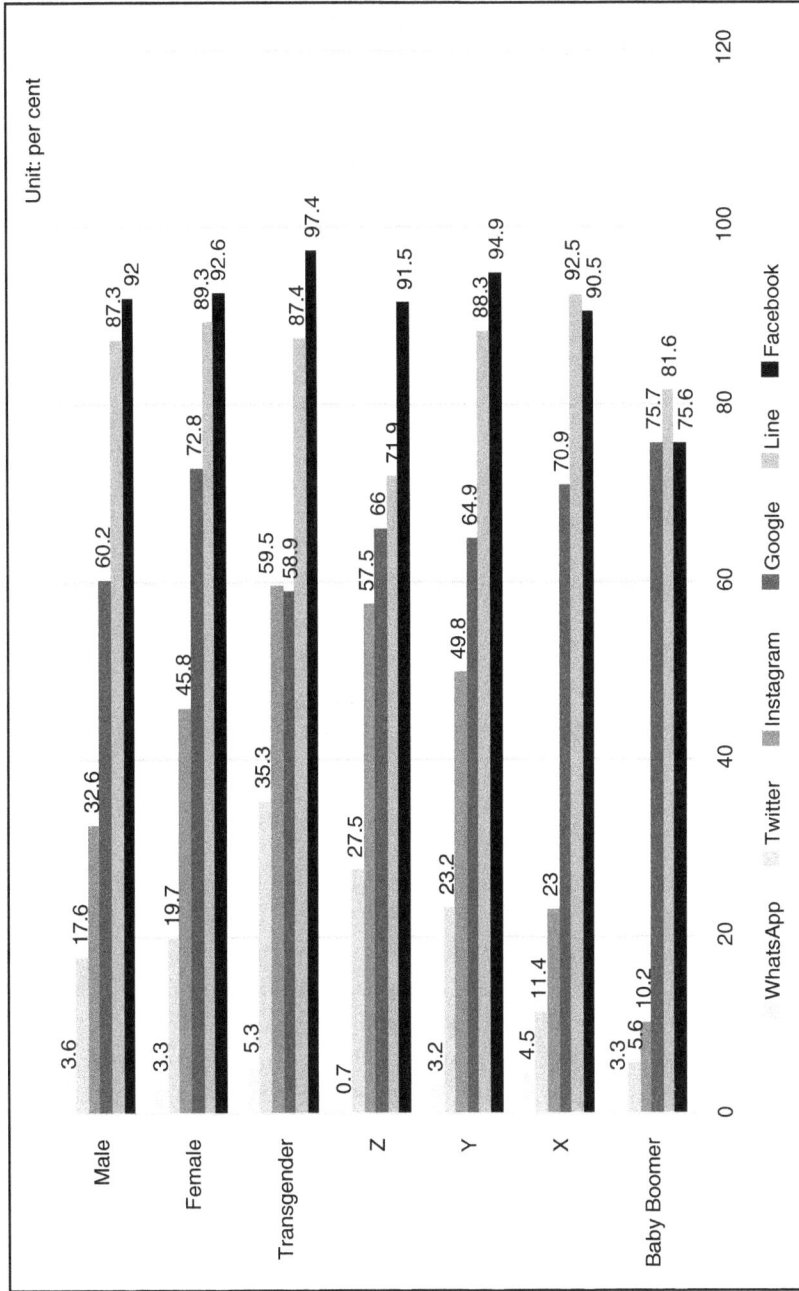

Unit: per cent

	WhatsApp	Twitter	Instagram	Google	Line	Facebook
Male	3.6	17.6	32.6	60.2	87.3	92
Female	3.3	19.7	45.8	72.8	89.3	92.6
Transgender	5.3	35.3	59.5	58.9	87.4	97.4
Z	0.7	27.5	57.5	66	71.9	91.5
Y	3.2	23.2	49.8	64.9	88.3	94.9
X	4.5	11.4	23	70.9	92.5	90.5
Baby Boomer	3.3	5.6	10.2	75.7	81.6	75.6

Source: ETDA (2015a).

for their first choice of social media sites, followed by Generation Y internet users, Generation X internet users, and baby boomer internet users.

According to all genders, Facebook is the most preferred social media site. Moreover, 97.4 per cent of transgender internet users use Facebook as their primary social media site, followed by 92.6 per cent of female internet users and 92.0 per cent of male internet users. In addition, Line app is the second most widely used social media site for all genders. About 89.3 per cent of female internet users prefer to use this social media app, followed by 87.3 per cent of male internet users and 87.4 per cent of transgender internet users. Google+ is the third most widely used social media app for all genders, except transgender internet users. More specifically, 72.8 per cent of female internet users prefer to use this social media app, followed by 60.2 per cent of male internet users and 58.9 per cent of transgender internet users.

Comparing among genders, 59.5 per cent of transgender internet users refer to use Instagram, followed by 45.8 per cent of female internet users and 32.6 per cent of male internet users. Moreover, 35.3 per cent of transgender internet users prefer to use Twitter app, followed by 19.7 per cent of male internet users and 17.6 per cent of transgender internet users.

Payment Systems for Online Purchases

For all types of e-commerce, access to competitive payment solutions is an important facilitator (UNCTAD 2015). Unlike brick-and-mortar retail stores, online retailers often require payment from buyers before completing their sale. Payment systems facilitate the payment for goods and services by consumers and corporate buyers.

For account-based payments systems, online payment systems involve payment through an existing personalized account such as (i) credit cards which are the dominant form of online payment in developed countries, (ii) debit card payments which are directly withdrawn from a personal bank account, (iii) electronic money transfer through a payment intermediary (e.g. PayPal) that is linked to e-shoppers' credit, debit or bank accounts, (iv) mobile payment and telephone account systems, and (v) online banking which enables buyers of a bank (or financial institution) to make their payment through the financial institution's website.

For electronic currency systems, buyers are able to make their payment as long as they have an adequate amount of electronic currency. This type has two forms as follows: (i) smart card systems which are used for buyers to pay small amounts within organizations and (ii) online cash systems which are software-only electronic money instruments based on signed money such as prepaid cards (UNCTAD 2015). According to the survey on Thai internet users' profile conducted by the ETDA (2015a), buyers are able to pay for goods and services purchased through online channels such as electronic cards and via offline channels such as bank transfer, ATM terminals, and cash payment on delivery.

According to Table 5.1, most online buyers are likely to use offline payment channels to pay for goods and services purchased online. Payment at bank counter service is the most important payment channel, accounting for over 65 per cent, followed by payment via ATM terminals at 31.2 per cent. This implies that online buyers still do not trust online payment channels. The third preferred payment for buyers is online payment by credit cards, accounting for 26.4 per cent.

TABLE 5.1
Buyers of Goods/Services Online, Classified by Payment Channel

Online Payment Channels	%	Offline Payment Channels	%
Credit card	26.40	Bank counter service	65.50
Online banking service	18.50	ATM terminal	31.20
Payment service provider	8.40	Cash payment on delivery	18.80
Debit card	6.50	Cash payment at service counter	12.70
Top-up card	1.30	Payment to vendor in person	7.30
Cash card	1.10		

Source: ETDA (2015a).

FIGURE 5.12
Buyers of Goods/Services Online, Classified by Generation,
Based on Payment Channels

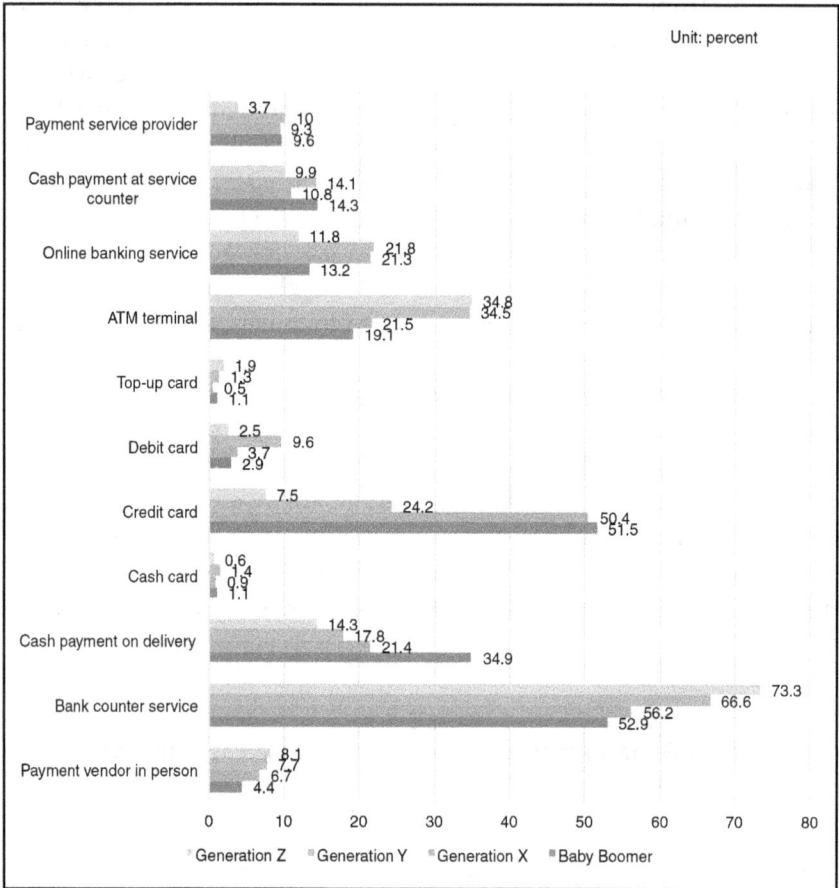

Unit: percent

Payment channel	Generation Z	Generation Y	Generation X	Baby Boomer
Payment service provider	3.7	10	9.3	9.6
Cash payment at service counter	9.9	14.1	10.8	14.3
Online banking service	11.8	21.8	21.3	13.2
ATM terminal	34.8	34.5	21.5	19.1
Top-up card	1.9	1.3	0.5	1.1
Debit card	2.5	9.6	3.7	2.9
Credit card	7.5	24.2	50.4	51.5
Cash card	0.6	1.4	0.9	1.1
Cash payment on delivery	14.3	17.8	21.4	34.9
Bank counter service	73.3	66.6	56.2	52.9
Payment vendor in person	8.1	6.7	4.4	

Source: ETDA (2015*a*).

In terms of the utilization of payment channels by age group, it is found that baby boomers and Generation X buyers are likely to pay by credit cards than other age groups—51.5 per cent of baby boomers and 50.4 per cent of Generation X buyers. Generations Z and Y buyers are likely to pay at bank counter service and ATM terminals than other age groups. This implies that Generations Z and Y buyers are more concerned about the risk of payments for goods and services purchased online than other age groups. However, baby boomers and Generation X buyers are less concerned about risks associated with purchasing goods and services through online payment channels such as credit cards.

Delivery Systems

Delivery systems of goods and services play a crucial role in promoting the country's e-commerce, since weaknesses in the delivery infrastructure can seriously impede its e-commerce, especially for goods (UNCTAD 2015). Consumers prefer e-commerce due to the convenience of having physical goods delivered to their homes and the ease of downloading digital goods from the internet (UNCTAD 2015). For B2C e-commerce the quality of the internet connection is an important factor for online delivery of digital products such as music, computer software, books, and videos. Postal and parcel express delivery networks are important for the delivery of physical products. In addition, buyers can also pick up their products ordered through a central retail website at a post (or parcel) office. Buyers might also access delivery lockers to pick up their goods.

According to the survey on Thai internet users' profile conducted by the ETDA (2015) as indicated in Table 5.2, more than 87 per cent of goods and services ordered online are delivered by parcel post, followed by courier service (30.7 per cent), product pick-up by the buyers (12.4 per cent), and other channels including e-Coupons or e-Tickets for redemption (3.8 per cent) (ETDA 2015). However, there are three main problems found from the survey such as: (i) delayed delivery of ordered goods, reported by 58.7 per cent of respondents, (ii) items received not matching the descriptions shown on websites, reported by 29.9 per cent of respondents, and (iii) damaged or defective goods, reported by 24 per cent of respondents. In addition, 79.7 per cent of online buyers in the survey prefer filing their complaints to websites of such goods and services, followed by complaints through online social media (25.7 per cent), complaints through government agencies (3.6 per cent), and complaints lodged with the police (1.5 per cent).

TABLE 5.2
Delivery Channels, Problems Encountered, and Complaint Channels for Goods and Services Purchased Online

Delivery Channels	Per Cent	Problems Encountered from Purchasing Goods and Services Online	Per Cent	Complaint Channels	Per Cent
Parcel post	87.4	Delayed delivery of ordered goods	58.7	Product/service websites	79.7
Courier service	30.7	Goods received not matching descriptions shown on websites	29.9	Social media	25.7
Product pick-up by buyers	12.4	Damaged/defective goods	24	Government agencies	3.6
Others	3.8	Goods not received despite payment	9.6	Complaint lodged with police	1.5
		Quantity of goods received lower than quantity ordered	6.4	Others	8.2
		No refund after return of goods	2.8		
		Others	9.1		

Source: ETDA (2015a).

4. E-commerce Laws in Thailand

Security and trust can help create an environment conductive to e-commerce (UNCTAD 2015). The adoption of laws is essential for e-commerce sustainable growth even though they may not be a prerequisite for e-commerce to take place (UNCTAD 2015). Therefore, a supportive legal environment for e-commerce can reduce online fraud and data breaches which are growing concern for consumers and enterprises. According to the research conducted by UNCTAD, the laws relevant to e-commerce include: (i) e-transaction laws, (ii) consumer protection laws, (iii) privacy and data protection laws, and (iv) cybercrime laws. Such laws are generally adequately implemented in developed countries but less so in other parts of the world (see Table 5.3).

In the case of Thailand, the country's main consumer protection law, the Consumer Protection Act of B.E. 2522, was enacted in 1979. The law is aimed at protecting consumers against false, misleading and unfair advertising of goods and services (Panuspatthna 2013). This Act also guarantees that consumers will have the same right regardless of whether the transaction is carried out electronically or by traditional means. In addition, this Act had been amended in 1998 and 2013. Similarly, Direct Selling and Direct Market Act of B.E. 2545 has also been enacted since 2002 to ensure that electronic transactions, which fall under the term "direct marketing", will be complied with the provisions of the Act. For example, consumers will have their right to terminate the contract within a cooling-off period. In addition, documents regarding the purchase of goods and services must contain statements that are easy to understand.

Thailand's cybercrime law is the Computer Crime Act of B.E. 2550 which was enacted in 2007. The law supports the country's ICT infrastructure by ensuring the security and building confidence of all parties involved with electronic transactions. This Act deals with computer-related offences (Panuspatthna 2013). It covers offences related to computer data, and offences related to providing of tools used in committing a computer crime. The law also imposes obligations and liabilities on internet service providers (ISPs). In addition, the Computer Crime Act of B.E. 2560 (the 2nd Act) was enacted since 23 January 2016. More severe penalties have been applied for the 2nd Act.

TABLE 5.3
Share of Economies with Relevant E-commerce Legislation by Region, 2014 (%)

	Countries (Number)	E-transaction Laws (%)	Consumer Protection Laws (%)	Privacy and Data Protection Laws (%)	Cybercrime Laws (%)
Developed economies	42	97.6	85.7	97.6	83.3
Developing economies					
Africa	54	46.3	33.3	38.9	40.7
Asia and Oceania	48	72.9	37.5	29.2	56.3
Latin America and the Caribbean	33	81.8	54.5	48.5	63.6
Transition economies	17	100	11.8	88.2	70.6
All economies	**194**	**74.7**	**47.4**	**55.2**	**60.3**

Source: UNCTAD (2015).

Thailand's e-transaction law, the Electronic Transactions Act of B.E. 2544, was enacted in 2001. The goal of this Act is to provide legal recognition of electronic transactions so that they would have the same legal effect as that provided to traditional paper transactions. The Act promotes the reliability of electronic commerce by recognizing: (i) data messages which are treated as the message made in writing as well as an original document under the law, (ii) methods of dispatch and receipt of data messages, (iii) the use of electronic signatures, and (iv) evidential admissibility of data messages (Panuspatthna 2013). This Act also applies to all commercial transactions which are performed by the use of a data message, except those that are related to family matters and succession (Panuspatthna 2013). In addition, this Act monitors electronic transactions in the public sectors, which are made in accordance with the rules and procedures prescribed by the Royal Decree Prescribing Rules and Procedures of Electronic Transactions in the Public Sectors of B.E. 2549 (2006).

Currently, there has been personal data protection for specific Acts such as Telecommunications Business Act B.E.2544 (A.D. 2001), Official Information Act B.E. 2540 (A.D. 1997), and Credit Data Business Operation Act B.E. 2545 (A.D. 2002). Despite the enactment of these laws covering particular areas of personal data protection, there has not been any rule, mechanism, or measure regulating personal data protection existing as a matter of general principles for the Thai people. The Ministry of Digital Economy and Society has finished conducting public hearings on the draft Personal Data Protection Act thus far, and the Thai Cabinet has already approved this draft Act on 22 May 2018. There are six chapters in this Act as follows: (i) Personal Data Production Committee, (ii) Personal Data Protection, (iii) Practice on Personal Data Protection, (iv) Complaints, (v) Civil Liabilities, and (vi) Penalties. According to Section 5 in this Act, "Personal Data" means any data pertaining to a person, which enables the identification of such person, whether direct or indirect. Unlike the General Data Protection Regulation (GDPR), this Act does not provide the means on how to identify an individual directly or indirectly. According to GDPR, an individual can be identified directly by his or her name, identification number, location data, and an online identifier (IP addresses and cookie identifiers which may be personal data) or identified indirectly from that information in combination with other information from another source.

This Act also provides a civil claim for compensation for any damage caused to the data owner as a result of any operation in relation to personal data as stated in Section 42.[5] Moreover, if the personal data administrator fails to comply with the orders of the personal data committee as stated in Section 43, he/she will be liable to a fine not exceeding two hundred thousand baht, and to an additional fine at a daily rate not exceeding five thousand baht until due compliance with legal requirements. According to Section 44, if the personal data administrator violates or fails to comply with Section 22 paragraphs 1, 24, 25, 26, 27, 30, 31, and 32, he/she will be subject to imprisonment for a term of not exceeding six months, or to a fine not exceeding three hundred thousand baht, or to both. However, if the personal data administrator commits to unlawfully benefit himself/herself or another person, or to cause damage to another person, he/she will be subject to imprisonment for a term of not exceeding two years, or to a fine not exceeding two million baht, or to both. Moreover, as indicated in Section 45, if any person who knows the personal data of another person as a result of performing duties under this Act and discloses it to any other person will be liable to imprisonment for a term not exceeding one year, or to a fine not exceeding twenty thousand baht, or to both. However, comparing with the GDPR, the penalties which are charged to the personal data administrator or any person who fails to comply with the law are not relatively significant.

According to Article 83, the GDPR will impose a substantial fine up to €10 million or 2 per cent of annual turnover of the previous year, whichever is higher, on data controllers and data processors for non-compliance in case of breaches of controller or processor obligations, but they will be liable to a fine up to €20 million or 4 per cent of annual turnover of the previous year, whichever is higher, for breaches of the data subject's rights and freedoms (Information Commission's Office 2018).

This Act also does not differentiate between the data controller and the data processor as defined by the GDPR. It just defines the data administrator as "a person having the powers and duties to make decisions regarding the management of personal data, including its collection, use, and disclosure under this Act". The question is that the owner of the company might not have legal liability when his/her workers fails to comply under this Act. Unlike Thailand's Personal Data Protection Act, the data controller, who determines the purposes and means of processing personal data, is not relieved of any obligations in which a data processer, who is responsible for processing personal data on behalf of a controller fails to comply under the law, is involved. In addition, a decision can be solely made by automated means without any human involvement.

Moreover, this Act does not define or mention about the rights of a data owner with regards to automated decision making, including profiling. This might lead to the broad interpretation of this Act and the complication of the law enforcement in the future. However, the GDPR also has provisions on automated individual decision-making, such as an online decision to award a loan and a recruitment aptitude test which uses pre-programmed algorithms and criteria. The GDPR also addresses the rights of individuals as follows: (i) the right to be informed about the collection and use of the personal data, (ii) the right to access their personal data, (iii) the right to have their inaccurate personal data rectified, or completed if it is incomplete, (iv) the right to have their personal data erased, (v) the right to request the restriction or suppression of their personal data, and (vi) the right to receive and reuse their personal data for their own purposes across different services (data portability).

This Act also covers most of the individual rights, but it might be different from the GDPR when it is practically enacted. For the case of Thailand's Personal Data Protection Act, the process of the data erasure seems to be lengthy because the personal data administrator must firstly fail to comply with the rules under this Act, and then the data owner has to obtain approval from the Personal Data Protection Committee. For example, if the personal data administrator does not comply with the rules under this Act, the data owner may request the Personal Data Protection Committee to order the personal data administrator to destroy, or temporarily suspend the use of the personal data, or convert the personal data into a form with anonymity.

However, in the case of the GDPR, the data owner can directly request the data processor to erase his/her personal data. For instance, the data owner can request the data processor to erase his/her personal data in case that (i) the personal data is not necessary for the purpose which the data processor originally collected or processed it for, or (ii) the data processor uses the personal data for direct marketing purposes and the data owner objects the processing of his/her personal data.

One of the differences between Thailand's Personal Data Protection Act and the GDPR is that the right to data portability addressed in the GDPR will allow the data owner to move his/her personal data from one service provider to another. This will help start-ups and smaller companies to access data markets dominated by large digital companies, and also increase the confidence of buyers when purchasing any goods and services in the market. Nevertheless, this cannot be found under Thailand's Personal Data Protection Act.

As mentioned earlier, this Act can instill confidence in consumers, especially those who purchase their goods and services in the online marketplace. However, there might be some concern over the enforcement of this Act. This is due to the broad interpretation of this Act which provides more legal authorities for the Personal Data Protection Committee to exercise control over this Act. Therefore, it might be time-consuming for the data owner to request the Personal Data Protection Committee to order the Personal Data Administrator under this Act. In addition, the civil penalties under this Act are quite low compared with the international standard. Due to the qualifications of the chairperson and qualified members under this Act,[6] it is recommended that they should not be involved with any company that is under their investigation. For instance, they should not be appointed as the committee or the shareholder of the investigated company due to their conflicts of interest.

In preparing to serve the data sharing economy, the rights of the data owner must be strengthened to be in line with the international standard, especially the right of data portability. Thus, if this can be compatible with the rapid evolution of big data, it could increase e-commerce transactions in the future, which could finally stimulate economic growth. This is because it can make it easier for potential customers to transfer their personal data between service providers, allowing them to exercise their power over their personal data. It also fosters more competition among firms, and attracts more new firms to the marketplace.

5. Determinants of E-commerce Activities: An Empirical Analysis

This section examines the factors affecting each type of e-commerce engagement as classified into (i) business-to-consumer (B2C), (ii) business-to-business (B2B), and (iii) business-to-government (B2G). Data for this analysis is from the survey on e-commerce conducted by the ETDA in 2015. Before discussing the methodology and empirical models used in this study, it is important to review a literature relating to this study.

A Review of Literature

Theoretical studies suggest that the development of e-commerce can lead to lower search and head-to-head comparison costs (Konings and Roodhooft 2002). Konings and Roodhooft (2002) also suggested that the internet through e-procurement helps firms to search for the cheapest supplier and to realize the decrease in transaction costs with suppliers resulting in a reduction in total production costs and higher production efficiency. However, there are a number of recent studies suggesting that the growth of e-commerce may result in monopolistic pricing behaviour. Geyskens et. al. (2000) found that competent firms with fewer direct channels achieve greater gains in financial performance than less competent firms with a broader direct channel offering. This implies that enterprises engaging in e-commerce are not likely to perform better than more traditional enterprises.

According to Anderson et al. (2003), in the case of electronic retail (e-retail), buyers can visit a website and search for goods displayed via text and graphic information. The buyers can pay electronically using a credit card or electronic payment. The goods purchased are shipped to the address which the buyer provides. In addition, a shipping charge may be applied according to geographical ranges or the charge may be included into the selling price of the goods. However, in conventional goods retailing, buyers must travel to a store searching for a particular item. The choice of the store depends on personal experience, advertising, or interpersonal communication with other shoppers. Buyers can actually transport the goods home, but the store may deliver the goods to their home if the goods are bulky. Therefore, a shift from conventional retail to e-retail can reduce consumers' time and capital inputs. E-commerce retailers can achieve much higher turnover rates of goods and enjoy lower inventory carrying costs than brick-and-mortar retailers. Anderson et al. (2003) also pointed out that a substitution of e-retail for brick-and-mortar retail can entail the substitution of personal transportation for freight transportation of goods. Therefore, courier services have benefitted from the rapid growth in both B2C and B2B e-commerce.

Focusing on the impacts of globalization on e-commerce adoption and firm performance, Kenneth et al. (2006) found that globalization as indicated by the degree to which firms conduct business internationally and face international competition leads to both greater scope of e-commerce use and higher levels of performance for ten countries (Brazil, China, Denmark, France, Germany, Japan, Mexico, Singapore, Taiwan, and the United States). This implies that highly global firms are in a better position to benefit from e-commerce because they can achieve economies of scale and global reach. In addition, they can employ resources and capabilities enhanced throughout their global operations to develop business operations and technologies such as e-commerce. Also, they find that globalization leads to different effects on B2B and B2C e-commerce. Highly global enterprises are more likely to engage in B2B e-commerce, but they tend to engage less in B2C, since upstream business activities (B2B) are more global while downstream business activities (B2C) are more local or multi-domestic (Kennet et al. 2006).

In addition, firm size has been identified in various research as a crucial factor in determining IT diffusion and use. Kenneth et al. (2005) revealed that a firm's size has a significant and positive correlation with its coordination which includes both lower procurement and inventory costs and proven coordination with suppliers, but significant evidence is not found for other dimensions as measured by its efficiency and market. Similarly, Kuan and Chau (2001) empirically evaluated the electronic data interchange (EDI) adoption of 575 small firms and found that 46 per cent of them have adopted technology. In other words, larger firms are likely to adopt ICTs as they own greater resources and have the knowledge to invest in and implement technology (Kenneth et al. 2005).

Prior to the emergence of the internet, consumers were not able to seek information by browsing web pages, through search engines and via social media platforms (Luo et al. 2013). Today, social media sites have become increasingly popular among consumers. As a result, firms are seeking to transform their businesses using social media and capitalize on its financial value (Luo et al. 2013). Social media platforms can improve a firm's business in terms of managing customer relationships, brand assets, and business processes, which ultimately enhance its performance. Luo et al. (2013) found that social media-based metrics (web blogs and consumer rating) are significantly and positively related to firm equity value. They also suggested that conventional online behavioural metrics (Google search and web traffic) are found to be significant, but substantially weaker predictive association with firm equity value than social media metrics. In addition, they found that social media has a faster predictive value (shorter or wear-in time) than conventional online media (Luo et al. 2012).

Besides the emergence of website and social media, the e-marketplace has increasingly been important to the firm's procurement and sales activities, which is a place for customers and suppliers to conduct trade in a more efficient way. The e-marketplace is known as an organizational platform that allows participants to exchange information about prices and offerings (Chang and Wong 2010). Chang and Wong (2010) found that firms which had adopted e-procurement were more likely to participate in the e-marketplace. Participating in e-marketplace can improve a firm's performance (efficiency, sales performance, customer satisfaction, and relationship development).

Focusing on the use of e-commerce channels related to different types of e-commerce engagement, Michaelidou et al. (2011) investigated the effect of Social Networking Sites (SNS) on B2B e-commerce engagement of a sample of 1,000 UK B2B SMEs. Their empirical results interestingly suggest that 27 per cent of B2B SMEs in the UK are currently employing SNS to achieve their brand objectives, especially for attracting new customers. More specifically, the majority of SMEs in the survey use Facebook (77 per cent of total SNS) as their platform to meet their B2B e-commerce, followed by LinkedIn, Twitter, and MySpace. They also provide the main reasons why SMEs in the UK use SNS, which can be identified as follows: (i) to attract new customers (91 per cent), (ii) to increase awareness of their brand (82 per cent), (iii) to communicate their brand online (73 per cent), (iv) to receive customers' feedback (46 per cent), and (v) to interact with suppliers (14 per cent). However, those SMEs who do not use SNS to support their brand strategies suggest that SNS are not important for their industries, accounting for 61 per cent of the reasons. In addition, 44 per cent of SMEs are not sure as to whether SNS can help their brands.

However, the use of social media is widely popular for B2C domain, since it can reach millions of customers with brand-related content and communicate with customers (Iankova et at. 2018). According to the study of Iankova et al. (2018), they investigate the implicit assumption that social media is fundamentally different in B2B companies than in the extant B2C literature. Focusing on the use of social media, Iankova et al. (2018) found a significant difference, with B2B organizations having significantly lower users than B2C organizations and mixed B2B/B2C organizations which refer to businesses that sell products to both other businesses and individual consumers. Therefore, B2B organizations perceive social media as a channel that has a lower overall effectiveness, and identify it as less important for relationship-oriented usage than other business models such as B2C and mixed B2B/B2C. More specifically, they also find a significant difference for the case of social networks (Facebook, Google+), with B2B organizations having significantly lower users than the other business models such as B2C, mixed B2B/B2C, and B2B2C.[7] However, they found an insignificant difference for website PR compared to all other business models (B2C, mixed B2B/B2C, and B2B2C).

Moore et al. (2013) use a sample of 395 salespeople in B2B and B2C markets to examine the utilization of relationship-oriented social media applications. They find that the adoption rate of social media sites such as Classmates, Facebook, LinkedIn, MySpace, and Ning is far greater for B2B as opposed to B2C. In addition, their results show that B2B salespeople are likely to use social media targeted at professionals through LinkedIn, but their B2C counterparts are likely to employ more social media sites targeted to the general public such as Facebook and MySpace for engaging one-to-one dialogues with their customers. In addition, B2B professionals are likely to employ relationship-oriented social media techniques more than B2C professionals for prospecting, handling objections, and after sales follow-up.

With respect to industry effects, e-commerce adaptation is likely to vary across industries. For instance, Kenneth et al. (2005) found that service-based industries such as distribution and finance are likely to make heavier use of B2C e-commerce than the manufacturing industry. This implies that distribution and finance are involved with downstream activities which require relatively more interaction with consumers, but manufacturing is more business focused.

After a review of the literature in this section, the methodology and empirical models used in this study will be discussed in the next section.

Methodology and Empirical Models

Model Specification

The e-commerce activities of firms can be analysed by the differentiating modes of e-commerce utilization such as B2C, B2B, and B2G.[8] When the dependent variable is defined as the e-commerce sales percentage of B2C, B2B, and B2G, there are relatively large numbers of observations with zero per cent and 100 per cent values, implying double truncation. Under such circumstances, applying the method of ordinary least squares (OLS) will lead to biased and inconsistent estimators, since the OLS method is likely to predict values greater than one (Kumbhakar and Lovell 2000; Coelli et al. 2005). Therefore, the maximum likelihood estimation for a two-limit tobit model is well-suited to the data of this study, which can be expressed as follows:

$$y_i^* = \beta_0 + \sum_{j=1}^{j=n} \beta_i x_i + \varepsilon_i \tag{1}$$

$$y_i = \begin{cases} L_1 & if\ y_1^* \le L_1 \\ y_i^* & if\ L_1 < y_i^* < L_2 \\ L_2 & if\ y_i^* \ge L_2 \end{cases} \tag{2}$$

where y_i^* = Unobserved dependent variables of firm i
y_i = Observed dependent variables of firm i
L_1 = The lower limit of the censored distribution
L_2 = The upper limit of the censored distribution
β_i = Unknown parameter to be estimated for each independent variable of firm i
x_i = Independent variables of firm i
ε_i = Random error ($\varepsilon_i \sim N(0,\ \sigma_\varepsilon^2)$)

Applying the maximum estimation of a Tobit model for firm performance as measured by the percentage of sales for each type of e-commerce engagement (B2C, B2B, and B2G), the maximum likelihood estimation for a two-limit Tobit model is adopted and provided as follows:

$y_i^* =$ (medium$_i$, large$_i$, pure internet company$_i$, Bangkok$_i$, e-marketplace$_i$, website$_i$, social media$_i$, manufacturing$_i$, information & communication$_i$, art, entertainment, and recreation$_i$, other sectors$_i$)   (3)

$y_i^* =$ (medium$_i$, large$_i$, pure internet company$_i$, central$_i$, e-marketplace$_i$, website$_i$, social media$_i$, manufacturing$_i$, information & communication$_i$, art, entertainment, and recreation$_i$, other sectors$_i$)   (4)

$y_i^* =$ (medium$_i$, large$_i$, pure internet company$_i$, north$_i$, e-marketplace$_i$, website$_i$, social media$_i$, manufacturing$_i$, information & communication$_i$, art, entertainment, and recreation$_i$, other sectors$_i$)   (5)

$y_i^* =$ (medium$_i$, large$_i$, pure internet company$_i$, northeast$_i$, e-marketplace$_i$, website$_i$, social media$_i$, manufacturing$_i$, information & communication$_i$, art, entertainment, and recreation$_i$, other sectors$_i$)   (6)

$y_i^* =$ (medium$_i$, large$_i$, pure internet company$_i$, south$_i$, e-marketplace$_i$, website$_i$, social media$_i$, manufacturing$_i$, information & communication$_i$, art, entertainment, and recreation$_i$, other sectors$_i$)   (7)

$$y_i = \begin{cases} 0 & if \ y_i^* \leq 100 \\ y_i^* & if \ 0 < y_i^* < 100 \\ 100 & if \ y_i^* \geq 100 \end{cases} \qquad (8)$$

where y_i^* = unobserved dependent variables, representing the proportion of e-commerce sales classified into (i) B2C e-commerce, (ii) B2B e-commerce, and (iii) B2G e-commerce; y_i = observed dependent variables of firm i.

Data Source and Data Classification

This study employs the survey on e-commerce conducted by the ETDA in 2016. From a population frame comprising 527,324 entrepreneurs, a total of 2,520 e-commerce entrepreneurs were sampled using the Yamane's formula. In the survey, 2,659 e-commerce firms with sales not exceeding 50 million baht were sampled using the online questionnaire and face-to-face interviews. Due to some missing data, 2,657 e-commerce firms were used to conduct the empirical analysis of this chapter. According to the survey, the e-commerce sector is classified into five sub-sectors as follows: (i) manufacturing, (ii) information & communication, (iii) art, entertainment, and recreation, (iv) retail & wholesale, and (v) other sectors. Data descriptive statistics are also provided in Tables 5.4 and 5.5.

Empirical Results

With respect to each type of e-commerce engagement as indicated in Tables 5.6–5.10, medium-sized enterprises are likely to engage more in B2B e-commerce than small-sized enterprises. This indicates that larger firms are likely to engage in upstream activities which require relatively more business focus, but smaller firms are more likely to engage in B2C e-commerce, since they are likely to be involved with downstream activities with consumers as suggested by Kenneth et. al. (2005). This empirical study is consistent with the findings of Kenneth et. al. (2005) and Kuan and Chau (2001) which suggest that larger firms are likely to adopt more ICTs than smaller firms due to greater resources and IT knowledge as these can result in more engagement in B2B e-commerce.

There is a significant and positive correlation between domestic sales and B2C e-commerce. This result implies that firms which greatly rely on the domestic market are likely to engage more in B2C e-commerce. This chapter, however, finds a significant and negative association between domestic sales and B2B e-commerce as well as B2G e-commerce.[9] The empirical evidence of this study also suggests that e-commerce enterprises which have high levels of domestic sales tend to engage less in B2B and B2G e-commerce. In other words, those firms with high foreign sales are likely to engage more in B2B ecommerce as well as B2G e-commerce which is business and government focused, respectively. This is because those firms which are connected to foreign markets are likely to engage more in B2B e-commerce as well as B2G e-commerce, since their business expertise might be more superior than those which have less collaborations with foreign partners due to the learning by exporting experience.

Therefore, those firms with higher levels of foreign sales are likely to engage more in B2B e-commerce which is business focus, especially in foreign markets. Therefore, e-commerce enterprises that need to participate in foreign markets may focus on B2B e-commerce. Similarly, those firms which participate in foreign markets can engage more in

TABLE 5.4
Variable Definitions and Summary Statistics (Continuous Variables)

Variable	Definition	N	Mean	S.D	Min	Max
Bangkok$_i$	The proportion of a firm's sales to the Bangkok metropolitan region relative to its total sales.	2,656	68.8811	31.6846	0	100
central$_i$	The proportion of a firm's sales to the central region relative to its total sales.	2,653	16.0894	20.7585	0	100
north$_i$	The proportion of a firm's sales to the northern region relative to its total sales.	2,653	5.6221	13.7493	0	100
northeastern$_i$	The proportion of a firm's sales to the northeastern region relative to its total sales.	2,653	4.7771	13.3288	0	100
south$_i$	The proportion of a firm's sales to the southern region relative to its total sales.	2,653	4.6656	12.8990	0	100
sales$_i$	Logarithm of a firm's total sales	2,657	12.1129	2.2199	3.4340	22.8148
B2C$_i$*	The proportion of a firm's business to consumer sales relative to its total e-commerce sales.	2,657	80.0106	35.4504	0	100
B2B$_i$**	A firm's proportion of business to business sales relative to its total e-commerce sales.	2,657	15.0631	30.3273	0	100
B2G$_i$***	A firm's proportion of business to government sales relative to its total e-commerce sales.	2,657	4.9263	18.9541	0	100

Notes:
* There are 1,814 firms which have only B2C sales accounting for 100 per cent of total e-commerce sales, but there are 290 firms which do not have any B2C sales accounting for 0 per cent of total e-commerce sales.
** There are 195 firms which have only B2B sales accounting for 100 per cent of total e-commerce sales, but there are 1,891 firms which do not have any B2B sales accounting for 0 per cent of total e-commerce sales.
*** There are 69 firms which have only B2G sales accounting for 100 per cent of total e-commerce sales, but there are 2,397 firms which do not have any B2G sales accounting for 0 per cent of total e-commerce sales.

Source: The survey on e-commerce (2016).

TABLE 5.5
Variable Definitions and Summary Statistics (Categorical Variables)

Variable	Definition	N	No. of "1"	No. of "0"	Min	Max
small$_i$	Dummy variable takes a value of 1 for a firm employing between 1 and 50 workers, or 0 otherwise	2,657	2,576	81	0	1
medium$_i$	Dummy variable takes a value of 1 for a firm employing between 51 and 200 workers, or 0 otherwise	2,657	44	2,613	0	1
large$_i$	Dummy variable takes a value of 1 for a firm employing more than and equal to 201 workers, or 0 otherwise	2,657	37	2,620	0	1
pure internet company$_i$	Dummy variable takes a value of 1 for a firm only selling its products and services via the internet (click & click sales), or 0 otherwise (click & mortar sales)	2,657	2,105	552	0	1
e-marketplace$_i$	Dummy variable takes a value of 1 for a firm selling its products and services via the e-marketplace, or 0 otherwise	2,657	1,628	1,029	0	1
social media$_i$	Dummy variable takes a value of 1 for a firm selling its products and services via the social media, or 0 otherwise	2,657	1,836	821	0	1
website$_i$	Dummy variable takes a value of 1 for a firm selling its products and services via the website, or 0 otherwise	2,657	2,017	640	0	1
manufacturing$_i$	Dummy variable takes a value of 1 for a firm in the manufacturing sector, or 0 otherwise	2,657	197	2,460	0	1
information & communication$_i$	Dummy variable takes a value of 1 for a firm in the information & communication sector, or 0 otherwise	2,657	63	2,594	0	1
retail & wholesale$_i$	Dummy variable takes a value of 1 for a firm in the retail & wholesale sector, or 0 otherwise	2,657	2,211	446	0	1
Art,entertainment, and recreation$_i$	Dummy variable takes a value of 1 for a firm in the art, entertainment, and recreation sector, or 0 otherwise	2,657	50	2,607	0	1
other sectors$_i$	Dummy variable takes a value of 1 for a firm in other sectors, or 0 otherwise	2,657	148	2,509	0	1

TABLE 5.6

Significant Sources Affecting E-commerce Engagement, Classified by Type of E-commerce Use (Geography: Bangkok)

Independent Variable:	B2C		B2B		B2G	
	Coef.	Robust Std. Err.	Coef.	Robust Std. Err.	Coef.	Robust Std. Err.
Enterprise's size:						
Medium	−36.0658*	(15.8715)	42.6957*	(13.5315)	3.2449	(21.5750)
Large	−32.6956	(21.8467)	25.1952	17.5044	29.5573	(31.4211)
Company's sale:						
Domestic sales	1.1848*	(0.1005)	−0.9315*	(0.0837)	−0.7355*	(0.1435)
Pure internet company	74.0150*	(6.4399)	−58.4929*	(5.3262)	−68.1832*	(10.1735)
Geography:						
Bangkok	0.7888*	(0.0919)	−0.5330*	(0.0753)	−0.8699*	(0.1500)
Central						
North						
Northeast						
South						
E-commerce channel:						
E-marketplace	−19.0078*	(6.2879)	24.4508*	(5.1698)	18.3480**	(10.3647)
Website	33.2968*	(6.8171)	−28.3527*	(5.7714)	−11.1887	(11.1760)
Social media	10.5537**	(6.0027)	−0.1705	(4.8649)	−34.3787**	(10.0122)

Industry (Base category: retail & wholesale):

Manufacturing	-11.8716	(9.7156)	10.0507	(8.2531)	5.1166	(16.2108)
Information & communication	-37.6735*	(17.4419)	28.1301**	(15.7379)	2.4709	(26.5406)
Art, entertainment, and recreation	-52.0230*	(18.2958)	41.5191*	(16.2955)	0.2327	(32.7443)
Other sectors	-26.9313*	(11.8868)	13.3981	(9.9134)	14.0674	(20.5191)
Constant	-72.4973*	(13.6039)	109.2322*	(11.0534)	11.6665	(18.9192)
/sigma	109.1804	4.40671	89.00174	3.65034	130.5227	9.850336
Left-censored obs. (B2C<=0)	284		1,886		2,379	
Uncensored obs.	544		562		189	
Right-censored obs. (B2C>=100)	1,809		189		69	
Number of obs.	2,637		2,637		2,379	
F statistics	37.0600		34.0300		13.1200	
Prob>F	0.0000		0.0000		0.0000	
Pseudo R2	0.065		0.0604		0.0506	

TABLE 5.7
Significant Sources Affecting E-commerce Engagement, Classified by Type of E-commerce Use
(Geography: Central)

Independent Variable:	B2C		B2B		B2G	
	Coef.	Robust Std. Err.	Coef.	Robust Std. Err.	Coef.	Robust Std. Err.
Enterprise's size:						
Medium	-36.5410*	(15.0028)	42.6470*	(12.9477)	3.3268	(22.2066)
Large	-41.1734**	(22.1682)	30.4630**	(17.7352)	37.2608	(31.3351)
Company's sale:						
Domestic sales	1.2701*	(0.1022)	-0.9853*	(0.0847)	-0.8368*	(0.1434)
Pure internet company	81.7579*	(6.5479)	-63.4281*	(5.3690)	-76.7512*	(10.1832)
Geography:						
Bangkok						
Central	0.4520*	(0.1493)	-0.2412*	(0.1208)	-0.3956**	(0.2257)
North						
Northeast						
South						
E-commerce channel:						
E-marketplace	-18.6418*	(6.4531)	24.4756*	(5.2619)	18.2251**	(10.4611)
Website	31.1912*	(6.9433)	-27.0463*	(5.8129)	-8.6740	(11.3200)
Social media	15.8118*	(6.1443)	-3.6653	(4.9061)	-40.1685*	(10.1804)

Industry (Base category: retail & wholesale):

Manufacturing	−9.5329	(10.0289)	8.8168	(8.4235)	1.8370	(16.4023)
Information & communication	−34.9488*	(16.2517)	26.3573**	(14.4535)	5.8597	(27.5184)
Art, entertainment, and recreation	−57.2282*	(20.0680)	45.4975*	(16.9609)	8.3569	(34.9907)
Other sectors	−29.5408*	(11.8561)	15.1969	(9.8512)	15.8506	(20.4083)
Constant	−41.0972*	(12.9218)	86.7171*	(10.4417)	−24.1985	(18.2160)
/sigma	111.8214	(4.5011)	90.19921	(3.6875)	133.3444	(9.91407)
Left-censored obs. (B2C<=0)	284		1,886		2,379	
Uncensored obs.	541		559		189	
Right-censored obs. (B2C>=100)	1,809		189		69	
Number of obs.	2,634		2,634		2,634	
F statistics	33.8200		31.8500		11.3800	
Prob>F	0.0000*		0.0000*		0.0000*	
Pseudo R2	0.057		0.0546		0.0402	

Note: Robust standard errors are in parentheses, * indicates 5 per cent level of significance, ** indicates 10 per cent level of significance.

Source: Authors' estimation.

TABLE 5.8
Significant Sources Affecting E-commerce Engagement, Classified by Type of E-commerce Use
(Geography: North)

Independent Variable:	B2C		B2B		B2G	
	Coef.	Robust Std. Err.	Coef.	Robust Std. Err.	Coef.	Robust Std. Err.
Enterprise's size:						
Medium	−38.1522*	(15.2693)	43.8551*	(13.1222)	6.5350	(21.5355)
Large	−40.1565*	(21.6982)	30.2289**	(17.6045)	37.2046	(30.3723)
Company's sale:						
Domestic sales	1.2413*	(0.1023)	−0.9719*	(0.0851)	−0.7915*	(0.1426)
Pure internet company	75.4743*	(6.5205)	−60.2188*	(5.3965)	−69.1596*	(10.1186)
Geography:						
Bangkok						
Central						
North	−1.4257*	(0.2183)	0.7703*	(0.1738)	1.4401*	(0.2940)
Northeast						
South						
E-commerce channel:						
E-marketplace	−18.8529*	(6.3663)	24.6183*	(5.2413)	18.6357**	(10.3613)
Website	30.8018*	(6.8316)	−26.9639*	(5.7775)	−8.6515	(11.1420)
Social media	12.0250*	(6.0813)	−1.5914	(4.9131)	−35.6543*	(10.0428)

Industry (Base category: retail & wholesale):

Manufacturing	−11.8987	(9.8618)	9.9993	(8.3313)	5.7226	(16.2560)
Information & communication	−27.4314	(17.8742)	21.9853	(15.7672)	−9.8929	(27.7909)
Art, entertainment, and recreation	−58.2650*	(19.4151)	45.7042*	(17.0875)	5.9079	(32.9777)
Other sectors	−32.3748*	(11.6994)	16.9568**	(9.7943)	20.5970	(19.9748)
Constant	−15.1325	(12.7387)	72.7395*	(10.4933)	−50.3685*	(18.7862)
/sigma	110.2591	(4.4658)	89.84766	(3.6930)	130.7597	(9.7148)
Left-censored obs. (B2C<=0)	284		1,886		2,376	
Uncensored obs.	541		559		189	
Right-censored obs. (B2C>=100)	1,809		189		69	
Number of obs.	2,634		2,634		2,634	
F statistics	34.0800		31.9200		12.0100	
Prob>F	0.0000		0.0000		0.0000	
Pseudo R2	0.0624		0.057		0.0477	

Note: Robust standard errors are in parentheses, * indicates 5 per cent level of significance, ** indicates 10 per cent level of significance.

TABLE 5.9
Significant Sources Affecting E-commerce Engagement, Classified by Type of E-commerce Use
(Geography: Northeast)

Independent Variable:	B2C		B2B		B2G	
	Coef.	Robust Std. Err.	Coef.	Robust Std. Err.	Coef.	Robust Std. Err.
Enterprise's size:						
Medium	-36.5850*	(15.4998)	43.1851*	(13.3426)	3.9569	(21.6969)
Large	-36.2066**	(21.2479)	27.9405	(17.0316)	35.8369	(30.6150)
Company's sale:						
Domestic sales	1.1456*	(0.1012)	-0.8974*	(0.0837)	-0.7394*	(0.1464)
Pure internet company	77.6496*	(6.4937)	-60.7224*	(5.3418)	-74.8561*	(10.0892)
Geography:						
Bangkok						
Central						
North						
Northeast	-1.9082*	(0.2406)	1.3019*	(0.1848)	1.3373*	(0.2782)
South						
E-commerce channel:						
E-marketplace	-17.1475*	(6.3177)	23.4434*	(5.1841)	17.5799**	(10.4203)
Website	31.9556*	(6.7990)	-27.4071*	(5.7564)	-9.2664	(11.2294)
Social media	13.0152*	(6.0020)	-2.0930	(4.8230)	-38.5510*	(10.0711)

Industry (Base category: retail & wholesale):					
Manufacturing	-9.1970	(9.5845)	8.4131	(8.1806)	2.0092	(16.0637)
Information & communication	-39.1249*	(16.3856)	29.4079*	(14.7721)	7.8615	(26.8720)
Art, entertainment, and recreation	-47.8367*	(19.1644)	37.1041	(16.9693)	-2.7336	(35.2591)
Other sectors	-24.3775*	(11.9041)	11.3710	(9.8514)	11.9293	(20.8669)
Constant	-11.1106	(12.5391)	66.9174*	(10.3142)	-46.7443*	(18.5556)
/sigma	108.9722	(4.4207)	88.6058	(3.6514)	131.8326	(9.8826)
Left-censored obs. (B2C<=0)	284		1,886		2,376	
Uncensored obs.	541		559		189	
Right-censored obs. (B2C>=100)	1,809		189		69	
Number of obs.	2,634		2,634		2,634	
F statistics	36.3900		34.2300		12.4000	
Prob>F	0.0000		0.0000		0.0000	
Pseudo R2	0.0664		0.0620		0.0462	

Note: Robust standard errors are in parentheses, * indicates 5 per cent level of significance, ** indicates 10 per cent level of significance

Source: Authors' estimation.

TABLE 5.10
Significant Sources Affecting E-commerce Engagement, Classified by Type of E-commerce Use
(Geography: South)

Independent Variable:	B2C		B2B		B2G	
	Coef.	Robust Std. Err.	Coef.	Robust Std. Err.	Coef.	Robust Std. Err.
Enterprise's size:						
Medium	-34.4198*	(15.4216)	41.5599*	(13.2198)	1.1302	(21.7707)
Large	-37.3728**	(21.4541)	28.4466**	(17.1971)	35.0155	(30.8779)
Company's sale:						
Domestic sales	1.1930*	(0.1035)	-0.9348*	(0.0859)	-0.7541*	(0.1464)
Pure internet company	75.5330*	(6.4911)	-59.4852*	(5.3798)	-70.7651*	(10.2949)
Geography:						
Bangkok						
Central						
North						
Northeast						
South	-1.5194*	(0.2709)	0.9964*	(0.2044)	1.3258*	(0.2925)
E-commerce channel:						
E-marketplace	-17.7173*	(6.4330)	23.6956*	(5.2830)	17.1194	(10.4264)
Website	33.0691*	(6.9225)	-28.1792*	(5.8355)	-10.7971	(11.2403)
Social media	13.1444*	(6.0527)	-2.2311	(4.8770)	-37.7779*	(10.0099)

Industry (Base category: retail & wholesale):

Manufacturing	−10.0669	(9.9324)	9.0792	(8.3513)	2.5545	(16.3229)
Information & communication	−39.8980*	(16.2322)	29.6886*	(14.5073)	11.3538	(27.0310)
Art, entertainment, and recreation	−54.5587*	(19.0060)	43.3352*	(16.2147)	5.0942	(35.5028)
Other sectors	−27.1888*	(12.0919)	13.5800	(10.1386)	12.4485	(20.4940)
Constant	−15.4040	(12.7819)	70.7874*	(10.5472)	−47.4106*	(18.6817)
/sigma	110.5081	(4.4547)	89.64448	3.6768	132.0745	(9.9060)
Left-censored obs. (B2C<=0)	284		1,886		2,376	
Uncensored obs.	541		559		189	
Right-censored obs. (B2C>=100)	1,809		189		69	
Number of obs.	2,634		2,634		2,634	
F statistics	33.2200		31.9700		12.1300	
Prob>F	0.0000*		0.0000*		0.0000*	
Pseudo R2	0.0619		0.0582		0.0454	

Note: Robust standard errors are in parentheses, * indicates 5 per cent level of significance, ** indicates 10 per cent level of significance.

Source: Authors' estimation.

B2G e-commerce, since they must be qualified in order to meet the minimum criteria before successfully getting government projects. This empirical result is similar to the findings of Kenneth et al. (2005) which suggests that international competition via exports can lead to greater scope of e-commerce engagement and upstream business activities (B2B) are more global while downstream business activities (B2C) are more local or multi-domestic.

Comparing between click-and-click companies (pure internet companies) and click-and-mortar companies with respect to the different scopes of e-commerce, this study finds a significant and positive association between click-and-click companies and B2C e-commerce. This result, therefore, suggests that click-and-click companies which focus only on online operations are likely to engage more in B2C e-commerce than click-and-mortar companies which focus on both online and offline operations. This is because dealing with consumers do not require much reliability compared to dealing with other firms. Physical stores, therefore, are not really important for B2C e-commerce. This finding is also similar to the suggestion of Anderson et al. (2003) that e-commerce retailers can gain higher turnover rates of goods and benefit from lower inventory carrying costs than brick-and-mortar retailers which only have physical stores or focus only on offline operations, leading to more engagement in B2C e-commerce which can be found in e-commerce retailers.

However, this study finds a significant and negative association between click-and-click companies and B2B e-commerce as well as B2G e-commerce. This empirical result implies that when firms prefer to run businesses with other firms or the government, physical stores or offices can play an important role besides their online operations to build up their creditability and reliability. According to different geographical regions of Thailand, the Bangkok metropolitan region is found to be an important region for e-commerce sources of income. This implies that consumers in the Bangkok metropolitan region are likely to buy more goods and services through electronic commerce than consumers in other regions.

Focusing on different types of e-commerce engagement in each geographical region, it is found that firms which sell in the Bangkok metropolitan and central regions are likely to have higher levels of B2C e-commerce, but a significant and positive result is not found in the case of B2B and B2G e-commerce. This implies that consumers in the Bangkok metropolitan region as well as the central region are likely to be the major source of income for B2C e-commerce. This finding is also consistent with the suggestion of ETDA (2015a) that the IT infrastructure in Bangkok metropolitan region is more readily available than that in other provinces. However, the Bangkok metropolitan and central regions are not major sources of income for B2B and B2G e-commerce as shown in Tables 5.6 and 5.7.

For Tables 5.6–5.10 it is found that the northern, northeastern, and southern regions are likely to be the major sources of income for B2B and B2G e-commerce, but these regions are not the major sources of income for B2C e-commerce. This is because B2B e-commerce is involved with upstream activities which are typically processes dedicated to obtaining raw materials from supplies found in the northern, northeastern, and southern regions. These regions might be suitable for upstream supply chains due to suitable locations for setting up factories, abundant raw materials, and enough labour supply. In addition, the government is likely to promote the upcountry development throughout the country, and therefore B2G e-commerce might not be obviously found in the Bangkok metropolitan region, but might be found in the northern, northeastern, and southern regions of Thailand.

Focusing on different types of e-commerce engagement, e-marketplace is found to be significantly and positively related to B2B and B2G e-commerce, but it has a significant and negative relationship with B2C e-commerce. This is because B2B and B2G e-commerce are likely to be transacted through e-marketplace where product or service information is provided by multiple sellers. In addition, website and social media are found to be significantly and positively associated with B2C e-commerce. This implies that consumers are interested in buying products and services through website and social media. In addition, it is found that there is a significant and negative association between website and B2B e-commerce and between social media and B2G e-commerce. This result suggests that the transactions of B2B and B2G e-commerce are found less in website and social media, respectively.

Comparing between industries, B2C e-commerce firms in the art, entertainment, and recreation sector perform the worst, followed by firms in the information and communication sector and those in other sectors. With respect to B2B e-commerce, it is found that firms in the information and communication sector perform the best, followed by firms in the art, entertainment, and recreation sector and those in the retail and wholesale sector. However, there is no significant evidence among industries for the case of B2G e-commerce.

6. Conclusions and Policy Implications

Conclusions

E-commerce is important to Thailand's economy, accounting for 43.47 per cent of the country's total sales value of goods and services and 16.59 per cent of GDP in 2015. B2B e-commerce is found to be the most important type of e-commerce engagement due to its highest e-commerce value, followed by B2C and B2G e-commerce. According to the importance of e-commerce classified by industrial sectors, accommodation was the most important industry for Thailand's e-commerce, followed by (i) retail, and wholesale trade, (ii) manufacturing, and (iii) information and communication. In addition, B2B e-commerce is the predominant type of e-commerce engagement in the manufacturing sector, followed by the information and communication, and retail and wholesale sectors. However, B2C e-commerce is predominantly found in the art, entertainment, and recreation sector, followed by (i) transportation and storage, and (ii) other services. However, this study found that B2G e-commerce is not important in any industrial sector.

In addition, large enterprises are found to play a dominant role in Thailand's e-commerce market. This is because SMEs still lack awareness of the full range of their potential in applying ICT for a variety of commercial and production-related purposes. Comparing Thailand's e-commerce size with other countries, it is found that Thailand's B2C e-commerce per capita is still smaller than some other countries such as the United States, Japan, South Korea, Singapore, China, and Malaysia. Thailand's B2C e-commerce per capita, however, is higher than Vietnam, the Philippines, and Indonesia.

This chapter also reviews a number of factors influencing the development of e-commerce as suggested by the UNCTAD (2015), such as (i) internet access, (ii) delivery system, and (iii) payment system. The internet usage in Thailand has increasingly become important for the access of the country's e-commerce. This is because of the change of internet usage behaviour of the Thai people. Generation Y internet users spent on average the longest hours on the internet, followed by Generation X internet users, Generation Z internet users, and baby boomer internet users. In addition, internet users, who reside in Bangkok metropolitan region, spent on average the longest hours on the internet, followed by those residing outside municipal areas in other provinces and those residing inside municipal areas in other provinces. For social media sites, Facebook is the most popular site for Thai internet users, followed by Line, Google+, Instagram, Twitter, and WhatsApp.

According to the survey on Thai internet users' profile conducted by the ETDA in 2015, buyers can make their payments when purchasing their goods and services through online channels such as electronic cards and via offline channels such as bank transfer, ATM terminals, and cash payment on delivery. Most online buyers are likely to use offline payment channels to pay for online purchased goods and services. In addition, payment at bank counter service is the most important payment channel, followed by payment via ATM terminals. This implies that online buyers still do not trust online payment channels. In addition, it is found that more than 87 per cent of goods and services which are ordered online are delivered by parcel post, followed by courier service, product pick-up by the buyers, and other channels including e-Coupons or e-Tickets for redemption.

This chapter also employs the survey on e-commerce conducted by the ETDA in 2016 to investigate firms' e-commerce engagement. It finds that medium-sized enterprises are likely to engage more in B2B e-commerce than small-sized enterprises, since larger firms are likely to engage in upstream activities with suppliers or business counterparts, but smaller firms tend to engage more in B2C e-commerce, since they are involved with downstream activities with consumers through the finished product. In addition, firms with higher levels of foreign sales are likely to engage more in B2B e-commerce, which is business focus, and B2G e-commerce, especially in foreign markets. Comparing between click-and-click companies and click-and-mortar companies, click-and-click companies are likely to engage more in B2C e-commerce than click-and-mortar companies, but click-and-mortar companies tend to engage more in B2B and B2G e-commerce. Moreover, this chapter finds that firms which sell in the Bangkok metropolitan and central regions are likely to have higher levels of B2C e-commerce. This evidence is also similar to the report of ETDA (2015) that internet users residing in Bangkok metropolitan region spent on average the longest hours on the internet and the IT infrastructure in these provinces is more readily available than that in other provinces. With respect to different types of e-commerce engagement, e-marketplace can increase firms' B2B and B2G e-commerce, but this is not the case for B2C e-commerce. In addition, website and social media can help increase firms' B2C e-commerce.

Policy Implications

The empirical results from this study indicate that Thai consumers prefer firms or companies which have both physical and online stores (click-and-mortar companies) for B2C e-commerce. The reliability of the sellers' e-commerce sites, online sales and protection of consumer rights are important to promote online operations of click-and-click companies, especially for those who focus on B2C e-commerce. Thus, Thailand's new personal data protection act which has recently been approved by the Thai Cabinet can increase the confidence of customers when buying products and services online. This study finds that website is still the most used e-commerce site for buyers. E-marketplace can increase a firm's B2B and B2G engagement. Moreover, website and social media can help increase a firm's B2C engagement. Therefore, security and trust can help create an environment conductive to e-commerce. The adoption and enhancement of e-commerce related laws is essential for the country's e-commerce growth. The relevant laws include e-transaction laws, consumer protection laws, privacy and data protection laws, and cybercrime laws (UNCAD 2015).

It is found that large enterprises play an important role in promoting Thailand's e-commerce market, especially for B2B e-commerce. The government, therefore, can promote large firm size through credit financing or equity financing from venture capital firms or the Market for Alternative Investment (MAI) or the Stock Exchange of Thailand (SET). More specifically, policies in promoting large firm size should focus on firms which deal mainly on B2B e-commerce. In other words, policies that promote upstream supply chains which are typically processes committed to receiving raw materials from supplies should be focused on.

Due to great reliance on the domestic market of Thai e-commerce enterprises, especially B2C e-commerce, relevant government agencies such as the Ministry of Digital Economy and Society and the National Electronics Computer Technology Center, the Department of Business Development, and the International Trade Promotion can support the establishment of e-commerce businesses in Thailand and build up the confidence for e-commerce business operators, leading to more reliability for foreign partners. More importantly ETDA, which was established by the Ministry of Information and Communication Technology (MICT), can play a vital role in enhancing electronic transactions in Thailand to create trust for foreign counterparts. The ETDA's main objectives are as follows: (i) to conduct studies and research related to e-commerce, (ii) to establish necessary infrastructure aimed at increasing the country's value and volume of electronic transactions, and (iii) to provide technical services or other practical services related to Thailand's economic transactions (ETDA 2017). The Thailand E-commerce Plan 2017–2021 aims to increase the country's value of electronic transactions. More specifically, this e-commerce plan aims at enhancing all e-commerce systems from business process to supply chain, establishing e-commerce standards for linking back-end data, building trust and good experience, making e-commerce more accessible and convenient for buyers and sellers, and building e-commerce collaboration between private and public sectors. To meet its missions, five strategies relating to this e-commerce plan will be implemented as follows: (i) to develop e-commerce capacities of entrepreneurs and enterprises, (ii) to develop trade facilitation, (iii) to promote ecosystem development in supporting e-commerce, (iv) to create opportunities and experiences for both sellers and buyers via e-commerce, and (v) to build trust and confidence for consumers (online consumer protection) (ETDA 2017b).

Finally, the empirical results indicate that the Bangkok metropolitan region is an important region for B2C e-commerce engagement. Therefore, policies promoting adequate internet service coverage, fast internet service, and internet security and privacy for online customers should be considered in promoting the country's e-commerce, especially for those residing in northern, northeastern, and southern regions.

NOTES

1. The narrow definition of e-commerce transactions states that "an internet transaction is the sale or purchase of goods or services, whether between businesses, households, individuals, governments, and other public or private organizations, conducted over the Internet. The goods and services are ordered over the Internet, but the payment and the ultimate delivery of the good or service may be conducted on or off-line. To be included are orders received or placed on any Internet application used in automated transactions such as web pages, Extranets and other applications that run over the Internet, such as EDI over the Internet, Minitel over the Internet, or over any other web enabled application regardless of how the web is accessed (e.g. through a mobile or a TV set, etc.). To be excluded are orders received or placed by telephone, facsimile, or conventional e-mail" (OECD 2011, p 72).
2. E-commerce is defined according to the Organisation for Economic Co-operation and Development's (OECD) narrow definition of e-commerce (ETDA 2015a, p. 91).
3. E-auction refers to the value of total government procurement under the e-Auction system from the Comptroller's General Office (ETDA 2015a, p. 52).
4. Generation X or Gen X refers to people who are born between 1965 and 1980. Generation Z or Gen Z refers to people who are born from 2001 onwards. Baby boomers refer to people who are born between 1946 and 1964 (ETDA 2015a).
5. Section 42: The Personal Data Administrator shall compensate for any damage caused to the Data Owner as a result of any operation in relation to personal data, regardless of whether the Personal Data Administrator is acting intentionally or negligently in such operation, except where the Personal Data Administrator proves that such operation was a result of: (1) a force majeure; (2) an action taken in compliance with an order of the government or a government official; (3) an act or

omission of the person concerned or another person; (4) an action taken in full compliance with the practice on personal data protection issued by the Personal Data Administrator. The compensation under Paragraph one includes all expenses borne by the Committee and government agencies in the prevention of such damage (Thai Netizen Network 2018; ETDA 2018).

6. According to Section 8 in this Act, the Chairperson and qualified members shall have the qualifications and not be under the prohibitions, as follows: (i) being of Thai nationality; (ii) not being bankrupt or having been dishonestly bankrupt; (iii) not being an incompetent or quasi-incompetent; (iv) not having been sentenced by a final judgment to imprisonment, except for an offence committed through negligence or a petty offence (Thai Netizen Network 2018; ETDA 2018).

7. B2B2C combines B2B and B2C e-commerce together to complete product or service transactions. B2B2C creates mutually beneficial service and product delivery channels by entering a B2B e-commerce with a firm whose expertise is selling online (B2C company). In return, the B2C firm can offer its customers more options. Therefore, a third party (a B2C company) serves as a middleman to move goods and services from the provider to the e-commerce vendor (or customers).

8. According to the survey collected by the ETDA, B2C refers to a firm's business to consumer sales relative to its total sales. B2B refers to a firm's business to business sales relative to its total sales. B2G refers to business to government sales relative to its total sales. However, according to the survey, only e-commerce enterprises were interviewed in the survey. This causes the sum of the percentages of B2C, B2B, and B2G to be equal to 100 per cent for each enterprise. In other words, the scope of this survey is to investigate the intensity of each e-commerce type (B2C, B2B, and B2G) for e-commerce enterprises. This chapter, therefore, cannot compare between a firm which engages one type of e-commerce and a firm which engages more than one type of e-commerce. This is because they are all e-commerce enterprises, and they are likely to engage in more than one type of e-commerce due to the data in the survey. This chapter, therefore, focuses on the intensity of each type of e-commerce, and investigates which factors significantly contribute to the intensity of each type of e-commerce.

9. This result is consistent with the finding of this chapter that medium-sized enterprises are likely to engage more in B2B e-commerce due to firm size effects, since larger firms tend to engage in upstream activities which require relatively more business focus, leading to more engagement in B2B e-commerce for larger firms.

REFERENCES

Anderson, William P., Lata Chatterjee, and T.R. Lakshmanan. "E-commerce, Transportation, and Economic Geography". *Growth and Change* 34, no. 4 (2003): 415–32.

ASEAN Secretariat. *ASEAN Economic Community Blueprint 2025*. Jakarta: ASEAN Secretariat, 2015.

AT Kearney and CIMB ASEAN Research Institute. "Lifting the Barriers to E-commerce in ASEAN". 2015. https://www.atkearney.co.uk/documents/10192/5540871/Lifting+the+Barriers+to+E-Commerce+in+ASEAN.pdf/d977df60-3a86-42a6-8d19-1efd92010d52 (assessed 1 December 2017).

Burkey, Jake and Thomas Harris. "Modelling a Share or Proportion with Logit or Tobit: The Effect of Out Commuting on Retail Sales Leakages". *The Review of Regional Studies* 33, no. 3 (2003): 328–42.

Chang, Hsin Hsin and Kit Hong Wong. "Adoption of E-Procurement and Participation of E-Marketplace on Firm Performance: Trust as a Moderator". *Information & Management* 47, no. 1 (2010): 262–70.

Chen, Qingyi and Ning Zhang. "Does E-commerce Provide a Sustained Competitive Advantage? An Investigation of Survival and Sustainability in Growth-Oriented Enterprises". *Sustainability* 7, no. 1 (2015): 1411–28.

CIMB ASEAN Research Institute. "AEC Blueprint 2025: An Analysis of the ASEAN Cooperation in E-Commerce". Working Paper Volume 1–Paper 19. Kuala Lumpur: CIMB ASEAN Research Institute, 2017.

Coelli, Timothy J., D.S. Prasada Rao, Christopher J. O'Donnell, and George Battese. *An Introduction to Efficiency and Productivity Analysis*. New York: Springer, 2005.

ECOMMERCEIQ. "The Country's Top Ecommerce Websites". 2017. https://ecommerceiq.asia/top-ecommerce-sites-thailand (assessed 2 November 2017).

ETDA (Electronic Transactions Development Agency). *Thailand Internet User Profile 2015*. Bangkok: Electronic Transactions Development Agency (Public Organization), 2015a.

———. *Value of E-commerce Survey in Thailand 2015*. Bangkok: Electronic Transactions Development Agency (Public Organization), 2015b.

———. *Thailand Internet User Profile 2016*. Bangkok: Electronic Transactions Development Agency (Public Organization), 2016a.

———. *Value of E-commerce Survey in Thailand 2016*. Bangkok: Electronic Transactions Development Agency (Public Organization), 2016b.

———. "Background and Mission". 2017a. https://www.etda.or.th/background-and-mission.html (assessed 15 November 2017).

———. "Thailand E-commerce Plan 2017–2021". 2017b. https://www.ccs.gov.sg/~/media/custom/ccs/files/education%20and%20compliance/events/

ccs%20iseas%20symposium/thailand%20country%20study_yot%20
amornkitvikai%20and%20jiraporn%20tangpoolcharoen.ashx (assessed
14 November 2017).

———. "Memorandum of Principles and Rationale of (Draft) Personal Data
Protection Act (in Thai)". 2018. https://ictlawcenter.etda.or.th/de_laws/
detail/de-laws-data-privacy-act (assessed 29 May 2018).

Geyskens, Inge, Katrijn Gielens, and Marnik G. Dekimpe. "Establishing the
Internet Channel: Short-term Pain but Long-term Gain?". eBusiness Research
Center Working Paper Volume 6-2000. Pennsylvania: eBusiness Research
Center, 2000.

Iankova, Severina, Iain Davies, Chris Archer-Brown, Ben Marder, and Amy Yau.
"A Comparison of Social Media Marketing between B2B, B2C and Mixed
Business Models". *Industrial Marketing Management*, 2018.

Information Commission's Office. "Guide to the General Data Protection
Regulation (GDPR)". 2 August 2018. https://ico.org.uk/media/for-
organisations/guide-to-the-general-data-protection-regulation-gdpr-1-0.pdf
(assessed 30 May 2018).

Konings, Jozef and Filip Roodhooft. "The Effect of E-business on Corporation
Performance: Firm Level Evidence for Belgium". Discussions Paper Series
(DPS) 00.26. Leuven: Katholieke Universiteit Leuven, 2000.

Kraemer, Kenneth L., Jennifer L. Gibbs, and Jason Dedrick. "Impacts of
Globalization on E-commerce Use and Firm Performance: A Cross-Country
Investigation". *The Information Society* 21, no. 5 (2005): 323–40.

Kshetri, Nir. "Barriers to E-commerce and Competitive Business Models in
Developing Countries: A Case Study". *Electronic Commerce Research and
Applications* 6, no. 4 (2007): 47–55.

Kuan, Kevin and Patrick Chau. "A Perception-based Model for EDI Adoption in
Small Business Using a Technology-O rganization-Environment Framework".
Information & Management 38, no. 8 (2001): 507–21.

Kumbhakar, Subal C. and C.A. Knox Lovell. *Stochastic Frontier Analysis*.
Cambridge, UK: Cambridge University Press, 2000.

Luo, Xueming, Jie Zhang, and Wenjing Duan. "Social Media and Firm Equity
Value". *Information Systems Research* 24, no. 1 (2013): 146–63.

Michaelidou, Nina, Nikoletta Theofania Siamagka, and George Christodoulides.
"Usage, Barriers and Measurement of Social Media Marketing: An Exploratory
Investigation of Small and Medium B2B Brands". *Industrial Marketing
Management* 40, no. 1 (2011): 1153–59.

Moore, Jesse N., Christopher D. Hopkins, and Mary Anne Raymond. "Utilization
of Relationship-Oriented Social Media in the Selling Process: A Comparison
of Consumer (B2C) and Industrial (B2B) Salespeople". *Journal of Internet
Commerce* 12, no. 1 (2013): 48–75.

OECD (Organisation for Economic Co-operation and Development). "Policy Brief: Electronic Commerce". Paris: Organisation for Economic Co-operation and Development, 2001.

———. "OECD Guide to Measuring the Information Society". Paris: Organisation for Economic Co-operation and Development, 2011.

Panuspatthna, Orabhund. "The Laws and Policies of Thailand in Supporting Electronic Commerce". *Thailand Law Journal* 16, no. 1 (2013): 1–2.

Thai Netizen Network. "Memorandum of Principles and Rationale of (Draft) Personal Data Protection Act". 2018. https://thainetizen.org/wp-content/uploads/2015/01/personal-data-protection-bill-20150106-en.pdf (assessed 29 November 2018).

UNCTAD (United Nations Conference on Trade and Development). *Information Economy Report 2010: ICTs, Enterprises and Poverty Alleviation.* Switzerland: United Nations Conference on Trade and Development, 2010.

———. *Review of E-commerce Legislation Harmonization in the Association of Southeast Asian Nations.* New York and Geneva: United Nations Conference on Trade and Development, 2013.

———. *Information Economy Report 2015: Unlocking the Potential of E-commerce for Developing Countries.* Switzerland: United Nations Conference on Trade and Development, 2015.

Virasin, Robert R. "Legality of E-Signatures in Thailand". *Sian Legal*, 2015. http://www.siam-legal.com/thailand-law/legality-of-e-signatures-in-thailand/ (accessed 12 March 2016).

6

E-COMMERCE DEVELOPMENT IN INDONESIA
Challenges and Prospects

Siwage Dharma Negara, Yose Rizal Damuri and Kathleen Azali

1. Introduction

In recent years, there have been both high expectations and stimulating development in e-commerce sector in Southeast Asia in general and in Indonesia in particular. High expectations come from both private and public sectors. For instance, Google-Temasek (2016) predicted that Southeast Asia will be the fastest growing internet market in the world (reaching around 480 million internet users by 2020). Moreover, they projected that Indonesia will become the fastest growing internet market in the world, with 19 per cent compound annual growth rate (CAGR) for the period of 2015–20. By 2025, Indonesia is expected to account for 52 per cent of e-commerce market in the Southeast Asian region. In addition to Google-Temasek's upbeat projection, McKinsey (2016) estimated that the value of the Indonesian e-commerce market will reach US$150 billion by 2025.

In November 2016, the Indonesian government released the 14th economic policy package, which aims to promote the country's e-commerce business environment. In this economic policy package, the government sets an ambitious target to create "1,000 technology entrepreneurs" with business valuation up to US$10 billion by 2020. Almost a year later, in August 2017, President Joko "Jokowi" Widodo signed a Presidential Regulation No. 74/2017 on the Roadmap for the National Electronic Commerce System 2017–2019 (Sekretariat Kabinet Republik Indonesia 2017). This regulation provides the required legal framework for e-commerce business operation in Indonesia.

Despite various upbeat projections on e-commerce prospect in Indonesia, there are many challenges facing the sector development in the country. Firstly, there is a limited pool of skilled workers trained in information and communication technologies (ICT) and in related fields, such as software engineers, coders, platform developers, and so on. Secondly, the internet penetration rate in the country is still low (at around 34 per cent), with internet speed still on the lowest end in the region (average 6.7 Mbps in 2016). Thirdly, the payment mechanism is still limited, also with more than 60 per cent of the population having no access to banking institutions. Fourthly, Indonesia's archipelagic-topographical structure creates additional challenge in terms of high logistical cost. This challenge is worsened by poor infrastructure and limited delivery options. And finally, there is still lack of trust with regards to online transactions, due to particularly high levels of fraud and cybercrime (Rahardjo 2017).

Nevertheless, with its huge, young population, Indonesia remains an attractive market for a number of global e-commerce companies. In 2017, there has been large investment inflows into the e-commerce sector in the Southeast Asia region, including Alibaba's US$1 billion additional investment in Lazada, the launching of Amazon Prime Now service in Singapore, Expedia's US$350 million investment in Traveloka, Tencent's US$100 million (and Google-Temasek's in 2018) investment in Go-Jek, and Alibaba's US$1 billion investment in Tokopedia. The Indonesian government has also initiated direct link-ups with the founder and CEO of Alibaba, Jack Ma, to be adviser for the country's e-commerce roadmap steering committee.

In future, with improved infrastructure and an increase in middle-class consumers, the e-commerce sector in Indonesia is likely to become a new growth motor. This sector development might have significant effects on the local economy and the people. This chapter explores the state of e-commerce sector development in Indonesia. It examines the population and the country's readiness to use ICTs through reviews of previous research and statistics. Then we analyse policy documents, particularly the sector roadmap, to identify key challenges and prospects for e-commerce sector development in Indonesia. We show some findings related to the use of ICTs and e-commerce for transactions based on a national survey carried out by ISEAS in May 2017 (Fossati, Hui and Negara 2017). The last section concludes and provides some policy recommendations.

2.   Population and ICT Readiness

Access to ICTs

Judging from its population size, Indonesia has the potential to be the largest e-commerce market in Southeast Asia. The country has a relatively large young population, with more than half aged below 30 years old, with median age at 28 years old (Indonesia-Investments n.d.). The young population is also increasingly becoming more connected to digital technology and internet, especially with the development of cheap mobile devices. Many urban Indonesians own two or more mobile devices. The country has significant number of users of social media apps, such as Facebook, Twitter, and Instagram.[1] McKinsey (2016) reported that even though "Indonesia's internet penetration is low—only 34 per cent of internet penetration rate, much lower if compared with Singapore (82 per cent), Malaysia (68 per cent), Thailand (56 per cent), and the Philippines (46 per cent)—but its connected citizens are tech savvy." The latter is measured based on: the time spent on internet via mobile device (Indonesian internet users on average spend 3.5 hours per day on internet via mobile device); the time spent on social media (Indonesian internet users on average spend 2.9 hours per day on social media); the percentage of internet users that visit Facebook (90 per cent of Indonesian internet users visit Facebook regularly); and the percentage of population that have made online purchases per active internet user (almost 80 per cent of Indonesian active internet users ever purchase online products or services).

Nevertheless, the amount of time spent on the internet or social media, or the frequency of doing online shopping, are not a good proxy of technological savviness. Even in the United States, studies on technological and digital literacy have shown that being "exposed to information or imagery through the internet and engaging with social media do not make someone a savvy interpreter of the meaning behind these artefacts" (Boyd 2015, p. 177).[2] Therefore, the assumption of tech-savviness of Indonesian-connected citizens should be interpreted with caution as it may overlook the highly uneven distribution of ICT access, literacy, and skills across the population. The latter is determined by various factors, such as age, gender, race, education, and socio-economic status. What can be achieved with a cheap mobile phone on an intermittent, prepaid subscription is vastly different from a laptop or desktop with a stable broadband connection. Moreover, wide disparity in terms of socio-economic conditions (see Figure 6.1) and ICT access, all these factors need to be considered in analysing the potential of digital economy in the country.

Figure 6.1 illustrates the wide regional disparity in Indonesia. West Java and East Java provinces have the highest concentration in terms of population, with 48 million and 39 million population, respectively. In contrast, provinces in the eastern part of Indonesia, such as Maluku and Papua have relatively much smaller population, less than 2 million. Moreover, provinces like Jakarta has a relatively high GDP per capita, much higher if compared with that of Maluku province, or even West and East Java, the two most populous provinces in the country. There is also wide disparity in terms of spending between urban and rural population. The average monthly spending per capita in urban areas is around 65 per cent higher than that of their counterparts in rural areas.

Within the Southeast Asian region, Indonesia's IT readiness indicators rank relatively low if compared with those of its neighbouring countries. According to the World Economic Forum's IT Network Readiness Index, Indonesia's IT network infrastructure, skills, network usage and economic impact scores are all lagging behind those of Malaysia, Thailand, and the Philippines (see Figure 6.2).

FIGURE 6.1
Regional Differences in Indonesia

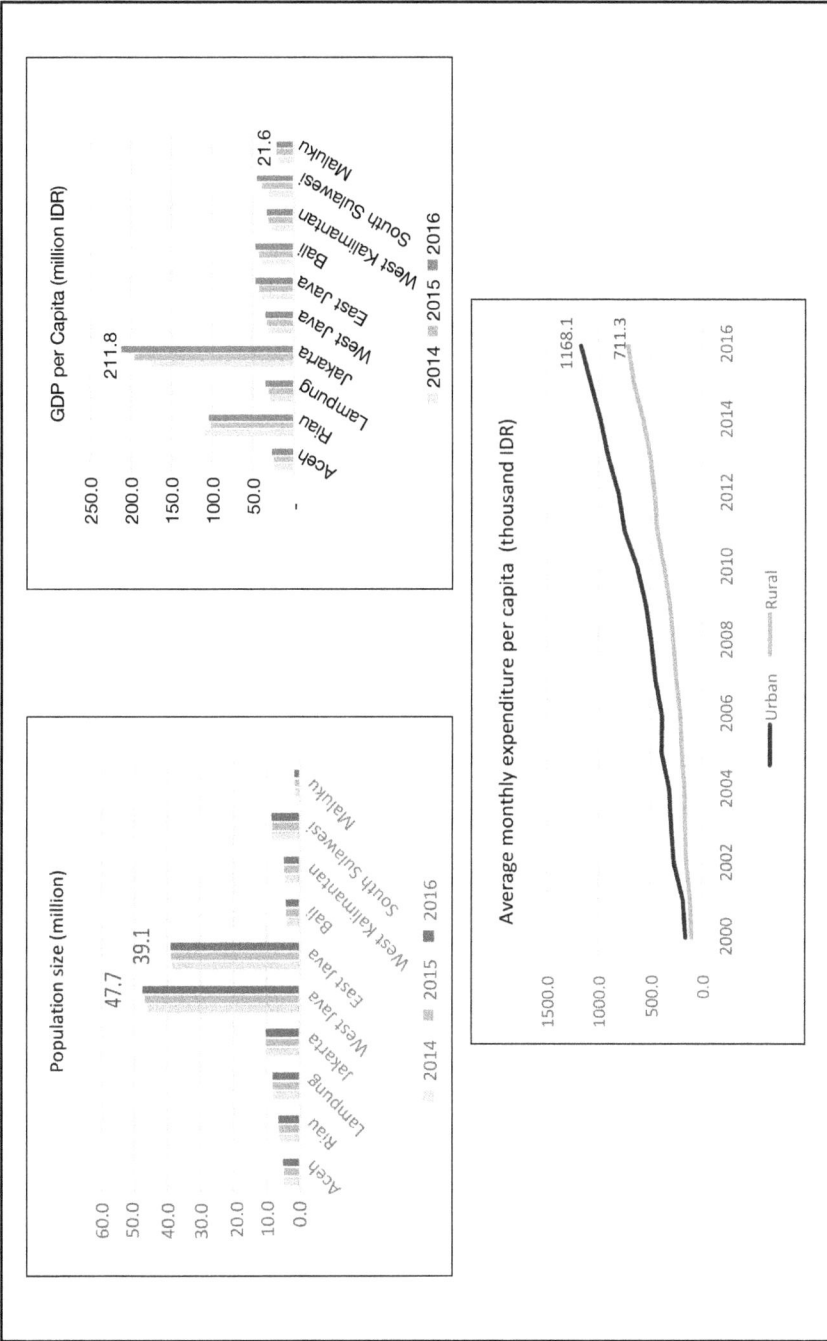

Population size (million)

GDP per Capita (million IDR)

Average monthly expenditure per capita (thousand IDR)

Source: BPS via CEIC.

FIGURE 6.2
ICT Readiness Index in Selected Countries, 2012–16

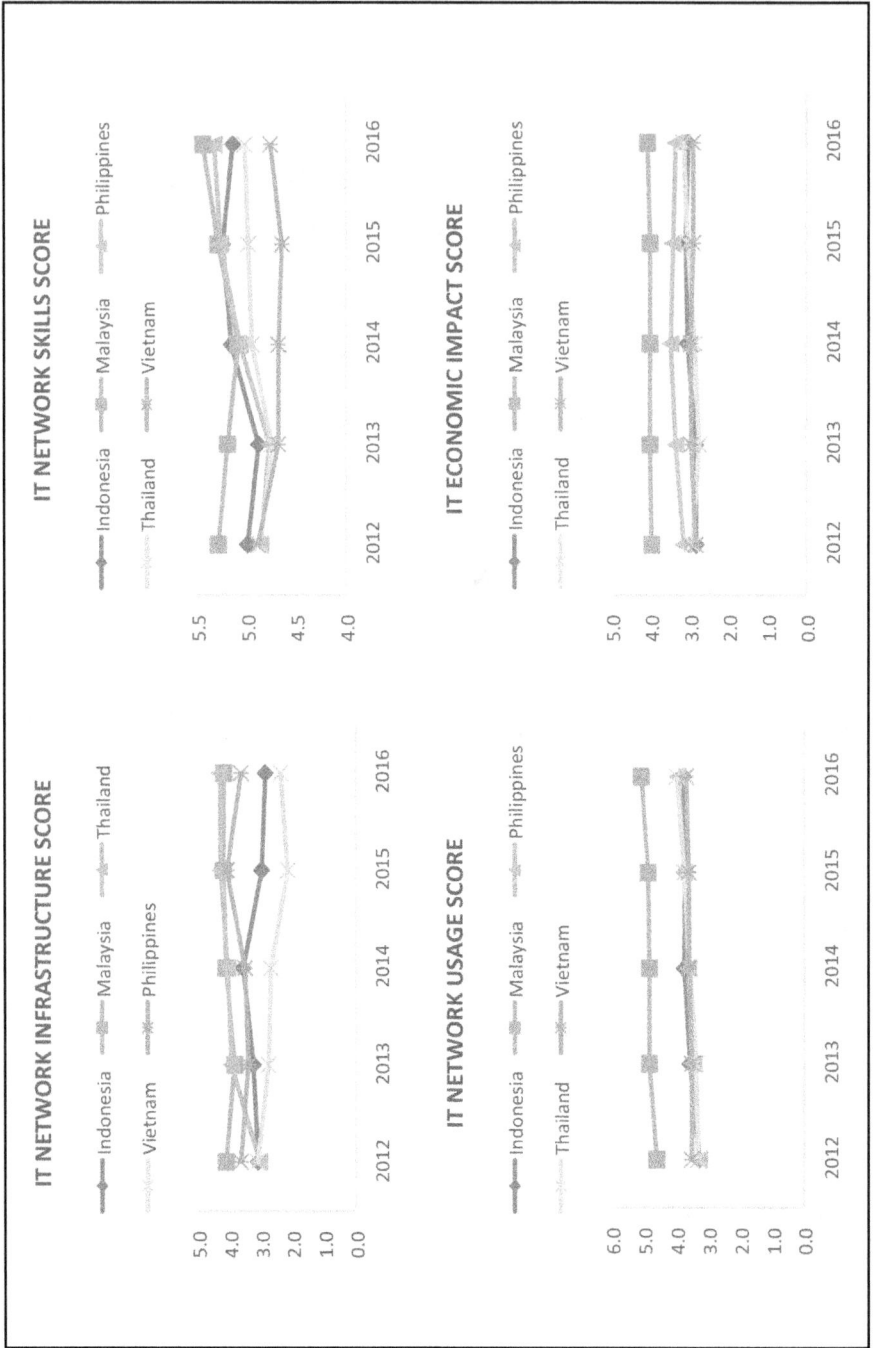

Source: World Economic Forum, via CEIC.

According to data from the ITU World Telecommunication, mobile cellular subscription in Indonesia has grown rapidly, reaching 132 per 100 inhabitants in 2015 (Azali 2017). This rapid growth in mobile subscription allows more and more people in getting internet access. In fact, in Indonesia, around 70 per cent of those who are connected to the internet did so via a mobile phone (Balea 2016). Yet while there are more mobile cellular subscriptions than people, Indonesia's mobile and internet teledensity remains low in the region (see Figure 6.3). This phenomenon indicates wide disparity in terms of internet access in the country. With penetration rate at only around 22 per 100 inhabitants in 2015, Indonesia has the lowest internet teledensity in Southeast Asia (see Figure 6.3).

It is worth mentioning that the vast majority of mobile subscriptions in Indonesia—up to 98 per cent—are prepaid SIM cards. SIM cards are cheap (can be purchased with Rp15,000 or around US$1), easy to acquire, swap, and discharge. However, the quality of mobile-data speed is low, the signal coverage is intermittent and unevenly distributed. Telkomsel, the state-owned telecommunication operator, generally has better coverage, but it charges consumers more for data packages. For example, in April 2017, Telkomsel's cheapest monthly subscription costs Rp52,500 for 600 MB data bundle, while its competitors Indosat charges Rp59,000 for 2 GB data package and XL charges Rp39,000 for 1 GB data package.[3] Moreover, the internet charges are differentiated by zones, in which areas with more cellular coverage enjoy cheaper prices, while those with less coverage area have to pay more. In short, cost-conscious users in Indonesia have to juggle multiple SIM cards to take advantage of promotions, better coverage quality, or better prices.

There are varying statistics about the state of ICTs and e-commerce in Indonesia. For example, the Association of Indonesia Internet Service Providers (APJII 2016) reported that the number of internet users in Indonesia increased from 34.9 per cent (88.1 million) in 2014 to 51.8 per cent (132.7 million) in 2016. This figure is significantly higher than the ITU figure of 22 per cent in 2015.[4] Moreover, in August 2017 the Nielsen Consumer and Media View reported that the internet penetration rate in the country has increased from 26 per cent in 2012 (ITU's figure for 2012 is 14.5 per cent) to 44 per cent in 2016. It is important to note that while Nielsen surveyed 17,000 respondents, the survey was done only in major cities (Diela 2017*b*). To further add to the confusion,

FIGURE 6.3
Mobile and Internet Teledensity in Selected Countries, 2005–15

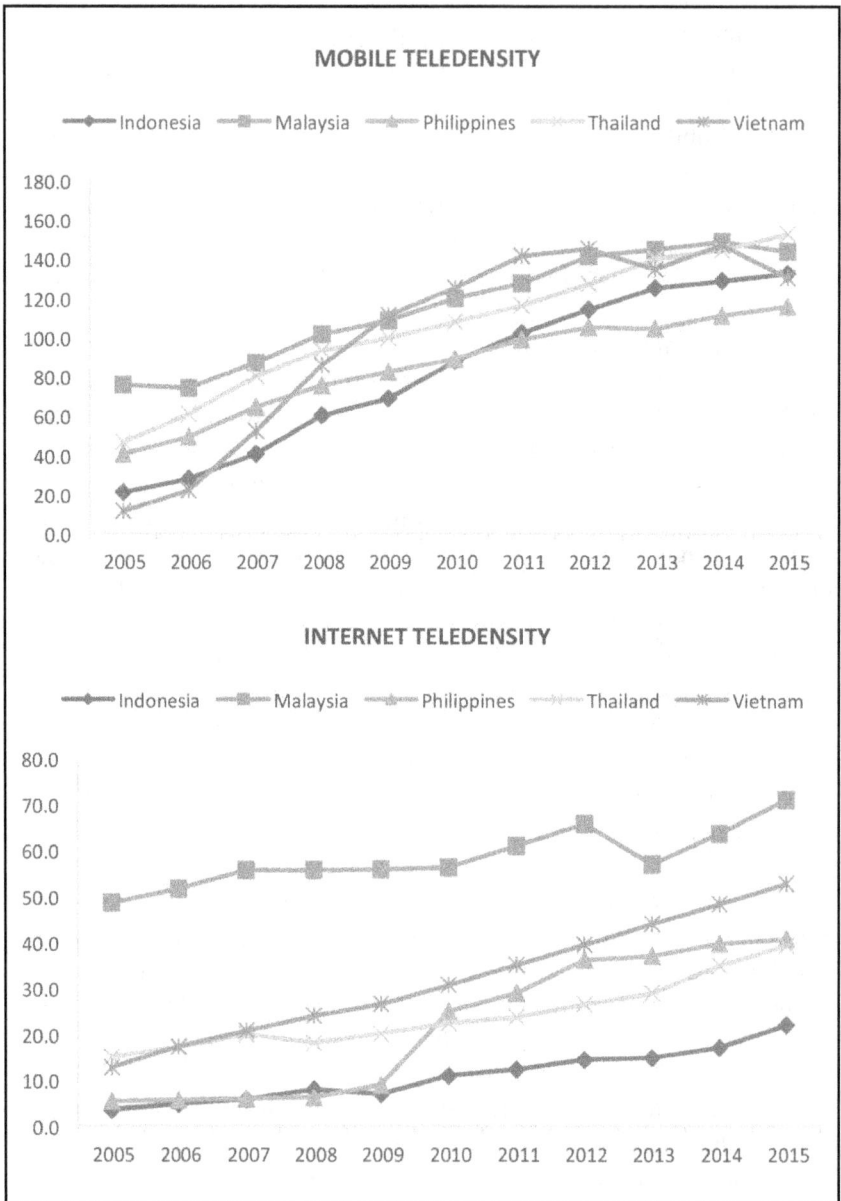

MOBILE TELEDENSITY

Indonesia ━━ Malaysia ━━ Philippines ━━ Thailand ━━ Vietnam

INTERNET TELEDENSITY

Indonesia ━━ Malaysia ━━ Philippines ━━ Thailand ━━ Vietnam

Note: Figures per 100 people.
Source: World Bank via CEIC.

up to 11 per cent—literally millions—of Indonesians when surveyed state that they use Facebook, but at the same time say that they do not use the internet.[5] This corroborates our point that being frequently exposed to the internet and social media does not necessarily translate to technological savviness. A nation-wide survey commissioned by ISEAS reveals that only about 31 per cent of Indonesians aged 17 and above used the internet. All things considered, we guesstimate that the internet penetration rate in Indonesia is likely to hover around 34–37 per cent.[6]

In terms of internet speed, the average internet speed in Indonesia has increased considerably from 3.2 Mbps in 2014 to 6.7 Mbps in 2016 (Trading Economics n.d.). However, this is still slower than the global and regional average.[7] The mobile 3G and higher connections still rely on existing infrastructure broadband and fibre optic, which will not be sufficient to support the growth of data traffic (expected to rise six-fold by 2020 according to McKinsey 2016). The ambitious Palapa Ring project to develop submarine fibre optic networks throughout Indonesia is still ongoing and if completed, it is expected to boost connectivity infrastructure (see Figure 6.8). However, the progress of this project, which was first initiated in 1998, is slow due to financing and geographical challenges, especially in the eastern part of the country.

Characteristics of Internet Users in Indonesia

In terms of age group, the younger population below 40 years old has the highest internet penetration rate, around 75 per cent (see Figure 6.4). This is consistent with the survey findings from APJII (2016). APJII's survey shows that internet penetration is 47.5 per cent among women and 52.5 per cent among men. The national survey conducted by ISEAS (INSP) revealed similar results, but two particular age groups showed noticeable differences. For 20–30 years old cohort, female internet users (35.6 per cent) is much higher than its male counterpart (23.7 per cent). Meanwhile for 30–40 years old group, there is a higher penetration among male population (29.8 per cent) compared with female (24.9 per cent). In addition, internet penetration is higher in the urban areas than rural areas (see Figure 6.4), indicating better ICT infrastructure in the urban areas. There is, however, an inverse pattern among gender groups in urban and rural areas. Internet penetration is about 5.5 per cent higher among women (36 per cent) than men (30.5 per cent) in rural areas, while in urban areas, it is the opposite,

FIGURE 6.4
Internet Users in Indonesia, by Gender, Age Group and Location, 2017

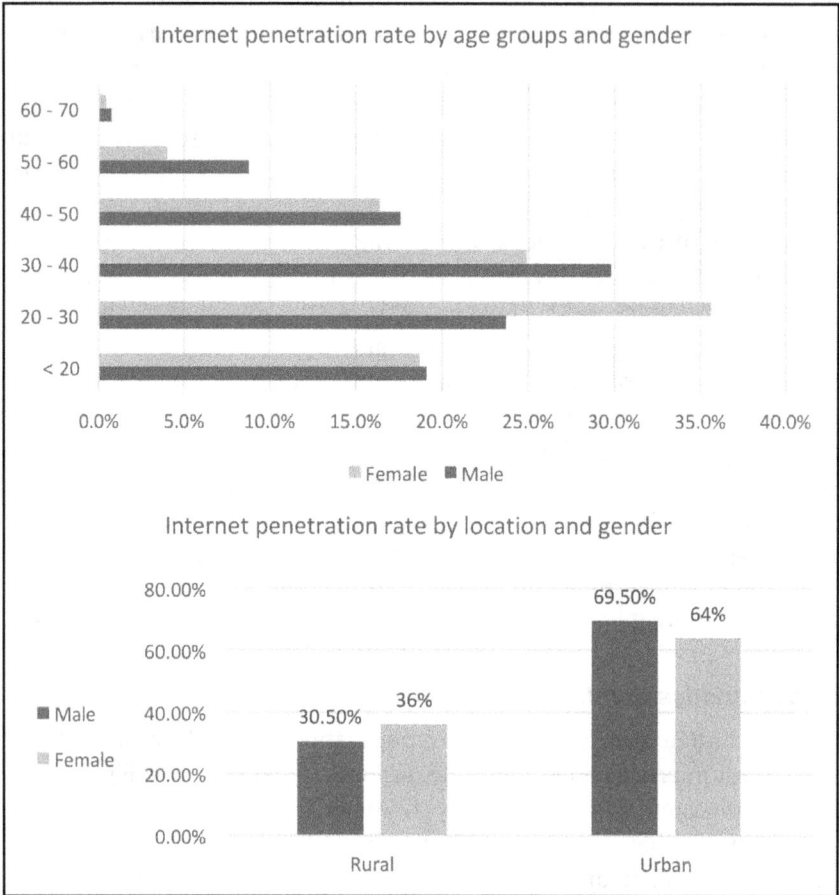

Internet penetration rate by age groups and gender

Internet penetration rate by location and gender

Source: INSP (2017).

with 5.5 per cent more penetration among men (69.5 per cent) than women (64 per cent).

The distribution of ICT infrastructure and cellular coverage is also very uneven across the country. Figure 6.5 shows where the concentration of cellular markets are, with 61.2 per cent internet penetration in Java, but less than a third in Sumatra (17.1 per cent), and even much lower in Kalimantan (7.8 per cent), Sulawesi (7 per cent), Bali and Nusa Tenggara (4.1 per cent) and Maluku and Papua (2.9 per cent).

FIGURE 6.5
Internet Penetration and Cellular Coverage in Main Islands

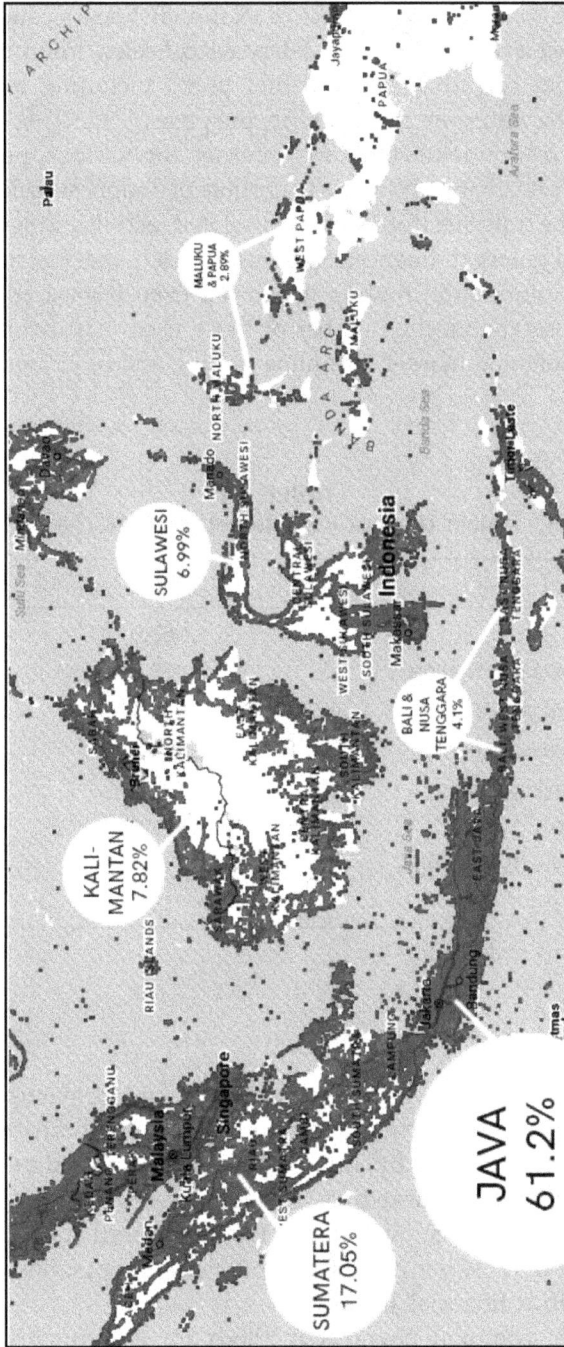

Source: The dotted area showed cellular (2G, 3G, 4G) coverage from OpenSignal (July 2017). The authors have added the rate of the internet penetration in Indonesian islands to the map based on the INSP (2017) results.

In addition, the 2015 and 2016 National Socio-economic Survey (*Survey Sosial Ekonomi National*, Susenas) collected information on the characteristics of Indonesia's internet users, including how intensive they use the internet for specific purposes.[8] Table 6.1 shows the portion of respondents that use internet for various purposes. The figures indicate that only a small portion of Indonesia's internet users has used the internet for economic-related activities, such as online trading and internet finance. Most users used the internet for social media and information finding. However, even from a relatively short two-year observation, the number of those users has increased rapidly, signalling potential market for online trading and other business-related activities.

TABLE 6.1
Main Uses of the Internet, 2015–16 (%)

	2015	2016
Social Media	82.0	85.8
Searching news/information	73.5	77.6
Entertainment/games	45.1	49.0
Doing school assignments	35.1	31.2
Sending/receiving email	27.8	27.7
Online trading	11.3	13.2
Financial facility (E-banking)	8.4	9.3
Others	3.9	3.9

Source: Susenas (2015, 2016).

Payment System

Indonesia's payment system is relatively underdeveloped and less sophisticated compared with those of its neighbouring countries. According to a research by Tufts University, sponsored by MasterCard (Chakravorti and Chaturvedi 2017), Indonesia is ranked 45th out of 60 countries for its digital evolution. Moreover, based on the 2014 World Bank Index, only 36 per cent of the Indonesian population has a formal account with a financial institution.

The most common payment methods for e-commerce transactions are bank transfer through ATMs and payment upon receipt or Cash on Delivery (COD). These create inefficiency for e-commerce businesses in the country. Internet banking, credit cards, SMS banking and e-money make up less than 15 per cent of the payment methods (see Table 6.2).

TABLE 6.2
Online Transaction Payment Mechanism

	Percentage	Number (million)
ATM	36.7	48.7
COD	14.2	18.8
Internet banking	7.5	9.9
Credit card	2.5	3.3
SMS Banking	1.6	2.1
E-money	0.7	0.93

Source: APJII (2016).

As of September 2017, there are 121 operators of ATM and ATM/debit card, 32 for credit card, and 26 for electronic money (e-money) in Indonesia.[9] There has been a significant increase in the use of cashless payment, e-money, and financial technology (fin-tech). Table 6.3 shows that cashless transactions have increased, mainly driven by debit card transactions. Meanwhile, credit card transactions have grown ssluggishly. This is mainly due to the regulation limiting credit ownership only to those with a monthly income of more than Rp3 million (*Kompas* 2014). However, e-money transactions have increased more than tenfold in both volume and value between 2010 and 2016, from their lower bases. Nevertheless, e-money transactions are mostly used for low-value (and high-volume) payments such as parking fees, toll road payments, and groceries purchases at mini-markets, such as Alfamart and Indomaret.

The government has campaigning the use of non-cash payment system. There is an effort to integrate this cashless payment system within the country's taxation system and other social service provision, such as for *Kartu Indonesia Pintar* (Indonesia Smart Card) and *Kartu Indonesia Sehat* (Indonesia Health Card). In September 2017, Bank

TABLE 6.3
Total Transactions Using Debit Cards, Credit Cards, and E-money

		2010	2011	2012	2013	2014	2015	2016
Debit card	Volume	1,812,076	2,262,299	2,824,108	3,510,209	4,077,696	4,574,388	5,196,512
	Value	2,001,853	2,477,041	3,065,080	3,797,370	4,445,073	4,897,794	5,623,913
Credit card	Volume	199,036	209,352	221,580	239,099	254,320	281,326	305,052
	Value	163,208	182,602	201,841	223,370	255,057	280,544	281,021
E-money	Volume	26,542	41,060	100,624	137,901	203,370	535,580	683,133
	Value	693	981	1,972	2,907	3,320	5,283	7,064

Note: Volume in thousand, value in billion.

Source: Bank Indonesia.

Indonesia issued a Regulation No. 19/2017 on the National Payment Gateway (NPG). The NPG regulation, scheduled to be implemented in April 2019, requires foreign principals (VISA, Mastercard, and so on) to work with local switching companies (*Artajasa Pembayaran Elektronis*, *Rintis Sejahtera*, and *Daya Network Lestari*, among others). The four major banks (Bank Rakyat Indonesia, Bank Mandiri, Bank Negara Indonesia, and Bank Central Asia), which represent 75 per cent of all domestic debit transactions, will act as the national principals switching companies (Diela 2017*a*). Henceforth, we foresee growing investment in developing cashless payment system.[10]

3. E-commerce Landscape

E-commerce market in Indonesia has been growing and taking a larger portion of the retail sector in the country. Figure 6.6 shows the estimated e-commerce transaction value in the country. It has grown rapidly from around a quarter billion dollars in 2012 to more than

FIGURE 6.6
E-commerce Transaction Value in Indonesia (US$ billion)

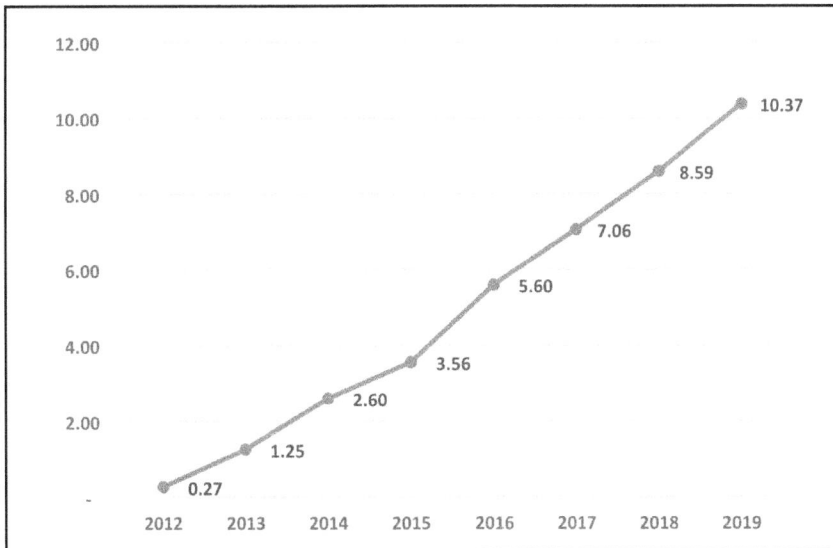

Note: 2018 and 2019 figures are estimated figures.

Source: Bank Indonesia, Statista, https://www.statista.com/statistics/280925/b2c-e-commerce-sales-in-indonesia/.

seven billion dollars in 2017. Considering its rapid growth, the Indonesian government has high expectations on the sector not only as a new growth motor but also a means to promote inclusivity in the economy (Julianto 2017). This is because e-commerce has opened up opportunities for many small and medium enterprises to promote their products and services.

Bede Moore, the co-founder and former Managing Director of Lazada Indonesia, stated that the flurry of programmes and funds invested in e-commerce in Indonesia was unimaginable couple of years ago, and many new players have emerged (Moore 2017, p. 268). He explained that the improvement of Indonesia's status in the global technology landscape was driven by two external factors. First, the 2008 global financial crisis (GFC) propelled many Western technology firms and venture capital to search for assets abroad, while Indonesia has navigated the GFC and at the same time maintained strong GDP growth. Second, the advancement of smartphone technology, whose cheap versions were quickly adopted in Indonesia around 2011 (where mobile penetration reached 100 per cent), followed with the popular spread of social media around the same period.

Table 6.4 indicates that Indonesia has the highest number of start-ups (2,033) in Southeast Asia, followed by Singapore (1,850) and Vietnam (1,541). Most of them are considered small start-ups with less than 10 million valuation. Only 16 ("little ponies") are valued between 10 and 100 million, and 7 ("centaurs") between 100 million and

TABLE 6.4
Summary of E-commerce Landscape in Selected ASEAN Countries

	Indonesia	Malaysia	Singapore	Philippines	Thailand	Vietnam
Small start-ups < US$10 million	2,010	749	1,807	377	348	1,529
Little ponies > US$10 million	16	7	27	7	8	9
Centaurs > US$100 million	7	3	12	1	2	3
Unicorns > US$1 billion	0	0	4	0	0	0

Source: Google-Temasek (2016), p. 14.

1 billion. Nevertheless, when Google-Temasek's report was released, all four "unicorns" (with more than US$1 billion valuation), i.e. Garena, Grab, Lazada, and Razer, were located in Singapore.

By July 2016, however, Go-Jek has become Indonesia's first billion-dollar start-up (Saiidi 2017). Starting out as a phone-based motorcycle ride-hailing services (*ojek*), Go-Jek now also operates in logistics (Go-Box), taxi (Go-Car), food delivery business (Go-Food), and mobile payment system (Go-Pay). In August 2017, Tokopedia, Indonesia's biggest online marketplace, received US$1.1 billion investment from China's e-commerce giant, Alibaba.

Four venture capital firms backed by the Indonesian powerful business families—Venturra Capital, Sinar Mas Digital Ventures, Convergence Ventures, and Emtek—have also invested in various large technology companies in the country, such as GrabTaxi, Bukalapak, KASKUS, DailySocial, BrideStory, PropertyGuru, MBDC Media, and so on (Moore 2017, p. 266).

There is an indication that a significant portion of online trading in Indonesia happens not through e-commerce platforms, but rather through social media. The findings from INSP provide rough estimation: while around 13.5 per cent of the respondents have used social media to buy and sell through the internet, only 7 per cent have used e-commerce platforms, e.g. Lazada, Tokopedia, etc. The popularity of social media among internet users as indicated above might be one reason behind it. Another reason might be related to the nature of social media and consumers' preferences. Transactions through social media require direct and more personal communications between buyers and sellers to select products and to settle for payment and delivery. That might be more suitable to consumers who are relatively new to online trading. This more personal approach is also preferable to many sellers and producers as they can maintain communications for promotional purposes while it is also easier to handle complaints more personally than through platforms (Damuri et. al. 2017).

Furthermore, the findings from INSP show that the most popular e-commerce transactions in Indonesia are for consumer goods, followed by ride-sharing, and travel and accommodation services (see Figure 6.7). This corroborates the findings of Pangestu and Dewi (2017).

TABLE 6.5
Key Local E-commerce Players

Company's Name	Product/Service	Type	Year of Establishment	Owner/Founder	Investor(s)
OLX	Online advertising	B2C, C2C	2005	Arnold Sebastian Egg and Remco Lupker	OLX group (Naspers)
FJB Kaskus	Online advertising	C2C	1999	Andrew Darwis, Ronald, and Budi	PT Darta Media Indonesia
Zalora Indonesia	Online shop	B2C	2012	Oliver Samwer, Hadi Wenas and Catherine Sutjahyo	PT Fashion Eservices Indonesia
Lazada Indonesia	Online shop	B2C	2012	Lazada Singapore	Alibaba
Bukalapak	Online marketplace	B2C, C2C	2010	Achmad Zaky	Emtek Group
Tokopedia	Online marketplace	C2C	2009	William Tanuwijaya and Leontinus Alpha Edison	Alibaba
Bhinneka	Online shop	B2C, C2C	1999	Hendrik Tio	
Blibli	Online shop	B2C, C2C	2010	Kusumo Martanto	PT Global Digital Niaga (Djarum)

Elevenia	Online marketplace	C2C	2014	James Lee	PT XL Axiata and SK Planet
Mataharimall	Online marketplace	B2C	2015	Goh Yiping	Lippo Group
Jualo.com	Online marketplace	C2C, B2C	2014	Chaim Fetter	
GOJEK	Motorcycle ride-hailing phone service		2010	Nadiem Makarim	Google, Temasek, Meituan-Dianping, Tencent
Traveloka	Hotels and ticket purchase online		2012	Ferry Unardi, Derianto Kusuma, and Albert Zhang	Expedia, JD.com, East Ventures, Hillhouse Capital Group, and Sequoia Capital
Tiket.com	Airways and railways ticket purchase online		2011	Wenas Agusetiawan	

Source: Authors' compilation.

FIGURE 6.7
What Did You Buy Online?

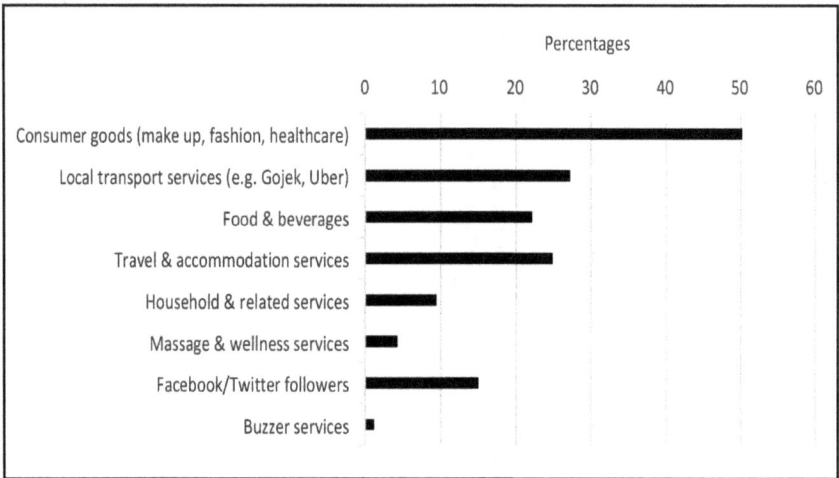

Source: INSP (2017).

In summary, Indonesia's e-commerce market has high growth potential. Future development of the sector will depend on several factors. First, Indonesia lacks in hardware manufacturing capacity and skilled workers. Second, Indonesia's commercial regulators started late in developing policy framework for e-commerce, when the country was already deeply embedded into Western technology backbone such as Facebook (including WhatsApp and Instagram), Microsoft, and Google (Moore 2017, p. 269). Third, compared to China's closed-environment model, Indonesia faces a much tougher competition in developing its own indigenous technological backbone. Clearly, local players will need to master the use of, and continue interactions with, existing foreign companies. However, given the country's ambivalent attitude towards foreign investment, it may be a challenge for Indonesia to compete with other neighbouring countries in attracting international e-commerce companies. In future, Indonesia needs to develop a more conducive ecosystem, including better consumer protection, taxation system, and fair competition policy, for its e-commerce sector to grow. Particularly, it is important to have clear regulations and codes of practice to enhance fair competition in the sector. As most players can often benefit from legal exemptions, this may reach certain limit until unfair competition happens. Therefore, the regulations must be effective to deter, detect and deal decisively with any mismanagement and wrongdoings. While currently, policymakers are still preparing various necessary regulations to support the sector development, it is useful to be mindful that the regulations must also be practical and allow some kind of flexibility to encourage innovation and ideas to flourish. In the next section, we turn to how the Indonesian government has been designing their policy framework under the national e-commerce roadmap.

4. E-commerce Policy in Indonesia

In November 2016, the Indonesian government released the 14th economic policy package on e-commerce roadmap. It states that Indonesia aims to create "1,000 technology entrepreneurs" with business valuation up to US$10 billion. It also sets a target for the country's e-commerce market to reach US$130 billion by 2020. Nine months later, a presidential regulation that governs the e-commerce roadmap implementation (2017–19) was signed by President Joko Widodo. The roadmap covers eight key areas: (1) funding, (2) taxation, (3) consumer protection, (4) education and human resources, (5) communication infrastructure, (6) logistics, (7) cybersecurity, and (8) the formation of committee for e-commerce roadmap implementation (*Sistem Perdagangan Nasional Berbasis Elektronik* or SPNBE). We will discuss some of the key policies below. The full list of the policies can be seen in Appendix 6.1.

General Policy Framework of Digital Platforms

All internet-related activities in Indonesia are regulated under the Law No. 11/2008 on Information and Electronic Transactions, which was partly revised by the Law No. 19/2016. The Law provides legal basis for all internet-based transactions, so that information and documents provided through the internet can be used as legal evidence. Despite the name, the Law does not provide specific measures for e-commerce or other internet-based economic transactions. Instead, what it means as "electronic transaction" is legal activities conducted through computer and computer network and other media. It focuses mainly on the contents of information in internet-based media, which may bring criminal conviction to related parties including platform providers.

There had been some confusion about the responsibility of marketplace providers on the information available in their platforms: whether the providers should be legally responsible for false information on products being sold there, or they just simply provide the platform for electronic transactions. While there is no significant legal event related to this, the confusion had a potential to hamper e-commerce development, since this legal responsibility might lead to criminal charges to platform providers. In order to clear up the issue, the Ministry of Communication and Informatics (MOCI) released a circular that provides "safe harbour policy" to e-commerce marketplaces. The policy provides greater certainty for marketplace providers as it limits the scope of liability of the parties involved, including the responsibility of providers on user-generated-contents in their platforms. This safe harbour policy, however, is only applicable to marketplace platforms, but not for social media.

There are several other unresolved policy issues that may affect the development of e-commerce and other digital applications. First, the Indonesian government has considered that all platforms should have representation in Indonesia, although it does not require the platforms to have legal establishment in the country; it can take the form of a representative agency or other types of representation. Second, there is an intensive discussion on data localization requirement. The government might require platforms to use domestic IP numbers and place servers or part of servers in data centres located in Indonesia based on the argument of data privacy and sovereignty. Internet-based platforms in Indonesia, however, have been trying hard to oppose such requirements on the basis that it might jeopardize data security and against international common practice of free flow of data. Third, there have been cases of dispute between network providers and digital platforms, where providers block or limit digital services from their network while giving preference to other similar services. The most prominent case is the blocking of Telkom to Netflix services in its network, while at the same time bundling its data package with entertainment services from its partner companies (*Jakarta Post* 2016a).

The government has been trying to provide general policy framework to resolve those issues. The MOCI has been circulating a draft regulation to deal with those issues since 2016, but has yet to come up with an arrangement due to diverse interests and overly ambitious purpose. The initial plan is to have an "umbrella" regulation to handle several basic issues of digital and online platforms. It turns out that the need for such policies is different from one online service to another.

Another important policy issue is the obligation for internet-based platforms to comply with sectoral-specific regulations. The case of ride-sharing services is an example of this issue. In respond to several conflicts between ride-sharing and traditional taxi providers, the Ministry of Transportation issued a regulation that requires ride-sharing providers to follow certain criteria comparable to traditional taxi providers, e.g. obtaining a special driving license, passing a roadworthy test, and operating in limited areas. The current regulation does not consider a ride-sharing platform as a transportation company, but there have been statements to consider it in the future (*Kontan.co.id* 2018). While there is no specific regulation at the moment in governing e-commerce marketplace, companies need to register their businesses with the Ministry of Trade, which is responsible for domestic commerce businesses. Such an approach would become more complicated and inapplicable given that an internet platform can extent its services to many other areas beyond its original business; for example, many marketplaces and ride-sharing platforms now also provide payment services for their customers.

Improving ICT Infrastructure

A reliable high-speed internet network is key for supporting rapid growth in e-commerce business (Pangestu and Dewi 2017, pp. 248–50). The Indonesian e-commerce roadmap only provides a single programme under the telecommunications infrastructure (see Appendix 6.1, Section E). This programme includes the provision of free domain and speed of internet access that support the growth of e-commerce, and the provision of broadband infrastructure, to be rolled out by July 2019. To support this programme, the Indonesian government has been developing the Palapa ring project (see Figure 6.8). This project aims to connect 514 regencies and cities through a broadband connection and provide faster communication services throughout the country by 2019 (Amindoni 2016). If completed, this project will address the huge digital divide in the country. In September 2016, the average download

FIGURE 6.8
Indonesia's Palapa Ring Project

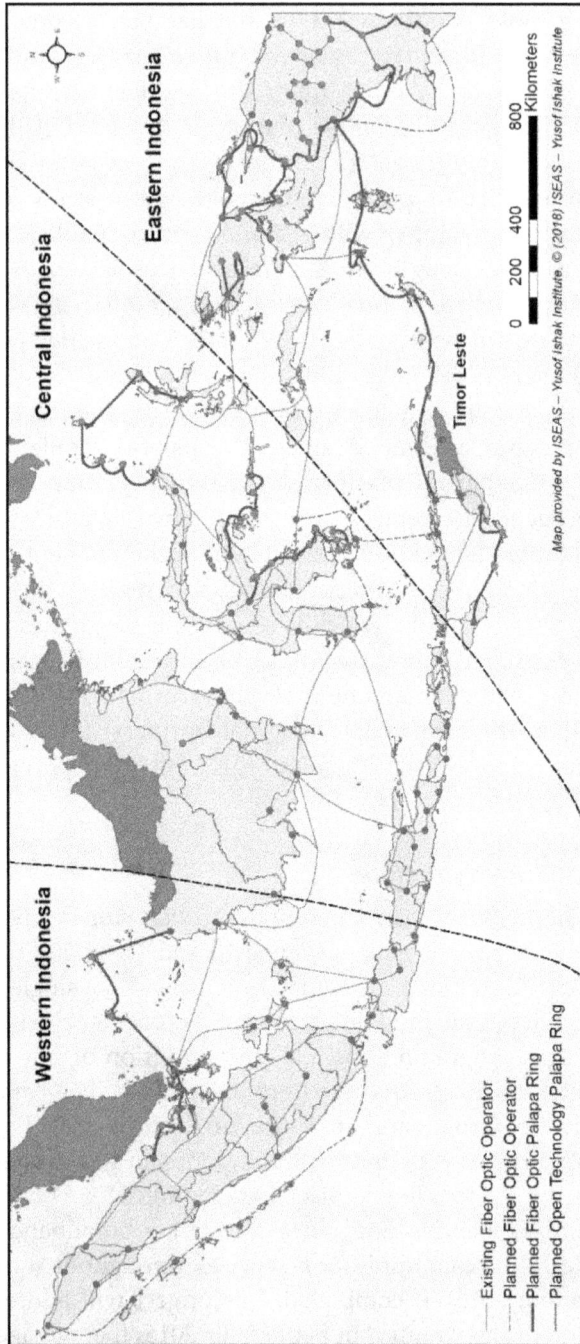

Source: Ministry of Communication and Informatics (Kominfo), http://www.pubinfo.id/beritapub-pemerintah-resmikan-proyek-palapa-ring-paket-tengah.html.

speed in Jakarta was about 7 Mbps. Meanwhile in Papua, the average download speed was only about 300 kilobits per second (Amindoni 2016). Not to mention that the people in Papua—similar to many less covered areas—have to pay higher price for internet and mobile subscriptions, as we have elaborated in the previous section. The Palapa ring project is estimated to cost around US$1.6 billion (Suprayitno 2017). It remains to be seen, however, whether the mega project can be completed on time, as it has been experiencing several interruptions since its conception in 1998.

In addition to the ambitious Palapa ring project, there have been a number of bottom-up strategies to build cellular networks in rural areas using open source technologies. However, the current regulations— which only allow large carriers to operate cellular networks—have made community-driven approaches legally difficult to operate, with potential closure by the police (Purbo 2017, p. 84). Moreover, developing the high-speed broadband network also needs to be supported with other infrastructure such as reliable supply of electricity and good transport networks. Here lies the biggest challenge in the country, which is to overcome the wide infrastructure gap between Java and other regions (Ray 2016).

Logistics

Closely related to the issue of infrastructure is the quality of logistics, which is crucial for a successful e-commerce business. Unfortunately, the logistics sector performance in Indonesia is relatively poor. Despite the country's long-standing aspiration to develop a comprehensive national logistics system (Sislognas), the speed and cost of distribution remains uncompetitive. One of the biggest obstacles is Indonesia's topographical structure with over 17,000 islands. In most part of the country, infrastructure, such as seaports, airports, roads, bridges, and railways are poorly developed. According to a media interview with a courier service and logistics company, PT Tiki Jalur Nugraha Ekakurir (JNE), there is no direct shipping line from Jakarta to Tanjung Selor in North Kalimantan, which is directly adjacent to the Malaysian border. To deliver a package from Jakarta to that area, JNE needs to send the package by plane to the nearest airport in Tarakan, North Kalimantan, then take a one-and-a-half-hour trip using a speed boat to take the package to Tanjung Selor (Singgih 2016).

Moreover, delivering goods outside Java can take more than ten days and sea freight costs can exceed US$1,000 for a 20 ft container (World Bank 2015). Given this reality, Indonesia's poor logistics sector has been blamed for the country's lack of competitiveness as a trading nation. In response to this challenge, the government has released the 15th economic policy package to reform the country's logistics sector. Realistically, it will take a long time to reform the country's lagging logistics sector. To start, the government must first address the inefficiency caused by regulatory and bureaucratic hurdles affecting the sector. For instance, the port handling process involves more than a dozen institutions and service providers apart from land transportation (Lingga 2017). Inefficient port handling and poor sea transportation hinder connectivity between the islands. This in turn prevents the least developed regions to connect with the growth centres in Java and Sumatera. Beyond investing in physical infrastructure, e.g. ports, airports and roads, Indonesia must also address its weak soft infrastructure, i.e. streamlining and untangling the complex bureaucratic and regulatory maze in its logistics system.

Payment System

To improve efficiency and security of online transactions, there is a need to develop a reliable and efficient digital payment mechanism. For Indonesia, it is challenging to transform 60 per cent of the un-bankable population, who prefer "cash on delivery" method, to use online payment system (*Jakarta Post* 2017). Part of the problem is that there is no widespread easy to use e-payment system, such as Alipay in China. Bank Indonesia has also launched a nation-wide non-cash payment programme, encouraging consumers to use e-money for daily transactions. While the motivation is good, however, the implementation is not easy as consumers strongly refuse to pay administrative fee for topping up credit in their accounts (Setiawan 2017). While there will be some resistance and difficulties, in the long run this "non-cash payment programme" will benefit the e-commerce industry, and especially the consumers. At the same time, there are also questions about how the cost burden of technological development and maintenance is going to be shared. For example, Bank Indonesia Regulation No. 19/2017 on the National Payment Gateway states that consumers must pay the administrative cost for any top-up of more than Rp200,000 (US$15). There has been strong consumers' rejection on this regulation. Henceforth, this will require public communication outreach and investment in banking and ICT infrastructure all over the country in order to minimize the cost for consumers.

Financing Schemes

Many local start-ups and small and medium-sized enterprises (SMEs) face funding constraint as capitals are concentrated on seed stage investments than in early stage investments. In the national e-commerce roadmap, the government states that it will allocate subsidized loans programmes (KUR) to support and protect local SMEs and start-ups (see Appendix 6.1, Section A). While providing funding for start-ups and SMEs in the early stage is critical, it is also important to ensure their sustainable growth and profitability. This requires continued innovation. Moreover, the government must ensure that the KUR programme helps sustain innovation within these start-ups and SMEs. It is important to note that Indonesia's market is similar to China's and India's, which is highly price-sensitive. The popular business model of most start-ups is relatively simple and may not be sustainable. Their business model relies on subsidizing customers in the short term, assuming it will lead to consumers' dependency that will continue even after the discounts disappear. However, in many occasions, once the company stops offering discounts, a substantial part of the customer base will stop buying the services offered. Therefore, the funding scheme needs to be complemented with incentives to promote innovative business models.

Pangestu and Dewi (2017, p. 249) highlight the need to "provide mechanisms not only to encourage people to invest in start-ups but also to allow them to exit their investments without too much difficulty, whether through the capital market or through mergers and acquisitions". This is because of "the uncertain role of financial capital in investments and the tax treatment of investors' capital gains" (p. 249). They also caution the government to find the right balance in ensuring a level playing field in terms of tax and regulatory compliance so as not to drive away large foreign technology companies such as Google and Facebook.[11]

Education and Human Resources

The ICT sector in Indonesia is projected to grow at an average of 17 per cent per year, while the value of digital economy is estimated to expand by six-fold to US\$130 billion by 2020 (*Jakarta Post* 2016*b*). However, there is a pertinent issue of lack of skilled human resources, especially engineers, coders, and platform developers (Pangestu and Dewi 2017, p. 249). According to a joint report by Singapore Management University and JP Morgan, unless skills training is dramatically improved, Indonesia could face a shortfall of about nine million skilled and semi-skilled ICT workers between 2016 and 2030 (Tan and Tang 2016).

In reality, the lack of skilled workers in Indonesia is widespread and affects not only the ICT sector but also other key economic sectors, including automotive, tourism, and many others. The issue is not because of a lack of fund, as the Indonesian government allocates at least 20 per cent of the annual expenditure for education. The fundamental problem is deep-rooted in the country's education and training system, with poor teacher quality, weak incentive system, lack of education training, lack of basic school facilities, low school retention rates, and so on.[12]

Under the national e-commerce roadmap, the government aims to promote education and human resources to support the sector (see Appendix 6.1, Section D). Specifically, there are several programmes to promote awareness and campaigns for the general public, consumers, SMEs, and the whole ecosystem of e-commerce (D13), such as:

a. Education programmes on the use of e-commerce and industry development;
b. Mechanism and taskforce for developing the contents and executing the programmes;
c. Socialization of the types of illegal e-commerce products within the jurisdiction of Indonesia;
d. National awareness campaign of e-commerce through online and offline media; and
e. Promotion through informal campaigns (among others via the National Online Shopping Day "Harbolnas").

Moreover, there will be briefings and education for policymakers to gain an understanding about e-commerce in their respective roles (see Appendix 6.1, Section D14). There is also an incubation programme dedicated for start-ups development (see Appendix 6.1, Section D15), led by the Head of the Creative Economy Agency (BEKRAF). The government will also provide some programmes for developing e-commerce education facilitators, led by the Ministry of Trade (see Appendix 6.1, Section D17).

Beyond the government's initiatives, in the last few years, there has been notable increase in the number of seminars, lectures, talk shows, training, and workshops focusing on digital technologies and literacies in Indonesia. However, most of them are unstructured, ad hoc, incidental, sporadic, and without any substantial evidence of long-lasting partnerships or continuation. For example, a research carried out in nine cities in Indonesia found that most digital literacy education programmes were "voluntary, incidental, sporadic". About 56.1 per cent of the programmes were organized through universities and lectures—note that less than 10 per cent of the Indonesian population achieves university-level education. There is no evidence of long-lasting structural partnerships between the organizers and their students (Kurnia and Astuti 2017). In short, to learn this supposedly urgently required ICT skills, Indonesians have to rely on sporadic, unstructured initiatives by various government and private institutions. In view of this, the government should ensure that its facilitation and incentives for ICT education are well structured and integrated within the curriculum, rather than relying on ad hoc, sporadic private initiatives.

In the national e-commerce roadmap, it is stated that at the formal education level (see Appendix 6.1, Section D16), the implementation of a curriculum covering subjects related to e-commerce at various levels of educational units is set to start in November 2017. Incentive schemes will also be provided for educational organizations or units focusing on e-commerce-related training and education in order to increase the number of ICT graduates. However, the challenge will be in the implementation stage. Especially, considering the complex problems within Indonesia's education system, including the lack of qualified educators and trainers across the country, it is hard to imagine that there will be any significant changes in the short term.

Cyber Security

Finally, there is a pressing need to improve cyber security system to support e-commerce businesses in the country. According to the Coordinating Ministry of Political, Legal and Security Affairs, between 2014 and 2015, the number of cyberattacks in Indonesia rose by 33 per cent, of which 54.5 per cent were aimed at e-commerce-related websites, causing systems to stop working (Amindoni 2016a). Due to high levels of fraud and cybercrimes, many potential consumers become reluctant to shop online. In view of this, there is a need for effective mechanism to improve the protection of systems, networks and data in cyberspace. This is a critical issue for e-commerce businesses. For this, the government must ensure the readiness of relevant institutions to master body of technologies, processes and practices designed to protect networks, computers, programmes and data from attack, damage or unauthorized access. In respond to this need, in May 2017, Jokowi signed a Presidential Regulation No. 53/2017 on the establishment of the Cyber Body and National Encryption Agency (BSSN).

This development is critical for the following reasons. First, it indicates the government's commitment to promote the country's digital economy while at the same time safeguarding national interests in cyberspace. Second, it shows national awareness of increasing risk of cyberattack, especially after the worldwide "WannaCry" ransomware attacks. Third, the regulation provides the needed legal framework for strengthening cyber security system in the country. It transforms the old National Encryption Agency (Lemsaneg) and combined it with the Directorate for Information Security under the Communications and Information Ministry into a special agency for dealing with cyber security (Gindarsah 2017).

The structure of BSSN indicates the government's intention to secure the vital communications network, to protect critical information and to safeguard the country's digital economy. The last objective clearly shows the government's aim to set the digital economy as the future pillar of the country's economy. For a start, BSSN will focus on protecting energy, financial, healthcare and transportation-related information systems, as well as public telecommunications networks (Gindarsah 2017). Nevertheless, there is a need to coordinate various policies and programmes to promote the national cyber security system. In this case, BSSN must collaborate with other relevant institutions, including Defence and Security Ministry, Indonesian Military (TNI), State Intelligence Agency (BIN), National Police, and Communication and Information Ministry. Over time, BSSN needs to develop mutual beneficial relationship between the public and private sectors.

5. Conclusions

After China and India, Indonesia is predicted to be the next e-commerce giant in Asia. Indonesia's "consuming class" is estimated to increase from 45 million in 2010 to 135 million by 2030 (Oberman et al. 2012).

Such a big market has attracted many big technology companies to venture into Indonesia. This happens despite the country is still developing its infrastructure and the ecosystem to support the digital economy and its e-commerce sector.

In the region, Indonesia has low internet penetration rate. However, its internet penetration rate has grown to 30 per cent, up a staggering 10 per cent from what experts were quoting in 2014 (Cosseboom 2015). A survey conducted by ISEAS finds that more than 80 million people are already online in the archipelago (the number is higher if we count people who only access the internet via mobile phones). Despite many challenges facing the e-commerce sector, there are a number of successful local e-commerce start-ups, which have transformed to be unicorns, e.g. Tokopedia and Traveloka.

Certainly, the e-commerce sector will bring changes to the Indonesian economy. The sector has the potential to empower many local SMEs and to create more jobs for the young tech-savvy generation. To support the e-commerce sector, the Indonesian government has passed several regulations and created some programmes to support local players. This includes the e-commerce roadmap and the taskforce to implement various programmes under the roadmap.

In order to achieve the development objectives stated in the roadmap, the taskforce must ensure good collaboration between the public and private sectors. This will require good coordination among various stakeholders, to avoid overlapping and conflicting regulations/programmes. This will not be an easy task as there are many institutions/agencies involved in different areas of the e-commerce ecosystem, with different interests/institutional goals. However, each institutional goal will be dependent on the other, hence a bottleneck in one area will be transmitted to other areas. Therefore, the role of the e-commerce taskforce becomes crucial to ensure that each subset within the e-commerce roadmap remains on the right track to promote a conducive e-commerce ecosystem in Indonesia.

Finally, Indonesia needs to have clear operational regulations and codes of practice to enhance fair competition in the e-commerce sector. The regulations must be effective to deter, detect and deal decisively with any mismanagement and offences. At the same time, the regulations must also be practical and should not create unnecessary rules/costs that demotivate the sector to flourish.

Appendix 6.1
Indonesia's E-commerce Roadmap, 2017–19

NO.	PROGRAMME	ACTIVITIES	OUTPUT	DEADLINE	INSTITUTION IN CHARGE	RELATED AGENCIES
A.	Funding					
1.	Funding and loan-financing schemes	a. Improving access to people's business credit (KUR) with credit risk assessment tailored to e-commerce business model	The procedures and guidelines for the distribution of KUR covering credit penalties, requirements documents, business feasibility assessments to be guaranteed by the guarantee company, and loan terms adjusted to the e-commerce business model.	Oct 2017	Coordinating Ministry of Economy	1. Ministry of Finance 2. Ministry of Cooperatives and SME 3. Financial Service Authority (OJK) 4. Central Bank (BI)
		b. Optimizing the bank/non-bank financial industry (IKNB) as a KUR distributor	a. Regulation by the Coordinating Minister of Economy governing the tenants developing the e-commerce platform to be the recipients of KUR funds disbursed by Bank/IKNB. b. Increasing the intensity of Program Laku Pandai and e-money to support financial inclusion.	Nov 2017	Coordinating Ministry of Economy	1. OJK 2. Bank Indonesia 3. Ministry of Communication and Informatics 4. Ministry of Cooperatives and SME 5. Creative Economy Agency
2.	Financing and grant-financing schemes (grants)/ subsidies	a. Develop a grant provision scheme for the development of business incubator	Grant schemes to develop and increase the capacity of business incubators in providing optimal assistance for	Nov 2017	Coordinating Ministry of Economy	1. Ministry of Communication and Informatics 2. Creative Economy Agency 3. Ministry of Trade

Appendix 6.1   (*continued*)

NO.	PROGRAMME	ACTIVITIES	OUTPUT	DEADLINE	INSTITUTION IN CHARGE	RELATED AGENCIES
			innovative entrepreneur actors in start-ups, including those in the e-commerce sector.			4. Ministry of Finance 5. Ministry of Research, Technology and Higher Education 6. Ministry of Cooperatives and SMEs 7. Association of E-commerce and Digital Economy (idEA)
		b. Establishment of grant schemes with sources derived from corporate social responsibility funds of SOEs and similar bodies	Grant provision schemes through the relocation of some corporate social responsibility funds (of SOEs and large companies) that support various life cycle stages of e-commerce business.	Nov 2017	Ministry of SOEs	1. Ministry of Finance 2. Ministry of Trade 3. Ministry of Communication and Informatics 4. Ministry of Industry
3.	Availability of alternative provision of financing and grant/subsidy financing schemes	Aligning grant schemes and subsidies to support the ecosystem of digital economy	a. The Ministerial Regulation on Communications and Information Technology that supports the utilization of Universal Service Obligation (USO) funds that is not limited to only the telecommu-nications sector alone, but may also be utilized for digital economic ecosystems, especially in Disadvantaged, Remote and Outermost Areas (3T).	Oct 2017	Ministry of Communica-tion and Informatics	1. Ministry of Cooperatives and SMEs 2. Ministry of National Planning/ National Development Planning Agency 3. Ministry of Finance

Appendix 6.1   (*continued*)

NO.	PROGRAMME	ACTIVITIES	OUTPUT	DEADLINE	INSTITUTION IN CHARGE	RELATED AGENCIES
			b. Public Service Agencies that can distribute Government/ Universal Service Obligation (USO) grants/ government subsidies to digital UMKM and start-up e-commerce platforms, especially in 3T areas as needed.			
4.	Availability of alternative provision of financing and financing schemes of angel capital/ seed capital	a. Achieve business matching between angel investors and venture capital firms with potential e-commerce companies	Capital investment scheme through angel capital/ venture capital	Nov 2017	Coordinating Ministry of Economy	1. Ministry of Communication and Informatics 2. Creative Economy Agency 3. Ministry of Trade 4. OJK 5. Association of Venture Capital/ Angel Capital 6. Association of E-commerce and Digital Economy
		b. Develop a scheme using the "Bapak Angkat" approach that can be used by businesses or industries that do not belong to the big Information and Technology (ICT) industry by providing seed capital and tech support to support start-up entrepreneurs.	Provision scheme of seed capital from "Bapak Angkat" as ICT business actors	Nov 2017	Coordinating Ministry of Economy	1. Ministry of Communication and Informatics 2. Creative Economy Agency 3. Ministry of Trade 4. OJK 5. Association of Venture Capital/ Angel Capital 6. Association of E-commerce and Digital Economy

Appendix 6.1   (*continued*)

NO.	PROGRAMME	ACTIVITIES	OUTPUT	DEADLINE	INSTITUTION IN CHARGE	RELATED AGENCIES
5.	Availability of alternative funding and financing schemes– crowdfunding	Developing a crowdfunding scheme as an alternative to funding, including a risk management framework to properly set up the crowdfunding scheme.	A fund-raising implementation scheme by adopting a successful fund-raising scheme, providing protection to investors, and reducing the risk of corporate funding, including through financial support from large firms.	Nov 2017	Coordinating Ministry of Economy	1. Ministry of Finance 2. OJK 3. Ministry of Industry 4. Ministry of Communication and Informatics 5. Ministry of SOEs 6. Ministry of Trade 7. Bank Indonesia 8. Creative Economy Agency 9. Association of E-Commerce and Digital Economy
6.	The opening of a tiered Negative Investment List (DNI)	Establish DNI related to e-commerce in the form of tiered openings with requirements	2 (Two) new standard classifications of Indonesian business sector (KBLI) on e-commerce that represent the businesses of e-commerce, marketplace, digital ads, on demand service, etc. a. Provider of electronic-based platform (including application and OTT), with investment value up to Rp 100 billion (maximum 49 per cent foreign ownership); b. Provider of electronic-based platform (including application and	Oct 2017	Coordinating Ministry of Economy	1. Ministry of Communication and Informatics 2. Ministry of Trade 3. Investment Coordinating Board 4. Central Bureau of Statistics

Appendix 6.1 (*continued*)

NO.	PROGRAMME	ACTIVITIES	OUTPUT	DEADLINE	INSTITUTION IN CHARGE	RELATED AGENCIES
			OTT) with investment value above Rp100 billion (foreign ownership up to 100 per cent).			
B.	**Taxation**					
7.	Simplifying the fulfillment of tax obligations	a. Simplify taxation procedures for e-commerce business entrepreneurs whose turnover is below Rp4.8 billion per annum.	Implementation of taxation rules for business actors with total business circulation up to Rp4.8 billion per year, applicable to e-commerce business actors whose turnover is below Rp4.8 billion per year.	Dec 2017	Ministry of Finance	1. Ministry of Cooperatives and SME 2. Ministry of Trade 3. Creative Economy Agency
		b. Establish tax incentives for trade investors	1) Incentive schemes for venture capital firms that invest capital in companies that meet certain criteria, including e-commerce companies.	Nov 2017	Ministry of Finance	1. Ministry of Cooperatives and SME 2. Ministry of Trade 3. Creative Economy Agency
			2) A tax incentive assessment document for angel investors and other funding sources that fund start-ups in the early stages.	Dec 2017	Ministry of Finance	1. Coordinating Ministry of Economy 2. Ministry of Communication and Informatics 3. Ministry of Cooperative and SME 4. Creative Economy Agency 5. Association of E-commerce and Digital Economy

Appendix 6.1 (*continued*)

NO.	PROGRAMME	ACTIVITIES	OUTPUT	DEADLINE	INSTITUTION IN CHARGE	RELATED AGENCIES
8.	Preparation of registration procedures for e-commerce business actors	Establish regulation of obligations of e-commerce business actors to register themselves, including foreign business actors.	Ministry regulation from the Ministry of Trade concerning the Provisions and Procedures for Registration and Issuance of Identity Number of Business Entities of Trade Transactions Through Electronic Systems (TPMSE).	Sep 2017	Ministry of Trade	1. Ministry of Finance 2. Ministry of Communication and Informatics 3. Association of E-commerce and Digital Economy
9.	Tax standardization	Arrange regulations that support the taxation of foreign and local e-commerce business actors in accordance with the provisions of the laws and regulations in the field of taxation.	Regulations from the ministry and the head of agencies of related sectors	Feb 2018	Coordinating Ministry of Economy	1. Ministry of Finance 2. Ministry of Trade 3. Ministry of Communication and Informatics
C.	**Consumer Protection**					
10.	Preparation of the Regulation for Trade Transactions Through Electronic Systems (TPMSE)	Completing the Draft of Government Regulation on Trade Transactions Through Electronic Systems (TPMSE)	Government Regulation on Trade Transactions Through Electronic Systems (TPMSE)	Oct 2017	Ministry of Trade	1. Coordinating Ministry of Economy 2. Ministry of Law and Human Rights 3. Ministry of State Secretariat
11.	Building Consumer Trust	Perform the harmonization of regulations that are to be applied consistently	A comprehensive legal framework that will accommodate: a. classification of e-commerce business actors;	Nov 2017	Coordinating Ministry of Economy	1. Ministry of National Planning Development/ National Planning Development Agency

Appendix 6.1 (*continued*)

NO.	PROGRAMME	ACTIVITIES	OUTPUT	DEADLINE	INSTITUTION IN CHARGE	RELATED AGENCIES
			b. electronic certification; c. accreditation process; d. payment mechanism policy; e. consumer and industry protection specific for e-commerce transactions; f. schemes for online dispute resolution; g. internalization of consumer protection specific for e-commerce into the national strategy of consumer protection; and h. e-commerce business information application system.			2. Ministry of Communication and Informatics 3. Ministry of Trade 4. Ministry of Law and Human Rights 5. Central Bureau of Statistics 6. Bank Indonesia 7. OJK 8. Association of E-commerce and Digital Economy
12.	Development of National Payment Gateway	Develop a gradual National Payment Gateway that can improve electronic retail payment services including e-commerce transactions	a. A payment system that accommodates the trade and spending of government goods/services through e-commerce.	Oct 2017	Ministry of Finance	1. The Procurement of Goods/ Services Policy Agency 2. Bank Indonesia
			b. Terms of Arrangement for the Payment Transaction Processor Facilities	Oct 2017	Governor of Central Bank (BI)	1. OJK 2. Ministry of Finance 3. Ministry of Communication and Informatics

Appendix 6.1   (*continued*)

NO.	PROGRAMME	ACTIVITIES	OUTPUT	DEADLINE	INSTITUTION IN CHARGE	RELATED AGENCIES
			c. Conceptual design development of Conceptual design development of National Payment Gateway including to support e-commerce	Oct 2017	Governor of Central Bank (BI)	1. OJK 2. Ministry of Finance 3. Ministry of Communication and Informatics
			d. Increased efficiency and protection in the utilization of existing payment systems			4. Association of E-commerce and Digital Economy 5. "Payment Gateway" companies
			e. Principles of setting up the National Payment Gateway	Apr 2019	Governor of Central Bank (BI)	Ministry of Communication and Informatics
			f. Implementation of National Payment Gateway			
D.	**Education and Human Resources**					
13.	Education awareness and education for consumers, SMEs, and the whole ecosystem of e-commerce	Providing education for the entire ecosystem of e-commerce	a. A continuing education programme to educate the public about the use of e-commerce and industry development. b. The mechanism and identification of the party who will be responsible for developing the content and executing the programme.	2017–19	Ministry of Communication and Informatics	1. Ministry of Education and Culture 2. Ministry of Research, Technology, and Higher Education 3. Ministry of Trade 4. Ministry of Cooperatives and SME 5. Association of E-commerce and Digital Economy

Appendix 6.1   (*continued*)

NO.	PROGRAMME	ACTIVITIES	OUTPUT	DEADLINE	INSTITUTION IN CHARGE	RELATED AGENCIES
			c. Socialization of e-commerce to communicate to the public about the types of illegal products within the jurisdiction of Indonesia.			
			d. National awareness campaign of e-commerce through online and offline media throughout Indonesia.			
			e. Promotion of e-commerce trading through informal campaigns (among others via National Online Shopping Day/Harbolnas).			
14.	Briefings for policymakers to gain understanding of e-commerce in accordance with the role of each stakeholder	Implement e-commerce education for policymakers so that stakeholders gain an understanding of e-commerce according to their respective roles	E-commerce material integrated into capacity building materials for policymakers	Sep 2017	Ministry of Trade	1. Ministry of Communication and Informatics 2. State Administration Agency
15.	Preparation of incubation programme for start-ups	Develop incubation programmes for startups to assist them in their development especially in the early stages	Business actors (private or state-owned) that support and manage "National Incubator Program" that will assist the development of	Sep 2017	Head of Creative Economy Agency	1. Ministry of Communication and Informatics 2. Ministry of SOE 3. Ministry of Industry 4. Ministry of Trade

Appendix 6.1 (*continued*)

NO.	PROGRAMME	ACTIVITIES	OUTPUT	DEADLINE	INSTITUTION IN CHARGE	RELATED AGENCIES
			start-up actors by providing management training and working spaces.			5. Indonesian Chamber of Commerce and Industry 6. Association of E-Commerce and Digital Economy
16.	Formal education for e-commerce talents	Preparing talent needs in order to maintain the sustainability of the ecosystem of e-commerce through formal education	a. Implementation of a curriculum covering subjects related to e-commerce at various levels of educational units. b. Incentive scheme for educational organizations or units focused on e-commerce-related training or education in order to increase the number of Information Technology graduates to drive industry growth significantly.	Nov 2017	1. Ministry of Education and Culture 2. Ministry of Research, Technology, and Higher Education	Ministry of Communication and Informatics
17.	Development of e-commerce education facilitators	Developing e-commerce education facilitators	a. Facilitators of e-commerce education b. Comprehensive education for the ecosystem of e-commerce by facilitators	Sep 2017	Ministry of Trade	1. Ministry of Communication and Informatics 2. Association of E-commerce and Digital Economy
E.	**Communication infrastructure**					
18.	Improved communications infrastructure (internet	Improve national communications infrastructure as the backbone of	a. Free domain and speed of internet access that support	Jul 2019	Ministry of Communication and Informatics	1. Coordinating Ministry of Political, Legal, and Security Affairs

Appendix 6.1 (*continued*)

NO.	PROGRAMME	ACTIVITIES	OUTPUT	DEADLINE	INSTITUTION IN CHARGE	RELATED AGENCIES
	speed, network and security)	the growth of e-commerce system industry	the growth of e-commerce b. Broadband infrastructure in order to increase internet speed throughout Indonesia			2. Ministry of National Planning Development / National Planning and Development Agency
F.	**Logistic**					
19.	Improvement in e-commerce logistics through the National Logistics System blueprint (Sislognas)	Utilizing Sislognas blueprint to improve the speed of e-commerce logistics delivery and reduce shipping costs	a. Implementation of Sislognas blueprint, including special elements that will provide benefits to the e-commerce sector b. Standardization of Electronic Data Exchange System for e-commerce and logistic business actors	Nov 2017	Coordinating Ministry of Economy	1. Ministry of Transportation 2. Ministry of Finance 3. Association of Indonesian National Shipping and Delivery Companies
20.	Implementation of the e-commerce logistics facility for MSMEs	Development of e-commerce logistics facilities, especially to support e-commerce development for MSMEs	a. Outsourcing mechanism, logistics for MSMEs b. E-commerce logistics facilities developed by logistics service providers	Oct 2017	Coordinating Ministry of Eocnomy	1. Ministry of Transportation 2. Association of Indonesian National Shipping and Delivery Companies

Appendix 6.1　(*continued*)

NO.	PROGRAMME	ACTIVITIES	OUTPUT	DEADLINE	INSTITUTION IN CHARGE	RELATED AGENCIES
21.	Increased capacity of local/national logistics service providers to meet shipping needs across Indonesia	a. Strengthen competitive local/national logistics service providers	a. Enhanced capacity of competent local/national logistics service providers in the national e-commerce system through the guidance and provision of capital access (KUR for MSMEs)	Oct 2017	Coordinating Ministry of Economy	1. Ministry of Communication and Informatics 2. Ministry of Finance 3. Ministry of Trade 4. Ministry of Cooperatives and SME 5. Ministry of Transportation 6. Association of Indonesian National Shipping and Delivery Companies
		b. Revitalization, restructurization and modernization of PT Pos Indonesia (Persero) as the national post service provider	Modern and competitive PT Pos Indonesia (persero)	Nov 2017	Ministry of SOE	1. Coordinating Ministry of Economy 2. Ministry of Communication and Informatics 3. PT Pos Indonesia (persero)
22.	Development of Logistic system from rural to urban areas	Developing logistic system from rural to urban areas	a. An e-commerce application that connects farmers/ fishermen/ business actors in the village with intermediating traders and/ or consumers b. Educate local businesses and traders on e-commerce systems	Apr 2019	Coordinating Ministry of Economy	1. Ministry of Trade 2. Ministry of Communication and Informatics 3. Ministry of Cooperative and SME 4. Ministry of Transportation 5. Ministry of Public Works and Housing 6. Ministry of Farming

Appendix 6.1 *(continued)*

NO.	PROGRAMME	ACTIVITIES	OUTPUT	DEADLINE	INSTITUTION IN CHARGE	RELATED AGENCIES
			c. Regional distribution centres and provincial distribution centres based on information systems d. Capital Access (KUR) e. Local logistics services/ branches of national logistics services f. Financial network (Bank/ IKNB) g. Rural ICT infrastructure h. Rural transport infrastructure i. Pilot projects in several cities for Village to Urban Logistics Program (Center for Onions, Chili and Vegetables)			7. Ministry of Industry 8. Ministry of Villages, Disadvantaged Regions, and Transmigration 9. Bank Indonesia 10. OJK
23.	Increased security for e-commerce activities	Increase the implementation of cyber security principles by online traders and/or operators	a. Increased consumer awareness to be able to detect and prevent the occurrence of cybercrime b. Standard Operational Procedure (SOP) for online traders and/or operators to implement the principles of caution and security	Nov 2017	Ministry of Communication and Informatics	1. Coordinating Ministry of Political, Legal, and Security Affairs 2. Ministry of Finance 3. Bank Indonesia 4. OJK 5. National Police

Appendix 6.1 *(continued)*

NO.	PROGRAMME	ACTIVITIES	OUTPUT	DEADLINE	INSTITUTION IN CHARGE	RELATED AGENCIES
24.	Development of a model of national oversight system in e-commerce transactions	Developing a model of national oversight system in e-commerce transactions	a. E-commerce transactions that already used national oversight system in e-commerce transactions b. Information technology and security surveillance systems for integrated electronic transaction activities	Jan 2018	Ministry of Communication and Informatics	1. Coordinating Ministry of Economy 2. Ministry of Finances 3. Ministry of Trade 4. Bank Indonesia
G.	The formation of acting management of e-commerce roadmap (SPNBE), 2017–19					
25.	Formation of the 2017–19 E-commerce Roadmap management	Forming the Acting Management of 2017–19 E-commerce Roadmap that is administratively under the Coordinating Ministry of Economy	a. Budgeting to support the Directing Committee, Executive Team, and Acting Management of 2017–19 National E-commerce Roadmap	2017– 19	Coordinating Ministry of Economic Affairs	1. Ministry of Finance 2. Ministry of Communication and Informatics 3. Ministry of National Planning Development/ Bappenas
			b. Standard cost required to implement the 2017–19 E-commerce Roadmap	Oct 2017	Ministry of Finance	1. Coordinating Ministry of Economic Affairs 2. Ministry of Communication and Informatics
			c. Ministerial Decree from the Coordinating Minister for Economic Affairs on the establishment of Acting Management of the 2017–19 National E-commerce Roadmap	Oct 2017	Coordinating Ministry of Economic Affairs	1. Ministry of Communication and Informatics 2. Ministry of Finance 3. The Procurement of Goods/ Services Policy Agency

Source: Annex, Presidential Regulation No. 74/2017 on the 2017–19 Roadmap of National E-commerce.

NOTES

1. According to Statista Q4 2016, Indonesia has the fourth largest number of active Facebook users, third largest for Twitter, and seventh largest for WhatsApp. The country ranks 12th worldwide but highest in Southeast Asia for active Instagram users.

2. Danah Boyd (2015) specifically focuses on youth and their use of social media, but (especially chapter 7) provides a more contemporary review and debates about how certain groups are assumed to be inherently more tech savvy than the older generation. For classical studies on digital media and internet literacies, see Livingstone (2004), Livingstone et al. (2005).

3. This issue received high-profile media attention after Telkomsel's website was defaced by hackers in April 2017 protesting their costly packages. See *Kumparan* (2017).

4. The 2016 APJII survey result was published by Polling Indonesia and APJII, using cluster probability random sampling (n = 1250), and provinces as analytical unit. It stated MoE ±2.8 per cent with 95 per cent confidence level.

5. Mirani (2015). This point is also frequently highlighted in Jurriëns and Tapsell, eds. (2017).

6. This estimate considers McKinsey's (2016) at 34 per cent whereas the Indonesian government's 14th economic policy package released in November 2016 cited 93.4 million, or around 36.4 per cent.

7. Google Temasek (2016, p. 29) states that the global average internet speed in 2016 was 23.3 Mbps.

8. Susenas is an annual large-scale multi-purpose socioeconomic survey covering a nationally representative sample typically composed of 200,000 households. It collects information such as household income and expenditure, labour force participation, education attainment and healthcare and nutrition. Since 2014 the survey also collects information on the use of internet.

9. For the list of operators of ATM and ATM/debit card: http://www.bi.go.id/en/sistem-pembayaran/informasi-perizinan/kartu-atm/Contents/Default.aspx; credit card: http://www.bi.go.id/en/sistem-pembayaran/informasi-perizinan/kartu-kredit/Contents/Default.aspx; e-money: http://www.bi.go.id/en/sistem-pembayaran/informasi-perizinan/uang-elektronik/Contents/Default.aspx.

10. For more discussions on cashless payment in Indonesia, see Stapleton (2013), Thomas (2013) and Azali (2016).

11. Both companies have been under investigation in 2016 for tax evasion in Indonesia, though similar things also happened in other countries. See *Kompas* (2016).

12. "The catalogue of qualitative defects in Indonesian primary schools is long, and includes poorly trained-teachers, high rates of teacher absenteeism, an

emphasis on rote learning, insufficient text-books, poor-quality buildings and a lack of toilets and running water." For more, see Suryadarma and Jones (2013).

REFERENCES

Amindoni, Ayomi. "Indonesia Sees Drastic Increase in Cybercrime: Jokowi". *The Jakarta Post*, 20 September 2016*a*. http://www.thejakartapost.com/news/2016/09/20/indonesia-sees-drastic-increase-in-cybercrime-jokowi.html.

———. "Palapa Ring Will Improve Connectivity in Indonesia: Jokowi". *The Jakarta Post*, 30 September 2016*b*. http://www.thejakartapost.com/news/2016/09/30/jokowi-says-palapa-ring-will-improve-connectivity-in-ri.html.

APJII (Asosiasi Penyelenggara Jasa Internet Indonesia). "Penetrasi & Perilaku Pengguna Internet Indonesia". Jakarta: Polling Indonesia & APJII, 2016. https://www.apjii.or.id/survei2016 (accessed 5 August 2017).

Azali, Kathleen. "Cashless in Indonesia: Gelling Mobile E-Frictions?" *Journal of Southeast Asian Economies* 33, no. 3 (2016): 364–86.

———. "Indonesia's Divided Digital Economy". *ISEAS Perspective* 70, 14 September 2017.

Boyd, Danah. "Literacy: Are Today's Youth Digital Natives?" In *It's Complicated: The Social Lives of Networked Teens*. New Haven and London: Yale University Press, 2015.

Chakravorti, Bhaskar and Ravi Shankar Chaturvedi. *Digital Planet 2017: How Competitiveness and Trust in Digital Economies Vary Across the World*. The Fletcher School, Tufts University, July 2017.

Cosseboom, Leighton. "No Country for Ecommerce Unicorns: Why the Word 'Bubble' May Not Apply to Indonesia". *Tech in Asia*, 16 July 2015. https://www.techinasia.com/indonesia-ecommerce-bubble-insights.

Damuri, Yose Rizal, Siwage Dharma Negara, and Kathleen Azali. "Indonesia's E-Commerce: A New Engine of Growth?". Presentation materials at Symposium on E-Commerce, ASEAN Economic Integration, and Competition Policy & Law, ISEAS - Yusof Ishak Institute, Singapore, 16 March 2017. https://asean-competition.org/research/uploads/admin-f88de83727/files/blogs/23092018/batch2/Indonesia%20Country%20Study_Damuri%20Negara%20Azali.pdf.

Diela, Tabita. "Bank Indonesia Issues National Payment Gateway Regulation". *Jakarta Globe*, 7 July 2017*a*. http://jakartaglobe.id/business/bank-indonesia-issues-national-payment-gateway-regulation/.

———. "Indonesian Netizens Hooked on 'Dual-Screening' Habit: Nielsen". *Jakarta Globe*, 27 July 2017*b*. https://jakartaglobe.id/context/indonesian-netizens-hooked-dual-screening-habit-nielsen.

Fossati, Diego, Hui Yew-Foong, and Siwage Dharma Negara. "The Indonesia National Survey Project: Economy, Society and Politics". *Trends in Southeast Asia* 10. Singapore: ISEAS – Yusof Ishak Institute, 2017.

Gindarsah, Iis. "New Cyber Security Agency: How Will It Operate?" *The Jakarta Post*, 21 June 2017. http://www.thejakartapost.com/news/2017/06/21/new-cyber-security-agency-how-will-it-operate.html.

Google-Temasek. "e-conomy SEA: Unlocking the $200 Billion Digital Opportunity in Southeast Asia", May 2016.

Indonesia-Investments. "Penduduk Indonesia", n.d. https://www.indonesia-investments.com/id/budaya/penduduk/item67? (accessed 22 December 2017).

Jackson, Steven J., Paul N. Edwards, Geoffrey C. Bowker, and Cory P. Knobel. "Understanding Infrastructure: History, Heuristics, and Cyberinfrastructure Policy". *First Monday* 12, no. 6 (2007).

Jakarta Post. "Telkom to Bring Netflix Rival to Indonesia", 28 March 2016a. http://www.thejakartapost.com/news/2016/03/28/telkom-bring-netflix-rival-indonesia.html.

———. "Talent Shortage Casts Shadow on Top Sectors", 1 November 2016b. http://www.thejakartapost.com/news/2016/07/22/govt-urged-play-leading-role-digital-awareness-campaign.html.

———. "RI Tops Digital Market in Southeast Asia: Bain & Co", 23 May 2017. http://www.thejakartapost.com/news/2017/05/23/ri-tops-digital-market-southeast-asia-bain-co.html.

Julianto, Pramdia Arhando. "Industri 'E-commerce' Diharapkan Menjadi Solusi Pemerataan Ekonomi". *Kompas*, 9 May 2017. http://ekonomi.kompas.com/read/2017/05/09/160100326/industri.e-commerce.diharapkan.menjadi.solusi.pemerataan.ekonomi (accessed 22 December 2017).

Jurriëns, Edwin and Ross Tapsell, eds. *Digital Indonesia: Connectivity and Divergence.* Singapore: ISEAS – Yusof Ishak Institute, 2017.

Kompas. "Pendapatan di Bawah Rp 3 Juta per Bulan Dilarang Memiliki Kartu Kredit", 1 October 2014. http://ekonomi.kompas.com/read/2014/10/01/174522526/Pendapatan.di.Bawah.Rp.3.Juta.per.Bulan.Dilarang.Memiliki.Kartu.Kredit (accessed 22 December 2017).

———. "Masalah Pajak yang Membelit Google di Indonesia", 19 September 2016. http://tekno.kompas.com/read/2016/09/19/09153207/masalah.pajak.yang.membelit.google.di.indonesia.

Kontan.co.id. "Pemerintah ubah aturan transportasi online", 2 April 2018. https://nasional.kontan.co.id/news/pemerintah-ubah-aturan-transportasi-online.

Kumparan. "Membandingkan Tarif dan Kuota Internet dari 5 Operator Seluler", 28 April 2017. https://kumparan.com/aditya-panji/membandingkan-tarif-dan-kuota-internet-dari-5-operator-seluler (accessed 27 September 2017).

Kurnia, Novi and Santi Indra Astuti. "Researchers Find Indonesia Needs More Digital Literacy Education". *The Conversation*, 25 September 2017. https://theconversation.com/researchers-find-indonesia-needs-more-digital-literacy-education-84570 (accessed 27 September 2017).

Lingga, Vincent. "Still Waiting for Long-Delayed Reform of Logistics Services". *The Jakarta Post*, 6 April 2017. http://www.thejakartapost.com/academia/2017/04/06/commentary-still-waiting-for-long-delayed-reform-of-logistics-services.

Livingstone, Sonia. "Media Literacy and the Challenge of New Information and Communication Technologies". *The Communication Review* 7, no. 1 (2004): 3–14.

Livingstone, Sonia, Magdalena Bober, and Ellen Helsper. "Internet Literacy among Children and Young People: Findings from the UK Children Go Online Project". *LSE Research Online* (2005), p. 25.

McKinsey & Company. "Unlocking Indonesia's Digital Opportunity", September 2016.

Mirani, Leo. "Millions of Facebook Users Have No Idea They're Using the Internet". *Quartz*, 9 February 2015. https://qz.com/333313/milliions-of-facebook-users-have-no-idea-theyre-using-the-internet/.

Moore, Bede. "A Recent History of the Indonesian E-commerce Industry: An Insider's Account". In *Digital Indonesia: Connectivity and Divergence*, edited by Edwin Jurriëns and Ross Tapsell. Singapore: ISEAS – Yusof Ishak Institute, 2017.

Oberman, Raoul, Richard Dobbs, Arief Budiman, Fraser Thompson and Morten Rossé. "The Archipelago Economy: Unleashing Indonesia's Potential". McKinsey Global Institute Report, September 2012. https://www.mckinsey.com/global-themes/asia-pacific/the-archipelago-economy.

Pangestu, Mari and Grace Dewi. "Indonesia and the Digital Economy: Creative Destruction, Opportunities and Challenges". In *Digital Indonesia: Connectivity and Divergence*, edited by Edwin Jurriens and Ross Tapsell. Singapore: ISEAS – Yusof Ishak Institute, 2017.

Purbo, Onno W. "Narrowing the Digital Divide". In *Digital Indonesia: Connectivity and Divergence*, edited by Edwin Jurriëns and Ross Tapsell. Singapore: ISEAS – Yusof Ishak Institute, 2017.

Rahardjo, Budi. "The State of Cybersecurity in Indonesia". In *Digital Indonesia: Connectivity and Divergence*, edited by Edwin Jurriëns and Ross Tapsell. Singapore: ISEAS – Yusof Ishak Institute, 2017.

Ray, David and Lili Yan Ing. "Survey of Recent Developments: Addressing Indonesia's Infrastructure Deficit". *Bulletin of Indonesian Economic Studies* 52, no. 1 (2016).

Saiidi, Uptin. "A Ride on Indonesia's First and Only 'Unicorn'". *CNBC*, 24 April 2017. https://www.cnbc.com/2017/04/24/a-ride-on-indonesias-first-and-only-unicorn.html.

Setiawan, Sakina Rakhma Diah. "Aturan Biaya 'Top Up' Uang Elektronik Terbit, Ini Rinciannya". *Kompas*, 21 September 2017. http://ekonomi.kompas.com/read/2017/09/21/131043226/aturan-biaya-top-up-uang-elektronik-terbit-ini-rinciannya.

Singgih, Viriya P. "Logistics Service Providers Gear up for E-commerce Boom". *The Jakarta Post*, 28 November 2016. http://www.thejakartapost.com/news/2016/11/28/logistics-service-providers-gear-up-for-e-commerce-boom.html.

Stapleton, Tim. "Unlocking the Transformative Potential of Branchless Banking in Indonesia". *Bulletin of Indonesian Economic Studies* 49, no. 3 (2013): 355–80.

Suprayitno, Dede. "Proyek Palapa Ring Mulai Dijalankan Tahun Ini". *Tribunnews*, 26 January 2017. http://www.tribunnews.com/techno/2017/01/26/proyek-palapa-ring-mulai-dijalankan-tahun-ini.

Suryadarma, Daniel and Gavin W. Jones, eds. *Education in Indonesia*. Singapore: Institute of Southeast Asian Studies, 2013.

Tan Kim Song and James Tang. "Managing Skills Challenges in ASEAN-5". SMU-JP Morgan, October 2016. https://socsc.smu.edu.sg/sites/socsc.smu.edu.sg/files/%5Bcurrent-domain%3Amachine_name%5D/news_room/Managing%20Skills%20Challenges%20in%20ASEAN-5_Final%20Report.pdf.

Thomas, Hugh. "Measuring Progress Toward a Cashless Society". MasterCard Advisors, 2013.

Trading Economics. "Indonesia Internet Speed", n.d. https://tradingeconomics.com/indonesia/internet-speed (accessed 8 April 2019).

World Bank. "Indonesia's Connectivity and Logistics Challenges: Findings from World Bank Advisory Work for IPC", 10 December 2015. http://isd-indonesia.org/wp-content/uploads/2015/12/Indonesia-Services-Dialogue-IPC-The-World-Bank.pdf.

Regulations

Bank Indonesia. "Peraturan Bank Indonesia No. 19/8/PBI/2017 tentang Gerbang Pembayaran Nasional (*National Payment Gateway*)", 6 July 2017. http://www.bi.go.id/id/peraturan/sistem-pembayaran/Pages/pbi_190817.aspx (accessed 17 September 2017).

Presidential Regulation No. 74/2017. "Peta Jalan Sistem Perdagangan Nasional Berbasis Elektronik (Road Map E-commerce) Tahun 2017–2019", 3 August 2017. http://www.peraturan.go.id/perpres/nomor-74-tahun-2017.html (accessed 4 August 2017).

Sekretariat Kabinet Republik Indonesia. "Inilah Perpres No. 74 Tahun 2017 tentang 'Road Map E-Commerce' Tahun 2017–2019", 10 August 2017. http://setkab.go.id/inilah-perpres-no-74-tahun-2017-tentang-road-map-e-commerce-tahun-2017-2019/ (accessed 11 August 2017).

7

DEVELOPMENT OF E-COMMERCE IN MALAYSIA

Tham Siew Yean

1. Introduction

According to OECD (undated), an e-commerce transaction is the sale or purchase of goods or services, conducted over computer networks by methods specifically designed for the purpose of receiving or placing of orders. The goods or services are ordered by those methods, but the payment and the ultimate delivery of the goods or services do not have to be conducted online. An e-commerce transaction can be between enterprises, households, individuals, governments, and other public or private organizations. This encompasses a broad range of commercial activities, including among others, business to business (B2B or e-commerce between companies), business to consumer (B2C, or between companies and consumers), consumer to consumer (C2C), or e-commerce between consumers. Transactions to be included are orders made over the web, extranet or electronic data interchange. The type of transaction is defined by the method of placing the order. Transactions to be excluded are orders made by telephone calls, facsimile or manually typed email.

The development of e-commerce has attracted the attention of developing countries due to its potential to contribute towards sustainable development. Transaction costs can be reduced with e-commerce as it can be used to lower barriers to entry by eliminating certain costs related to having a physical storefront (WTO/OECD 2017). This provides more opportunities especially for small and medium enterprises (SMEs) to enhance their market access in domestic and foreign markets, thereby increasing the scalability prospects of these enterprises. When more inputs can be delivered digitally, it will also facilitate the management of fragmented production networks and the operation of global value chains (GVCs). Since it enhances productivity, more firms can also shift to exports. It also provides enhanced opportunities for women entrepreneurs and rural traders thereby empowering the disadvantaged. Consumers can also benefit through lower prices, greater convenience, and more varieties to choose from.

Rillo and dela Cruz (2016) reported the findings from Qiang, Rossotto, and Kimura (2009), which showed that increased broadband access has accelerated economic growth due to the close link between information and communications technology (ICT) diffusion and firm level productivity. They further cited a McKinsey Global Institute study (2011) that found internet access has helped SMEs in eight developing countries to create 3.2 jobs for every job lost. China has also reportedly used e-commerce to support rural development when several villages successfully sold their agricultural products online (WTO/OECD 2017). Huang et al. (2018) found that e-commerce significantly spurred urban and rural entrepreneurship in China. In particular, e-commerce development encouraged new business start-ups while it helped to reduce the exit of incumbent business entities. Finally, e-commerce development also changed the sectoral choices of entrepreneurs, shifting them towards physical entities that are closely related to e-commerce operations such as wholesale, transportation, and information technology.

Although empirical evidence on the development impact of e-commerce is still evolving, developing countries, including Malaysia, are particularly keen to harness e-commerce for their development. The purpose of this chapter is to examine key government initiatives that have been undertaken to promote the use of e-commerce, the overall performance of e-commerce and the main outstanding challenges encountered by Malaysia in moving its e-commerce development forward.

2. Government Policies and Strategies to Promote E-commerce

The seeds of Malaysia's e-commerce initiatives can be traced back to the ICT plans of the country. ICT infrastructure was prioritized for development since the Seventh Malaysia Plan (7MP: 1996–2000) as the means to shift Malaysia from a production-based to a knowledge-based economy. The National IT Agenda (NITA), formulated in 1996, provided the framework for the development of an information and knowledge-based society by 2020. NITA mooted a National Strategic ICT Roadmap, which was later introduced in 2008 with the development of digital commerce included in it. E-commerce was subsequently inserted into the Ninth Malaysia Plan (9MP: 2006–10) and as e-business in the Tenth Malaysia Plan (10MP: 2011–15). The development of e-commerce continues to be emphasized in policy documents, with the government targeting a contribution of RM211 billion (or 6.4 per cent contribution) from e-commerce to the country's Gross Domestic Product (GDP) by 2020 in the latest five-year plan or the Eleventh Malaysia Plan (11MP: 2016–20).

A National eCommerce Strategic Roadmap was launched in October 2016, identifying six areas of focus for government intervention, namely: (i) accelerating seller adoption of e-commerce; (ii) increasing the adoption of e-procurement by businesses; (iii) lifting non-tariff barriers (such as e-fulfillment, cross-border, e-payment, consumer protection); (iv) realigning existing economic incentives; (v) making strategic investments in select e-commerce players; and (vi) promoting national brand to boost cross-border e-commerce.

Eleven government agencies are roped in to implement eleven prioritized programmes, as shown in Table 7.1.

TABLE 7.1
Malaysia's E-commerce Programmes, 2016

SME Corporation Malaysia	Malaysian Investment Development Authority
1. Promote and market e-commerce to SMEs 2. Improve the scale and effectiveness of SME e-commerce training and talent development 3. Create a one-stop e-business portal for SMEs	8. Transform Malaysia into a regional e-fulfilment hub
Ministry of Finance 4. Require government agencies to use e-procurement to buy goods and services 5. Encourage government-linked companies to use e-procurement	**Ministry of International Trade and Industry** 9. Reduce border clearance lead time for inbound and outbound parcels
Malaysian Communications and Multimedia Commission 6. Transform Malaysia's last-mile delivery network with best-in-class capabilities	**Bank Negara Malaysia** 10. Increase awareness of e-payment innovations, benefits, and security
Ministry of Domestic Trade, Co-operatives and Consumerism 7. Protect consumer rights	**Malaysia External Trade Development Corporation** 11. Promote Malaysian brands in international marketplaces

Source: MDEC (undated).

These plans indicate the need for ministries to work together for the implementation of an effective e-commerce strategy due to the nature of this form of business. Hence, each ministry is assigned a specific task based on the key functions of the ministry to facilitate the development of e-commerce.

Multimedia Development Corporation (MDEC)'s SME E-commerce Reward Programme

In this one-off programme, launched in June 2014, MDEC collaborated with several organizations such as Telekom Malaysia, MYNIC, the agency in charge of .my or the internet country code top-level domain (ccTD), and easyparcel.my to train 600 SMEs to create an online presence to generate traffic and sales lead. The top 25 SMEs among these 600, based on the highest revenue collected from e-commerce platform and the highest number of customers generated over the three-month programme, were rewarded with prizes worth up to RM175,000, as well as inclusion as Digital Malaysia's e-commerce success stories.

#MYCYBERSALE

This is an annual government-led online sale launched by MDEC in collaboration with the National ICT Association of Malaysia (PIKOM) in 2014 (https://www.mycybersale.my). It aims to increase Malaysia's e-commerce revenue by generating online shopping demand from consumers, to encourage sellers to be part of the e-commerce ecosystem, and to increase domestic and export e-commerce revenue.

In its debut year, it generated an increase of 75 per cent in Gross Merchandise Value (GMV) from RM67 million to RM117 million. In the 2017 sale, RM311 million in GMV was achieved, with an export revenue of RM39 million, and a total of 26 export countries (ecInsider 2017).

Digital Free Trade Zone (DFTZ)[1]

After the appointment of Jack Ma of Alibaba as the special economic adviser to the government in November 2016 and the announcement of the establishment of a DFTZ in the October budget of 2016 (Ho 2016), Malaysia accelerated its plans for the establishment of such a zone. In March 2017, the DFTZ was swiftly launched in partnership with Jack Ma's Alibaba, as a dedicated zone whereby the whole range of services which is needed to ensure the speedy delivery of goods is scheduled to be made available over a staggered timeline. The zone is also the first of Jack Ma's internet-based trading platform or electronic World Trade Platform (e-WTP) to be established outside China. It is meant to connect Malaysia's SMEs with other players in the countries along China's Belt and Road Initiative (BRI) that have been targeted for Jack Ma's global expansion plans, which will eventually lead to a Digital Silk Road (Tham 2018a).

Specifically, an e-fulfilment[2] hub, a satellite services hub and an e-services platform are being developed over two phases with the first phase undertaken by Pos Malaysia at a cost of RM60 million. This is used for upgrading and renovating the former Low Cost Carrier Terminal (LCCT) and it is already operational. The government budget for 2018, as announced in October 2017, also included an allocation of RM83.5 million for the development of this first phase.

The satellite services hub aims to be a premier digital hub for global and local internet-related companies that are geared towards the Southeast Asian market. This includes end-to-end services as well as networking and knowledge-sharing.

In the second phase, Cainiao Network, the logistic arm of Alibaba, is supposed to partner with Malaysia airports in a greenfield investment, which will be operational in 2020. Alibaba will reportedly host its regional e-fulfilment hub at Kuala Lumpur International Airport (KLIA) Aeropolis DFTZ Park. This park will build on existing air freight infrastructure to include sea freight via Port Klang and railway cargo to Bukit Kayu Hitam, that will support a regional multimodal transhipment hub. The hub will subsequently be linked to Alibaba's planned e-WTP hubs in other countries.

Alibaba's financial services will also be included eventually as two of Malaysia's financial services providers, Maybank and CIMB Bank Bhd., have entered into agreement with Ant Financial Services Group to establish the Alipay mobile wallet in Malaysia. Alibaba Cloud, the cloud computing arm of Alibaba group, is also reportedly planning to establish a data centre in Malaysia.

For the e-services platform, besides providing market access, integrated trade facilitation measures have reduced the time taken for cargo clearance time from six to three hours at the KLIA Air-Cargo Terminal 1 (KACT1), which is critical for the speedy delivery that is required in e-commerce transactions.

Overall, the DFTZ is expected to increase the contribution of e-commerce to GDP to RM211 billion by 2020, as stated in the Eleventh Malaysia Plan. It is also expected to double SMEs exports to RM160 billion (or US$38 billion) by 2025.

Incentives

The 2014 e-Trade Programme of Malaysia External Trade Development Corporation (MATRADE) provides an incentive to help SMEs participate in international leading marketplaces for increasing their revenue, including export revenue and reducing costs, with a special focus on the China market (MIDF 2016). SMEs, based on stipulated eligibility criteria (see Table 7.2) which qualify for participation in this programme, are given an e-voucher worth RM1,000. The voucher is meant to defray half of the expenses for subscribing to Alibaba e-Trade Global Supplier Package. The first phase of the programme focused on B2B, with plans to move to B2C in the next phase. According to MIDF (2016), 426 registrants were recorded under Alibaba's gold supplier programme, with these e-vouchers, as opposed to a targeted 1,000 companies.

TABLE 7.2
Eligibility Criteria for e-Trade Voucher

CRITERIA			
	Type	**Annual Sales Turnover (RM)**	**No. of Full-time Employees**
	Manufacturing	< 50 million	< 200
Definition of SMEs	Trading	< 20	< 75
	Services	< 20	< 75
	Professional Service Providers	< 20	< 75
Have at least 60 per cent Malaysia equity			
Incorporated under the Companies Act 1965			
Exporting made in Malaysian products and/or services			

Source: MATRADE.

Subsequently other online marketplaces were brought into collaboration with MATRADE such as Singapore E-commerce Pte. Ltd., eBay International AG, Amazon Asia-Pacific Holdings Pte. Ltd., TradeIndia.com and JinBaoMen. SMEs are also given the opportunity to be listed under the trade directory published by the respective online marketplace. In January 2017, the e-Trade incentive for approved SMEs has been upgraded; the amount has increased to RM5,000, with RM2,500 for listing/subscribing purposes and another RM2,500 for e-commerce expenses associated with e-marketplaces.

The e-Trade Programme also provides free training to equip SMEs acting as suppliers with the essential knowledge for marketing their products and services online. This includes, among others, the need to have dedicated staff to update information and images in a timely fashion, as well as handling online enquiries from potential buyers in real time. SMEs that managed to penetrate export markets through the e-Trade Programme were given the e-Trade Achievement Award together with an e-Trade incentive worth RM5,000 to enable them to subscribe to another marketplace of their choice as well as free promotional space on MATRADE website and Alibaba.com homepage.

A wide range of grants are available under SME Corporation Malaysia's joint programme with MDEC, or the Go eCommerce Programme — an online platform to empower SMEs to channel or diversify their businesses digitally (see Table 7.3). These include grants focusing on specific sectors such as agriculture and which facilitate exports as well as *bumiputera* participation.

TABLE 7.3
List of Grants Available under the Go eCommerce Programme

	Agency	Name of Grant	Amount (RM)
1.	SME Corp.	• SME Emergency Fund • Green LED	• Up to a maximum of 100,000 • Up to a maximum of 3 million
2.	Bumiputera Agenda in Teraju Unit (Unit Peneraju Agenda Bumiputera)	• New Bumiputera Entrepreneurs Scheme • Facilitation Fund	• Up to a maximum of 500,000 • Up to a maximum of 30 million
3.	Sarawak Economic Development Corporation	• Bumiputera Entrepreneur Development Program	• Not exceed 5,000

TABLE 7.3 (*continued*)

	Agency	Name of Grant	Amount (RM)
4.	National Entrepreneurs Corporation Ltd. (PUNB)	• SME Scheme	• 500,000–5 million
5.	National Corporation (PNS)	• Fund to aid the development of franchises • Local Franchise Product Development	• Up to a maximum of 100,000 • Not available
6.	MATRADE	• Marketing Development Grant • Service Export Fund	• 200,000 • 5 million
7.	Department of Agriculture, Sarawak	• SME Development (Entrepreneur Level 1) • SME Development (Entrepreneur Level 2) • SME Development (Entrepreneur Level 3) • Agriculture Entrepreneurial Project	• Not available • Not available • Not available • Not available
8.	National Film Development Corporation (FINAS)	• Assistance of short film/ short documentary/short animation	• Not exceed 30,000
9.	Cradle Fund Private Limited	• CIP300	• 300,000
10.	Bio-economy Corporation	• Biotechnology Commercial Fund	• Up to 3 million
11.	People's Trust Council (MARA)	• Micro credit finance scheme	• Not available

Note: Teraju is a strategic unit in the Prime Minister's department that aims to spearhead, spur and coordinate the participation of *bumiputera* in the economy in line with the National Transformation Plan (see http://www.teraju.gov.my/pengenalan/).

Source: http://www.matrade.gov.my/en/etrade.

There is unfortunately no data available to indicate the utilization of these grants as well as their effectiveness.

Legislations

Malaysia has a suite of laws that govern the conduct of online businesses. According to the Ministry of Domestic Trade, Co-operatives and Consumerism, all online businesses must be registered with the Companies Commission of Malaysia (SSM). Online business companies with foreign ownership of above 51 per cent and operating in Malaysia have to abide by the Guidelines on Foreign Participation in the Distributive Trade Sector in Malaysia; comply with the Consumer Protection Regulations (Electronic Trade Transactions) 2012; and all existing laws and regulations in Malaysia that are applicable to a physical business. This includes, for example, the Trade Descriptions Act 2011 (TDA), as it prohibits false trade descriptions and incorrect or misleading statements, conduct and practices in relation to the supply of goods or services, including goods supplied through electronic means; and the Sale of Goods Act 1957 (SGA), which governs contracts for the sale of goods in Malaysia.

There are, however, specific laws pertaining to online businesses. First and foremost is the Digital Signature Act 1997, which covers digital signatures and the Communications and Multimedia Act 1998 (CMA), as it regulates the multimedia and communications industry, including content applications service providers (such as website operators). Other important regulations include the Electronic Commerce Act 2006 (ECA) which pertains to the validity of electronic contracts and signatures; the Electronic Government Activities Act 2007 (EGAA), which applies similar rules for the government sector and the Personal Data Protection Act 2010 (PDPA), which governs the use of personal data, including that of website users.

The Consumer Protection Act 1999 (CPA), which protects consumers against a range of unfair practices and enforces minimum product standards, was amended in 2007 to cover electronic commerce transactions (export.gov undated). Subsequently in 2010, a new provision was introduced on the general safety requirement for services and the protection to consumers from unfair terms in a standard form contract.

Despite the new provision, the Royal Malaysia Police reported that there was a total of 24,314 cases of cybercrime from 2007 to 2012, leading to a total loss of RM286.2 million (Mahfuz undated). The top three highest number of cases reported were e-commerce fraud (online purchases), parcel scam and Voice over Internet Protocol (VOIP) scams with the latter being conducted by cross-border syndicates.

To further protect consumers and enhance their confidence to shop and trade online, a new act to regulate operators that supply goods or services through websites or online marketplaces was subsequently enacted, namely the Consumer Protection (Electronic Trade Transactions) Regulations 2012 (ETT Regulations) (ecInsider 2014). The regulation came into force on 1 July 2013. Under this regulation, an online marketplace operator is required to, among others, provide their full details, terms of conditions of sale, rectification of errors and maintenance of records.

There are also guidelines on the scope of charge, tax liabilities, treatment of server and website as well as an examination of business models in the Guidelines for Taxation, provided by the Inland Revenue Board of Malaysia (export.gov 2017).

3. E-commerce Market and Performance

The Department of Statistics (DOS) has put out two publications on e-commerce in Malaysia, from the macro and micro perspectives. The ICT Satellite Account (ICTSA) measures the contribution of ICT and e-commerce in Malaysia. As shown in Table 7.4, the contribution of e-commerce has increased steadily since 2011. Based on the sectoral breakdown, e-commerce from non-ICT sectors contributes more than those from ICT sectors throughout the period.

TABLE 7.4
Contribution of E-commerce Gross Value Added by
Industry to GDP, 2011–16

Contribution (%)	2011	2012	2013	2014	2015	2016
ICT industry	0.9	0.9	1.0	1.2	1.2	1.2
ICT manufacturing	0.4	0.4	0.4	0.5	0.5	0.6
ICT trade	0.2	0.2	0.2	0.2	0.2	0.2
ICT services	0.3	0.3	0.4	0.4	0.4	0.5
Content and media	0.0	0.0	0.0	0.0	0.0	0.0
Non ICT industry	4.0	4.2	4.4	4.6	4.7	4.8
Total	4.0	4.2	4.4	4.6	4.7	4.8

Note: E-commerce transactions are defined as sales or purchases of goods or services, conducted over computer networks by methods specifically designed for the purpose of receiving or placing orders.

Source: DOS (2017*a*); ICTA (2016).

However, the rate of growth in gross value added in e-commerce averaged at 10.9 per cent per annum from 2011 to 2016. This is close to MITI and AT Kearney (undated)'s projected growth of 11 per cent for the period 2012–20, except that the growth has moderated from a peak of 15.2 per cent in 2014 to 9.3 per cent in 2016. But it shows that the aspired acceleration in growth of 20–25 per cent that is needed to enable Malaysia to leap up the e-commerce ladder towards the growth of the likes of Singapore, Taiwan, and China has yet to be achieved.

Based on DOS's Economic Census on the usage of ICT by businesses and e-commerce (DOS 2017b), there was a total of 47,556 establishments engaged in e-commerce transactions in 2015 (see Table 7.5). However, this constitutes a mere 5.2 per cent of the total number of establishments in the country. SMEs constitute 91.4 per cent of the total number of establishments that are engaged in e-commerce. The services sector has the largest number of e-commerce establishments, be it at the overall or SME level. At the overall subsectoral level, wholesale and retail trade is the largest service subsector with the greatest number of establishments.

TABLE 7.5
Number of E-commerce Establishments, 2015

	Agriculture	Mining & Quarrying	Manufacturing	Construction	Services	Total
Overall	81	53	3,856	272	43,294	47,556
SMEs	36	34	2,474	245	40,671	43,460

Source: DOS (2017b).

Despite the dominance of establishments in services, the share of income derived from e-commerce is bigger for manufacturing at the overall and SME levels (see Table 7.6).

TABLE 7.6
Share of Income from E-commerce Transactions, 2015 (%)

	Agriculture	Mining & Quarrying	Manufacturing	Construction	Services	Total
Overall	0.0	1.7	69.3	0.1	28.9	100.0
SMEs	0.0	0.2	52.2	0.1	47.5	100.0

Source: DOS (2017b).

Domestic transactions dominate e-commerce income as shown in Table 7.7. In particular, only 5.9 per cent of SMEs' income from e-commerce is derived from international transactions, which includes imports as well (see Table 7.7). The services sector is the largest contributor to international income from e-commerce transactions. Therefore, not many SMEs on board e-commerce platforms are able to generate export revenue, with most of them focusing on the domestic market as in the traditional offline SMEs.

TABLE 7.7
Income of E-commerce Transactions by Type of Market, 2015
(RM; % in parenthesis)

Sectors	SMEs	
	Local	International
Agriculture	3 million (0.0)	0 million (0.0)
Mining & Quarrying	Nil (0.0)	194 million (3.7)
Manufacturing	46.5 billion (54.8)	556 million (10.6)
Construction	58 million (0.1)	0 million (0.0)
Services	38.4 billion (45.2)	4.5 billion (85.7)
Total	84.9 billion (94.1)	5.3 billion (5.9%)

Source: DOS (2017*b*).

By type of customers, the highest income is derived from B2B, with a share of 79.2 per cent, followed by B2C (18.5 per cent), and B2G (2.3 per cent) (DOS 2017*b*). Likewise, for SMEs, the highest income is obtained through B2B (RM68.9 billion; 76.4 per cent), followed by B2C (RM17.0 billion; 18.9 per cent); and lastly by B2G (RM4.2 billion; 4.7 per cent).

The DFTZ has attracted about 2,072 export-ready Malaysian SMEs to the e-commerce platforms available in the zone thus far (MITI 2018). Selangor, Federal Territory of Kuala Lumpur and Melaka are the three states with the biggest number of SMEs participating in the DFTZ (69 per cent), while the top three products preferred by Malaysian SMEs on Alibaba are food and beverages, others, and beauty and personal care, which are mostly consumer products (see Table 7.8).

TABLE 7.8
Top Ten Categories of Products Preferred by Malaysian SMEs on Alibaba

Industry	No. of Companies
Food & Beverage	385
Others	225
Beauty & Personal Care	196
Furniture	116
Health & Medical	84
Packaging & Printing	76
Apparel	63
Agriculture	61
Rubber & Plastics	59
Automobiles & Motorcycles	58

Source: MITI (2018).

Due to the lag between data collection and publication, as well as the time lag for policies to affect actual change, the data above cannot fully capture the impact of the recent e-commerce policies and strategies of the country. Nevertheless, the relatively low contribution of B2C indicates that Malaysia's e-commerce market has yet to catch up with countries like India, Singapore, Taiwan and China. Frost and Sullivan (2016) estimated internet retail as a percentage of retail sales in Malaysia to be the lowest at 0.7 per cent among the ASEAN-4 in 2014, with Indonesia taking the lead at 3.4 per cent, followed by Thailand (1.2 per cent) and Singapore (0.9 per cent). There is therefore substantial room for improvement in Malaysia's e-commerce development.

4. Outstanding Challenges

A review of the literature indicates several outstanding challenges remain in e-commerce development in Malaysia. These are online security, infrastructure support, logistics support, shopping malls and consumer preferences.

Online Security

Despite the new Consumer Protection (Electronic Trade Transactions) Regulations 2012, the percentage of online buyers who still do not trust giving their credit card information online stood at 52 per cent, which was more than the global average of 49 per cent in 2014 (MIDF 2016). The lack of trust is reflected in the preference of Malaysian consumers to pay cash on delivery when purchasing online goods (Handley 2016). Therefore, although Malaysia reportedly has 14 million of digital consumers, only 29 per cent of these digital consumers are converted to digital buyers. Instead these digital consumers use the internet to research on products and services. Furthermore, they prefer to buy products that are not available on the local market rather than local goods. Lack of trust has also constrained the development of mobile-commerce in the country, as reportedly only 0.3 per cent of online transactions were made on mobile in 2014 (ASEAN UP 2017).

MIDF (2016) reported that there were 2,960 cases recorded for fraud in 2015. Malaysia was also stated to be ranked number seven in a list of top twenty-five fraudulent countries in the world in 2015, based on a sampling of online transaction data conducted by a fraud fighting service provider called Sift Science. According to consumer complaints, e-commerce recorded the highest number of complaints received by the National Consumer Complaints Centre (NCCC) in 2016, registering 15.2 per cent of the total number of complaints (48,563) (*The Sun Daily* 2017). It would appear that both businesses and consumers do still have some concerns over the security of online transactions.

Existing regulations may need further improvements. Naemah and Roshazlizawati (2013)'s analysis show that the Consumer Protection Regulation (2012) deals primarily with pre-contractual disclosure of information while post-contractual issues such as confirmation of e-payment, maximum period of performance, cooling-off period, delivery and return of goods are not covered. NCCC further reported that out of the 7,371 complaints received, 34.4 per cent were related to issues faced on the delivery of the purchased goods, where vendors fail to live up to their promises, including on the delivery time (*The Sun Daily* 2017). Thus efforts to improve regulatory oversight need to be continued besides being more effective at building up consumer confidence, especially since compliance is an additional cost for sellers.

Infrastructure Support

Out of the fifteen surveyed Asia-Pacific countries by Akamai, Malaysia was just behind Singapore and Thailand in ASEAN-5 in terms of average connectivity speed in 2015. Despite improvements, by 2017, Malaysia is behind Singapore, Thailand and Vietnam (see Table 7.9). Likewise, in terms of broadband adoption, Malaysia is also lagging behind the ASEAN-5, with the exception of the Philippines (see Table 7.10).

TABLE 7.9
Average Connection Speed in the Asia-Pacific Countries, 2015 and 2017

2015			2017		
Global Ranking	Country	2015Q3 Av. Mbps	Global Ranking	Country	2017Q1 Av. Mbps
1	South Korea	20.5	1	South Korea	28.6
5	Hong Kong	15.8	4	Hong Kong	21.9
7	Japan	15.0	7	Singapore	20.3
17	Singapore	12.5	8	Japan	20.2
33	Taiwan	10.1	16	Taiwan	16.9
42	New Zealand	8.7	21	Thailand	16.0
43	Thailand	8.2	27	New Zealand	14.7
46	Australia	7.8	50	Australia	11.1
71	Sri Lanka	5.1	58	Vietnam	9.5
73	Malaysia	4.9	62	Malaysia	8.9
91	China	3.7	68	Sri Lanka	8.5
97	Vietnam	3.4	74	China	7.6
104	Indonesia	3.0	77	Indonesia	7.2
108	Philippines	2.8	89	India	6.5
116	India	2.5	100	Philippines	5.5

Sources: MIDF (2016); Akamai (undated).

TABLE 7.10
Broadband Adoption in the Asia Pacific, 2017

Global Rank	Country	% Above 4 Mbps
2	South Korea	98%
4	Thailand	97%
13	Taiwan	95%
17	Singapore	94%
20	Hong Kong	94%
28	Japan	93%
32	New Zealand	91%
49	Vietnam	86%
57	Sri Lanka	82%
59	China	81%
61	Australia	61%
71	Indonesia	76%
80	Malaysia	72%
104	India	42%
107	Philippines	39%

Source: Akamai (undated).

As noted by MIDF (2016), improvements in connectivity is essential to encourage internet users to engage in e-trade activities from demand to supply. Besides speed, cost makes a difference in facilitating e-trade activities. In this regard, Malaysia is disadvantaged against Singapore and Thailand but faces lower costs compared to Vietnam (see Table 7.11). Limited competition in Malaysia may be the cause of the relatively higher cost of fixed broadband services (World Bank 2018). Overall, Malaysia has a lot to catch up with Singapore and Thailand in both speed and cost.

TABLE 7.11
Cost of Broadband in ASEAN-6, 2017

Countries	Average Monthly Broadband Cost (USD)
Indonesia	76.00
Malaysia	44.88
Philippines	53.50
Singapore	39.06
Thailand	26.80
Vietnam	62.45

Source: Hanlon (2017).

Rural and urban access to telecommunication infrastructure differ to the extent that accessing the rural market is an issue due to poorer connectivity and last mile delivery. There are therefore regional disparities in the adoption of e-commerce. Since e-commerce can also bring development to rural entrepreneurs, improving access for the rural population is also important.

Logistics Support

Online consumers demand prompt delivery; in fact, increasingly same-day delivery is demanded and offered by some vendors. Consequently, strong logistics support is critical for a satisfactory fulfilment experience. A Logistics and Trade Facilitation Master Plan (2015–20) was launched in 2015 to improve logistics development. The plan has three phases of development: the first phase covers 2015–16 and focused on de-bottling the sector; the second phase (2016–19) works on enhancing domestic growth; while the third phase aims to create a regional footprint through the internationalization of logistics services.

The Ministry of Transport, which is tasked with the implementation of the plan, reported piecemeal changes that were made in the first phase (MOT 2017a). De-bottling was achieved through specific projects such as improving last-mile connectivity to Port Klang; addressing Padang Besar Container Terminal's bottlenecks; enhancing efficiency of import/export processes; regulating warehouse and off-dock depots development; enhancing road freight transport productivity; streamlining licensing and air freight processes and procedures; establishing national freight data programme; increasing quality of goods vehicle drivers; and reviewing Malaysian ship registry structure.

Similarly, the media announcement in 2017 on the second phase targeting domestic growth also shows a piecemeal approach as it is made up of a string of projects that are being developed, such as Pulau Carey Port-Industrial City Project, East Coast Rail Link (ECRL), DFTZ, Regional E-commerce and Logistics Hub in KLIA Aeropolis, 24-hour customs facilitation at the borders, and Sabah as the regional logistics hub for East ASEAN Growth Area (BIMP-EAGA) (MOT 2017b). Most of these projects are planned in collaboration with China, be it in terms of foreign direct investment or loans or technical advice. It remains to be seen if the projects funded by loans from China that are guaranteed by the government will be continued with the change in government as the newly elected Prime Minister Mahathir Mohamad in May 2018, had expressed concern over the debt incurred from such loans in his campaign trail.

But it is the governance of this sector that holds the key for improving logistics performance since logistics is a highly fragmented sector because it is made up of several subsectors that cover several modes of transport such as land, air, and water; warehousing and support facilities; and post and courier services. Since the goods handled pose different risks to society, regulatory intervention is necessary to overcome informational asymmetries, security, safety, health and environmental concerns. Consequently, there are different regulations governing different subsectors, leading to considerable complexities in the overall regulatory structure. But a complex regulatory structure also increases inefficiency as well as compliance costs, besides creating sometimes unintended barriers to trade such as the entry of new domestic and foreign service providers.

Malaysia has moved towards regulatory overhaul in an attempt to streamline the whole regulatory structure of the country and not just in logistics. But as noted by Tham (2018b), it remains to be seen whether the regulatory reviews that have taken place will be translated into lower regulatory burden or whether the regulatory reviews merely focus on form rather than substance. In other words, adopting a system of regulatory reviews without leading to substantial regulatory de-bottlenecking that can translate into lower logistics costs is a futile waste of time. This remains to be seen as there is as yet no mid-term review on changes in logistics costs and performance using comparable measurements over time, since the implementation of the plan.

Several players have emerged to provide last mile logistics support.[3] This includes Pos Malaysia, which has the advantage of having the widest reach in Malaysia, due to its status as the sole postal service provider in Malaysia. Reportedly, it commands about 40 per cent of the courier market, which has 30 competitors (Khairie 2017). It has also formed strategic alliances with other providers, such as Alibaba in the DFTZ, to provide integrated services. GD Express Carrier Berhad has also emerged as another strong contender in the express delivery segment, partnering Lazada and Astro.

Shopping Malls and Consumer Preferences

Malaysia is the home of shopping malls, including mega malls. It has been estimated that 1,000 shopping centres with 150 mil sq. ft. of retail space are available, with the majority of them located in Kuala Lumpur, Selangor, Penang and Johor (Tan 2018). It is also home to three of the biggest malls in the world in terms of retail space, namely One Utama, Mid Valley Mega Mall and Sunway Pyramid. This has encouraged a "weekend mall culture" where the whole family will spend the weekends at a mall as a recreational activity. Hence, online convenience and accessibility are deemed to be less urgent in Malaysia compared to other countries (Chua 2016). It has also contributed to the consumer preference to feel and try out an item before purchase especially for clothing (MIDF 2016) and pose an additional challenge to virtual malls in terms of providing a similar array of choices.

Online shops have attempted to meet consumers' preference by opening a physical outlet or providing temporary pop-up stores as a means of bringing the online experience offline (MIDF 2016). This also follows the global trend where offline complements online, with Amazon reportedly experiencing an increase in online shopping in regions where it has opened a physical store. MIDF (2016) asserts that e-commerce in Malaysia has to rise to the challenge of meeting omni-channel functionality by moving to clicks and bricks.

5. Conclusion

Malaysia has put in considerable efforts in terms of policy planning and strategies to enhance e-commerce adoption. This includes the collection of data to ascertain the extent to which e-commerce has contributed to the GDP of the country as well as data at the enterprise level. While these efforts are commendable, the World Bank (2018), nevertheless, concluded that Malaysia's performance in terms of digital adoption by businesses is closer to that of a lower middle-income country as only 62 per cent of business establishments are connected to the internet and only 28 per cent have some form of web presence.

The country still lags behind in terms of infrastructure support and the public's overall trust in online transactions. Limited international bandwidth and a smaller number of secure servers are also noted in the World Bank (2018)'s assessment of Malaysia's challenges in shifting towards more digital adoption by businesses. Efforts are being made to reduce the cost of broadband charges by the new government with the announcement of the implementation of the Mandatory Standard on Access Pricing on 8 June 2018 by the Malaysian Communications and Multimedia Commission (MCMC) (Wong 2018).

Improvements in some laws will be needed to foster greater confidence in increasing the share of online transactions, especially in the retail sector. Likewise, efficient logistics will shore up online transactions. But e-commerce has to compete against an ingrained physical mall culture, especially in the urban areas and consumers' preference for a "touch and feel" experience prior to making a purchase.

A lot of hopes are pinned on the DFTZ that was launched in 2017 to take e-commerce transactions to a higher level. The zone aims to provide a complete e-commerce ecosystem which will encompass e-commerce platforms, e-fulfilment, logistics, trade facilitation, payment and finance. It remains to be seen if SMEs are persuaded to invest time and money to put together a team to manage and market e-commerce transactions as well as to enhance their understanding on how to overcome cross-border regulatory barriers for exports. It should be noted that the DFTZ will also ease the import of goods. SMEs will further face greater competitive pressures due to the change in the *de minimis* or the minimum value of the goods below which no duties and taxes are being collected by the customs threshold, which also favour imports over exports.

NOTES

1. This section is based on Tham (2018*a*).
2. This encompasses warehousing, order fulfilment, shipping logistics and last mile delivery in an e-commerce value chain.
3. This refers to the movement of goods from a fulfilment centre to their final destination. In other words, the last mile is the last leg of the product's trip before it arrives on the customer's doorstep.

REFERENCES

Akamai. "Q1 2017 State of the Internet/Connectivity Report", undated. https://www.akamai.com/uk/en/about/our-thinking/state-of-the-internet-report/global-state-of-the-internet-connectivity-reports.jsp (accessed 16 May 2018).

ASEAN UP. "Mobile Internet and Social Media in Malaysia", 10 February 2017. https://aseanup.com/mobile-internet-social-media-malaysia/ (accessed 16 May 2018).

Chua Sue-Ann. "Why Malaysia Still Hasn't Had Its E-commerce Boom". *The Edge Weekly*, 29 November 2016. http://www.theedgemarkets.com/article/why-malaysia-still-hasn%E2%80%99t-had-its-e-commerce-boom (accessed 17 May 2018).

DOS (Department of Statistics). *Information and Communication Technology Satellite Account 2016*. Putrajaya: DOS, 2017*a*.

———. *Economic Census 2016: Usage of ICT by Businesses and e-Commerce*. Putrajaya: DOS, 2017*b*.

ecInsider. "Understanding E-commerce Legislation in Malaysia", 30 July 2014. http://www.ecinsider.my/2014/07/understanding-ecommerce-legislation-malaysia.html (accessed 11 May 2018).

———. "#MYCYBERSALE 2017 Results & Analysis in Infographic", 5 December 2017. http://www.ecinsider.my/2017/12/mycybersale-2017-results-analysis-infographic.html (accessed 13 May 2018).

export.gov. "How to Export", undated. https://www.export.gov/How-to-Export (accessed 11 May 2018).

Frost & Sullivan. "ASEAN Retail: Overview, Trends, and Outlook, with a Focus on SGX-listed Companies", 2016. http://www.iberglobal.com/files/2017/asean_retail.pdf (accessed 15 May 2018).

Handley, Harry. "An Introduction to e-Commerce in Malaysia". *ASEAN Briefing* (2016). https://www.aseanbriefing.com/news/2016/12/16/an-introduction-to-e-commerce-in-malaysia.html (accessed 16 May 2018).

Hanlon, Mike. "Broadband Bang per Buck: How Your Country Rates on Speed versus Cost". *New Atlas*, 27 November 2017. https://newatlas.com/broadband-speed-versus-cost-country-comparison/52346/ (accessed 17 May 2018).

Ho Wah Foon. "Najib: Alibaba Founder Jack Ma Agrees to be Advisor to Malaysian Government on Digital Economy". *The Star Online*, 4 November 2016. https://www.thestar.com.my/news/nation/2016/11/04/alibaba-founder-jack-ma-agrees-to-be-advisor-to-malaysian-govt-on-digital-economy/ (accessed 11 May 2018).

Huang, Bihong, Mohamed Shaban, Quanyun Song, and Yu Wu. "e-Commerce Development and Entrepreneurship in the People's Republic of China".

ADBI Working Paper Series No. 827 (March 2018). https://www.adb.org/sites/default/files/publication/411161/adbi-wp827.pdf (accessed 11 May 2018).

Khairie Hisyam Alirman. "E-commerce Delivering Growth to Pos Malaysia". *The Edge Malaysia*, 8 May 2017. http://www.theedgemarkets.com/article/ecommerce-delivering-growth-pos-malaysia (accessed 17 May 2018).

Mahfuz Bin Dato' Ab. Majid. "Cybercrime: Malaysia", undated. https://www.mcmc.gov.my/skmmgovmy/media/General/pdf/DSP-Mahfuz-Majid-Cybercrime-Malaysia.pdf (accessed 15 May 2018).

MDEC (Malaysia Digital Economy Corporation). "National Ecommerce Strategic Roadmap", undated. https://www.mdec.my/digital-innovation-ecosystem/ecommerce/nesr (accessed 9 May 2018).

MIDF (Malaysian Industrial Development Finance). "Unlocking the Potential of E-Trade in Malaysia". Kuala Lumpur: MIDF Investment Research, 2016. http://www.midf.com.my/images/Downloads/Research/EqStrategy/SpecialReports/E-Trade-MIDF-260416.pdf (accessed 13 May 2018).

MITI (Ministry of International Trade and Industry). "DFTZ", 2018. http://www.miti.gov.my/miti/resources/Media%20Release/Fact_Sheet_DFTZ_at_Malaysia_Digital_Economy_2018_SME_Fact_Sheet.pdf (accessed 26 February 2018).

MITI and AT Kearney. "National eCommerce Strategic Roadmap Overview", undated. http://www.miti.gov.my/miti/resources/Gallery_Walk.pdf (accessed 14 May 2018).

MOT (Ministry of Transport). *Logistics and Trade Facilitation Masterplan: Performance Report 2016*. Putrajaya: MOT, 2017a.

———. "Enhancing Domestic Growth Through Logistics Masterplan". Media Statement by Y. B. Dato' Sri Liow Tiong Lai, Minister of Transport, Malaysia. Putrajaya: MOT, 2017b. http://www.mot.gov.my/my/Kenyataan%20Media/Tahun%202017/Media%20Statement%20-%20Enhancing%20Domestic%20Growth%20Through%20Logistics%20Masterplan.pdf (accessed 16 May 2018).

Naemah Amin and Roshazlizawati Mohd Nor. "Online Shopping in Malaysia: Legal Protection for E-consumers". *European Journal of Business and Management* 5, no. 24 (2013): 79–86.

OECD (Organisation for Economic Co-operation and Development). "Glossary of Statistical Terms", undated. https://stats.oecd.org/glossary/detail.asp?ID=4721 (accessed 16 May 2018).

Qiang, Christine Zhen-Wei, Carlo M. Rossotto, and Kaoru Kimura. "Economic Impacts of Broadband". In *Information and Communications for Development: Extending Reach and Increasing Impact*. Washington, D.C.: The World Bank, 2009.

Rillo, Aladdin D. and Valdimir dela Cruz. "The Development Dimension of E-commerce in Asia: Opportunities and Challenges". *ADBI Policy Brief*

No. 2016-2 (June 2016). https://www.adb.org/sites/default/files/publication/185050/adbi-pb2016-2.pdf (accessed 11 May 2018).

Tan Hai Hsin. "An Oversupply of Retail Space in Malaysia". *StarProperty.my,* 5 April 2018. http://www.starproperty.my/index.php/articles/property-news/an-oversupply-of-retail-space-in-malaysia/ (accessed 17 May 2018).

Tham Siew Yean. "Digital Free Trade Zone (DFTZ): Connecting Malaysia's SMEs with the Digital Silk Road". *ISEAS Perspective* 17, 26 March 2018*a.*

————. "FDI Liberalization in Malaysia's Logistics Services". In *Services Liberalization in ASEAN: Foreign Direct Investment in Logistics,* edited by Tham Siew Yean and Sanchita Basu Das. Singapore: ISEAS – Yusof Ishak Institute, 2018*b.*

The Sun Daily. "Online Shopping Tops Number of Consumer Complaints in 2016", 29 August 2017. http://www.thesundaily.my/news/2017/08/29/online-shopping-tops-number-consumer-complaints-2016 (accessed 16 May 2018).

Wong Eee Ling. "Broadband to be At Least 25% Cheaper by End 2018". *The Edge Financial Daily,* 21 June 2018. http://www.theedgemarkets.com/article/broadband-be-least-25-cheaper-end-2018 (accessed 11 July 2018).

World Bank. *Malaysia Economic Monitor 2018: Navigating Change.* Washington, D.C.: World Bank, 2018. http://www.worldbank.org/en/country/malaysia/publication/malaysia-economic-monitor-navigating-change (accessed 11 July 2018).

WTO/OECD. "Harnessing E-commerce for Sustainable Development". In *Aid for Trade at a Glance 2017: Promoting Trade, Inclusiveness and Connectivity for Sustainable Development.* Geneva/Paris: World Trade Organisation/OECD Publishing, 2017. https://www.wto.org/english/res_e/booksp_e/aid4trade17_chap7_e.pdf.

8

E-COMMERCE IN SINGAPORE
Current State, Policies and Regulations

Kala Anandarajah, Tanya Tang and Zheng Xi

1. Introduction

Singapore has a highly developed and open economy. The country, which has the highest gross domestic product (GDP) per capita in Southeast Asia, is also well-known for its corruption-free environment. The main drivers of the growth of the Singaporean economy include the manufacturing, finance and insurance sectors (Ministry of Trade and Industry 2017). The Singapore population is highly educated and tech-savvy, with a literacy rate of 97.0 per cent amongst residents aged 15 years and above (Department of Statistics Singapore n.d.), and 84 per cent of the population are internet users in 2016 (IMDA 2018). The Singapore government has encouraged Singaporean businesses to venture into overseas markets by taking advantage of new opportunities in the digital economy and build strong capabilities in innovation and enterprise (Budget 2017). These conditions make

Singapore a conducive environment for the growth and development of e-commerce.

This chapter provides an analysis of the current state of e-commerce in Singapore from a number of perspectives. The outline of this chapter is as follows. After defining e-commerce in Section 2, the state of e-commerce infrastructure is discussed in Section 3. The size of Singapore's e-commerce is examined in Section 4. The evolution of e-commerce in terms of the major players in the industry is discussed in Section 5. Government policies, as well as the laws and regulations governing e-commerce in the country, are covered in Sections 6 and 7, respectively. Competition law and policy-related issues are discussed in Section 8. Factors that can impede and restrict the opportunities for e-commerce growth in Singapore are discussed in Section 9. Finally, Section 10 concludes by presenting policy recommendations for the further development of e-commerce in Singapore.

2. Defining E-commerce

E-commerce refers to the sale and purchase of goods and services over the internet and includes ancillary activities which support such transactions. E-commerce transactions can take place between businesses and consumers (B2C), between businesses (B2B) or between the government and businesses (G2B); between consumers (C2C) whereby consumers buy and sell directly to each other through platforms such as eBay; as well as between the government and citizens via the offering of e-Government services.

The primary feature of e-commerce is the use of the internet as a sales channel to reach out to customers. Some e-commerce businesses operate solely online (i.e., they do not have brick-and-mortar stores) whereas others operate through both online and offline sales channels. Many businesses also use the internet for marketing and advertising, which is attractive to businesses due to its wider reach, higher investment returns and ability to supplement traditional advertising methods. It is observed that the nature of online marketing has evolved, with social media playing a larger role in recent years.

3. State of E-commerce Infrastructure

Internet Quality and Cost

Based on statistics published by the World Bank, the percentage of internet users in Singapore in 2016 was 81 per cent (World Bank n.d.), compared to the global average of 46 per cent. Internet users in Singapore generally enjoy high quality internet access at affordable prices, with fibre broadband subscription plans starting from as low as S$29.00 (as of August 2019),[1] high upload and download throughputs, as well as low latencies.[2] In a 2017 market report published by Speedtest, Singapore was ranked second in the world for both its average fixed broadband download speed and its average mobile download speed.[3] This provides a good foundation for e-commerce to take off in Singapore.

As part of its iN2015 Infocomm Masterplan, the Singapore government co-funded the rolling out of a nationwide fibre broadband network to provide ultra-high speed broadband access of 1 Gbps and more to all businesses and homes in Singapore. The government has also worked with private sector operators under the Wireless@SG programme to offer free wireless broadband access in public areas of up to 5Mbps, with the aim of catalysing the growth of the wireless broadband market in Singapore and promoting a wireless broadband lifestyle among citizens.

Mobile Penetration Rate

According to statistics published by the Infocomm Media Development Authority of Singapore (IMDA), the mobile phone penetration rate in Singapore as at May 2019 was 154.1 per cent (IMDA, 7 August 2019). This means that a substantial number of individuals own two or more mobile phones in Singapore.

Mobile broadband plans are offered by mobile operators in Singapore on a post-paid and pre-paid basis. According to IMDA, the wireless broadband population penetration rate (including Wireless@SG subscriptions) was 185.6 per cent as at May 2019 (ibid.). Given the portability and convenience of mobile phones, it is no surprise that e-commerce transactions commonly take place through mobile phones. Based on a survey conducted by Bain & Company, in 2015, 26 per cent of online purchases and research in Singapore took place on mobile phones (Hoppe 2016)—this figure is expected to be much higher today.

Logistics

Singapore was ranked 7th in the Logistics Performance Index (LPI) published by the World Bank in 2018, above any other country in Southeast Asia (World Bank n.d.). This makes Singapore one of the most conducive countries for e-commerce businesses to operate in, as logistics constitute a crucial link between businesses and their customers in the e-commerce market. E-commerce logistics service providers not only link e-commerce players to customers located in Singapore, but also enable these players to expand their reach to customers in other Southeast Asian countries and beyond.

Riding on the growth of the e-commerce industry in Singapore, Singapore Post (SingPost) launched its regional e-commerce logistics hub in November 2016 at Tampines Logistics Park, a S$182 million facility representing its largest investment in e-commerce logistics in Singapore (SingPost 2016). Following this, in May 2017, Lazada, a leading online shopping destination in Southeast Asia, moved its entire warehouse operations in Singapore to the SingPost Regional eCommerce Logistics Hub, allowing it to work more closely with SingPost to serve customers in Singapore and in the region (SingPost 2017). The rise of e-commerce has also spawned new delivery service providers such as Ninja Van, which specializes in next day delivery for e-commerce clients. They join established global delivery companies such as DHL, which has ambitious plans for expansion in Southeast Asia (Lee 2016).

In Singapore, trials have also been underway for delivery via drones, or unmanned aircrafts, as companies seek a breakthrough in conventional methods of delivery. In October 2015, SingPost announced that it had completed a package drone delivery trial in a remote part of Singapore, claiming to be the world's first postage service to have used a drone for "point-to-point, recipient-authenticated" mail delivery (Lee 2015). During the trial, the drone flew 2 kilometres to a landing point in Pulau Ubin (an island of Singapore) and successfully delivered the package to the intended recipient. According to a spokesperson for SingPost, the key to the success of the trial was the cooperation from both the aviation and telecommunication regulators of Singapore (IMDA, 7 November 2017). Subsequently in April 2017, SingPost embarked on a project with Airbus to develop an aerial drone delivery system for urban environments like Singapore. As part of the project, the parties plan to conduct an initial trial involving transporting small packages around the National University of Singapore using drones by early 2018 (Lim, 18 April 2017).

In July 2017, Amazon introduced its express delivery service known as Prime Now in Singapore, which guarantees delivery within two hours after placing an order online (Kwang, 26 July 2017). The range of products available on Prime Now includes grocery items, electronics, toys and games, stationery and beauty products. With the formal entry of Amazon into Singapore, consumers are expected to benefit from a greater level of competition in the Singapore e-commerce market.

Online Banking and Payment Services

According to a report by McKinsey & Company, the digital banking penetration rate in Singapore in 2014 was 94 per cent (Barquin and Vinayak 2015). Singapore ranks third in the world for banking capabilities and second in the world for digital banking readiness (AT Kearney and EFMA 2013), suggesting that not only are Singapore banks well equipped to provide digital banking services, but that Singaporeans have also become more sophisticated and receptive towards the use of digital banking services. Digital banking is an important service ancillary to e-commerce, as the alternative payment method of cash on delivery is less efficient and could create problems such as refusal to pay or rejection of the ordered goods upon delivery.

Other than digital banking, there has also been a move in recent years for Singaporeans to go cashless. Not only have banks introduced mobile applications, such as DBS's Paylah! and OCBC's Pay Anyone, to allow convenient funds transfer using mobile phones, other merchants have also entered the race to go cashless (think GrabPay, Fave Pay, Singtel Dash and more). GrabPay, which was launched in Singapore in November 2016, had a user base of 4 million as of November 2017 and currently has over 4,000 merchants on-board in Singapore (Grab 2016, 2017 and 2019). With the launch of GrabPay in Thailand in November 2018, in partnership with Thailand's Kasikornbank, GrabPay is now available in six Southeast Asian countries (Tang 2018). With Singapore going cashless, e-commerce transactions would become more hassle-free, giving consumers more reason to turn to e-commerce.

In addition, financial technology (Fintech), which refers to the use of technology to provide financial services at lower prices and to offer innovative technology-driven solutions in the financial sector (PWC 2016), has gained considerable traction in Singapore. In 2018, Fintech investments in Singapore reached a total of US$365 million (approximately S$492.4 million), more than double the figure in 2017 (sgsme.sg 2019). The Monetary Authority of Singapore (MAS) remains the key driver behind Singapore's Fintech ecosystem. Fintech is expected to bring about innovative payments solutions that will stimulate growth of the local e-commerce industry.

4. Statistics on E-commerce

The e-commerce market in Singapore was estimated at US$1 billion (approximately S$1.412 billion) in 2015 and is projected to reach US$5.4 billion (approximately S$7.67 billion) by 2025 (Google and Temasek 2016). In 2016, the e-commerce penetration rate in Singapore was 51 per cent (Hootsuite and We are Social Singapore 2017) and the total value of the e-commerce market was US$3 billion (approximately S$4.04 billion) (ibid.). These numbers are expected to grow as the population becomes more accustomed to transacting online, and more buyers and sellers jump onboard the e-commerce bandwagon.

One of the major contributors to e-commerce in Singapore is the online hotels and airlines market, which is valued at US$4 billion in 2015 (approximately S$5.62 billion) (ibid.). This is the second largest market in Southeast Asia after Indonesia. As Singapore positions itself as the regional air hub in Asia, the online hotels and airlines market will continue to play an important role in the local e-commerce industry and is expected to experience more than two times growth by 2025.[4]

The local online advertisements market also continues to grow, from US$0.7 billion in 2015 to an estimated US$1 billion by 2025 (approximately S$0.99–1.42 billion) (ibid.). Currently, Singapore already has the highest rate of digital advertising in Southeast Asia, standing at 31 per cent of total advertising expenditure in 2015 (ibid.). Businesses are increasingly advertising their products and services on popular e-commerce platforms, so that they can reach out to potential consumers through the online channel. Thus, e-commerce players may capitalize on online advertisements as a potential source of revenue.

E-commerce businesses that are looking for investors may be encouraged to know that in 2015, venture capital investments in Singapore reached a total of US$820 million (approximately S$1.16 billion), topping the chart for Southeast Asian countries (ibid.). Looking at Southeast Asia as a whole, from 2010 to 2015, 61.4 per cent of all venture capital investments were in e-commerce and logistics (ibid.), paving the way for a larger and more vibrant e-commerce industry in the region.

5.   Major Players in E-commerce

The e-commerce market in Singapore, and in Southeast Asia generally, is highly fragmented, as seen from the fact that no online platform is the preferred platform for more than 20 per cent of any consumers in any country in Southeast Asia.[5] This could be partly attributed to consumers' habit of multi-homing (i.e. where users make use of multiple platforms offering comparable services) instead of relying on a single e-commerce platform. According to Bain & Company, this means that consumers are more likely to look to search engines rather than websites of specific retailers when searching for products and services online, and are more suited to shopping through social media platforms.

As a result of the lack of loyalty of consumers towards any online retail platform, e-commerce markets in Singapore are highly competitive. In order to attract consumers to shop on their online platforms, e-commerce players need to differentiate themselves in terms of product or service offerings, price, quality of products or services, customer service, ease of payment, security and other factors which will contribute to a pleasant online shopping experience for the consumers.

Based on an interactive e-commerce study conducted by iPrice, in the second quarter of 2019, the top ten e-commerce sites based on the total average monthly visits in Singapore are Lazada, Qoo10, Shopee, EZBuy, Zalora, eBay, Forty Two, Reebonz, Althea and Hipvan (iPrice, July 2019). Many of these are local websites, suggesting that Singapore consumers generally prefer to shop from local e-commerce players, possibly due to the latter's familiarity with the population's shopping habits and preferences.

Qoo10 is one of the most popular e-commerce platform in Singapore, with an average monthly traffic of 7.2 million in the second quarter of 2019 (ibid.). In 2015, Qoo10 raised US$82.1 million (approximately S$115 million) in funding, led by Singapore Press Holdings Ltd. (SPH), along with eBay, Saban Capital Group, UVM 2 Venture Investments LP, Brookside Capital and Oak Investment Partners (SPH 2015). The funding will be used to improve the technology used and the services provided by Qoo10, as well as to invest in new infrastructure and acquire fresh talent. With a strong following of 2.5 million registered users in Singapore, Qoo10 continues to lead the local e-commerce scene (Qoo10 n.d.).

Lazada entered the Singapore market in 2014, and has since established a strong local presence, evident from its 20.7 million followers on Facebook.[6] In April 2017, Lazada teamed up with online supermarket RedMart and other online services to offer the LiveUp membership programme, which offers members benefits such as rebates and discounts for purchases made. The LiveUp membership was launched in anticipation of the entry of Amazon and its Prime membership programme into Singapore. In June 2017, Alibaba Group Holding Ltd. invested an additional US$1 billion (approximately S$1.34 billion) to increase its stake in Lazada from 51 per cent to 83 per cent, buying out all investors other than the Lazada management and Temasek Holdings (Aravindan 2017). Following this, in August 2017, Alibaba entered into a strategic alliance with CapitaLand, who has since set up an online mall on Lazada Singapore.[7] E-commerce players in Singapore and Southeast Asia would be well advised to step up their games, given the aggressive entry of Alibaba into the region.

Another fast-growing e-commerce market in Singapore is the provision of online food ordering and delivery services. The well-known players in this market are Foodpanda Singapore (launched in 2012), Deliveroo (launched in 2015), and GrabFood (launched in 2018 following the acquisition of UberEats). As the market becomes more saturated, it is important for both incumbents and new entrants to come up with strategies to differentiate their services from those provided by other players, in order to compete effectively in the market. In this new age of digitalization, online food delivery service providers are increasingly leveraging on technology to improve the quality of their services. For example, Deliveroo invested in a new despatch algorithm tool which has reduced service times by 15 per cent, while Foodpanda recently acquired a similar tool, which tracks riders' locations and helps to maximize manpower resources and achieve greater efficiency (Cheok 2017).

Online grocery shopping has also become increasingly popular, given the convenience of having one's groceries delivered to the doorstep. This explains how local startups like RedMart (acquired by Lazada in 2016) and Honestbee came into the picture, and why large supermarkets such as Fairprice, Cold Storage, Giant and Sheng Siong have set up online platforms for grocery shopping and delivery services. In 2016, the online grocery market in Singapore was estimated to have a 1.2 per cent share of the Singapore grocery market, and is expected to grow more than 3 times by 2020 to 3.9 per cent (Institute of Grocery Distribution 2017).

Mobile taxi-booking and ride-sharing services have also taken off at a rapid pace in Singapore in recent years. The shake-up to the taxi industry arising from the entry of players such as Uber and Grab had led to several taxi operators re-considering and re-formulating their business models. In March 2017, the Land Transport Authority and the PTC approved proposals from taxi companies and Grab to introduce surge pricing, i.e. where the price of a taxi ride booked through a mobile application will vary according to the demand for such services (Lim, 17 March 2017).

6. Government Policies in Support of E-commerce

Various initiatives and incentives have been launched to further the government's efforts for Singapore to become a smart nation—harnessing the power of technology to change the way people live, work and play. Most of these initiatives are not specific to e-commerce. Rather, they are aimed more generally at encouraging businesses, especially small and medium enterprises (SMEs), to take advantage of the digital world to improve the way they run their businesses and serve their customers. As a consequence, more businesses may establish an online presence and enter the e-commerce market.

SMEs Go Digital Programme

In the Budget 2017 speech, the Singapore government introduced a new SMEs Go Digital Programme (SGDP), to encourage SMEs to make use of technology to develop their capabilities and be a part of the growing digital economy worldwide. The government sets aside a total of S$80 million to fund programmes under the SGDP.

The SGDP has since been implemented by the IMDA. SMEs can obtain assistance under the SGDP in the following ways:

(a) SME Digital Tech Hub (IMDA, 31 May 2019) provides specialized advice on areas such as data analytics, data protection, cybersecurity and Internet of Things. SMEs may also consult with experts at the SME Digital Tech Hub for guidance on technologies that they can use to transform their businesses and participate in workshops to improve their digital capabilities.

(b) Industry Digital Plan (IDP) (IMDA, 17 November 2017) provides step-by-step advice to SMEs on digital technologies at each stage of growth. For a start, the IDPs will focus on the retail, food services, wholesale trade, logistics, environmental services and security sectors. As of 17 November 2017, the IMDA has rolled out IDPs in the logistics and retail sectors.

(c) Pre-Approved Digital Solutions (IMDA, 3 November 2017) is approved by the IMDA to help SMEs improve their digital capabilities. The criteria for approval focuses on whether the solution meets SMEs' requirements, ease of use, affordability and the supplier's capability and capacity. As of 11 May 2017, fifty digital solutions for SMEs have been pre-approved by the IMDA.

Grants Provided by the IMDA

In addition to the above, the IMDA offers various grants to encourage SMEs to use technology to improve their productivity and efficiency and grow their businesses. For example, the iSPRINT (IMDA, 20 February 2017) programme was introduced in 2010 (and enhanced in June 2016) to incentivize SMEs to deploy technology-based solutions in their operations. Under iSPRINT, SMEs can get up to a 70 per cent grant on the costs of these solutions. SMEs can also receive a 50 per cent subsidy for their monthly fibre broadband subscription costs.

Wholesale Trade Industry Transformation Map

The Wholesale Trade Industry Transformation Map (ITM) was launched in September 2017 by then International Enterprise Singapore (IE Singapore). The aim of ITM is to help companies digitalize to enhance their productivity and growth, and to create 10,000 new jobs in Singapore by 2020. According to IE Singapore, the wholesale trade industry accounted for 9 per cent of Singapore's workforce and contributed S$47.3 billion to its GDP in 2016 (IE Singapore, 6 September 2017).

In order to ensure that the sector stays relevant, one of the strategies under the ITM is to build trade connectivity through digital marketplaces and platforms. In this regard, the key initiatives are as follows (ibid.):

(a) ASEAN Single Window (Chia 2018) facilitates cooperation amongst ASEAN logistics associations and customs clearance through a single window and allows for greater efficiency and cost-effectiveness in transporting goods within the region;

(b) Cross Border Cognitive Supply Chain Solution is a digital trade platform which enables 350,000 trading partners on IBM's Supply Chain Business Network to do automated customs declaration at eighteen customs nodes across the world, including Singapore, China, Indonesia, Thailand and the United States; and

(c) Collaborating with trade associations and private enterprises to help SMEs get listed on digital marketplaces, allowing SMEs to enter new markets and benefit from economies of scale through shared services.

Partnership between SPRING Singapore and SingPost

In 2015, then SPRING Singapore[8] entered into a partnership with SingPost to launch an integrated end-to-end e-commerce solution known as "ezyCommerce" (SingPost 2015). ezyCommerce is a user-friendly platform which allows SMEs to manage their online sales channels and inventory, provide automated ordering processing services and offer different modes of delivery to their customers. Under the Collaborative Industry Projects initiative, SMEs will be able to enjoy up to 70 per cent subsidy provided by SPRING Singapore for their use of ezyCommerce (SPRING Singapore 2015).

Assistance Programmes and Initiatives by IE Singapore

To support businesses, including e-commerce businesses, in their internationalization efforts, IE Singapore introduced the Market Readiness Assistance (MRA) programme and the Global Company Partnership (GCP) programme in 2015. Under the MRA, Singapore businesses are provided with knowledge resources and networking opportunities, as well as financial assistance to ease the process of entering overseas markets (IE Singapore n.d.*b*). Under the GCP, IE Singapore aims to help Singapore enterprises with business strategies for overseas expansion and funding for the purposes of capacity building, market access, manpower development and access to loans and capital (IE Singapore n.d.*a*).

Based on statistics published by IE Singapore (16 February 2017), in 2016, it had provided assistance to 37,000 companies, out of which 80 per cent were SMEs. A total of S$73.4 million in grants was given out to more than 10,000 companies. In addition, IE Singapore had approved 1,500 MRA grants in 2016, out of which 22 per cent were for activities in global online retail or e-commerce platforms, an 86 per cent increase from 2015.

In November 2017, IE Singapore initiated an alliance between Shopmatic, Red Dot Payment, and iCommerce Asia which sees an integration of the e-commerce solutions offered by each company (IE Singapore, 9 November 2017). The combined solution offered by these companies can assist companies seeking to enter the e-commerce market in Southeast Asia, by providing them with an e-commerce platform to host their goods and services, digital payment solutions for consumers, and logistics and supply chain management services. IE Singapore also encouraged more e-commerce solution providers to collaborate with one another to respond to the rapidly changing competitive landscape in e-commerce markets.

Monetary Authority of Singapore Fintech Regulatory Support

As noted above, Fintech has been an area of rapid growth and innovation in recent years, and e-commerce players benefit from developments in Fintech as they gain access to higher quality payment services at lower costs, which may be tailored to suit their individual business needs. To foster the growth of Fintech, in November 2017, MAS was engaged in various new initiatives, including:

(a) partnership with the Hong Kong Monetary Authority to create a cross-border platform for trade finance using distributed ledger technology, known as the Global Trade Connectivity Network;

(b) stronger supervision through the use of Supervisory Technology, which can, amongst others, detect trade syndicates in the stock market and analyse suspicious transaction reports made by financial institutions. In addition, to ease the burden of compliance, the MAS will eventually make all its information requests in machine readable templates;

(c) use of distributed ledger technology to enable cross border interbank payments to take place directly without the use of intermediaries, at lower costs and risks and with greater efficiency; and

(d) establishment of the ASEAN Financial Innovation Network which facilitates cooperation between banks and Fintech companies in ASEAN, and to improve access to digital financial services across ASEAN.

With strong support from the MAS, Fintech has taken off at an unprecedented pace in Singapore, and e-commerce would also benefit from the development of Fintech, which has the ability to generate greater cost savings, efficiency and security in cross-border payments and transactions.

e-Government

The government also leads by example in terms of encouraging electronic transactions with businesses and citizens.

In Singapore, all government procurement takes place on the GeBIZ platform, a one-stop e-procurement portal hosting all invitations for tenders and quotations from the public sector. E-government procurement promotes the growth of e-commerce in the following ways (ADB 2013):

(a) allows transactions to take place with lower costs for both the government and suppliers. In addition, the government's adoption of e-commerce in G2B transactions will accelerate suppliers' adoption of the same. The standards set by G2B transactions could become widespread in B2B and B2C transactions, for instance, in the use of e-catalogues, digital signatures, e-payment and electronic bank guarantees; and

(b) promotes cross-border transactions by offering access to information and opportunities locally, regionally, and even internationally. By allowing the full tender process to take place online, problems such as geographical barriers and information gaps can be addressed, thus encouraging participation from suppliers and potentially expanding the scope of the market.

Other than procurement, the government also encourages interactions between citizens and government agencies via the internet. Citizens typically transact with government agencies online via their SingPass (Singapore Personal Access) account. Over the years, SingPass has been enhanced to include an improved user interface, mobile-friendly features and stronger security capabilities, such as 2-Factor Authentication (also known as 2FA) for digital transactions involving sensitive data. In October 2018, the government launched the SingPass Mobile application to allow users to log in using their fingerprint, facial recognition or a passcode as a 2FA. When transactions with the government are completed online, payment for services provided by the government are also done electronically on a secured platform.

7.   Laws and Regulations on E-commerce

Singapore was one of the first countries in the world to recognize the challenges and legal issues which may arise out of e-commerce transactions, and has in place legislative measures to tackle these problems, largely by way of the Electronic Transactions Act.

Other than the Electronic Transactions Act which directly addresses the issues related to electronic transactions, the other relevant laws and regulations are not specific to e-commerce. The Personal Data Protection Act, the Computer Misuse Act and the Cybersecurity Act 2018 seek to create a trusted environment that facilitates e-commerce. The Competition Act is a generic law which seeks to maintain and enhance efficient market conduct and eliminate anti-competitive conduct by businesses, whether operating online or not. Additionally, laws such as the Consumer Protection (Fair Trading) Act and the Sale of Goods Act extend the protection offered to consumers in the brick-and-mortar space to the online space. Finally, the import and export of goods sold online to or from Singapore are regulated by the Regulation of Imports and Exports Act, as well as potentially other trade legislation which deal with controlled goods, permits and licensing. Goods sold via e-commerce would also be subject to local laws on taxation.

As the government generally takes a very pro-business approach, the regulatory environment in Singapore is designed to facilitate rather than restrict the growth of e-commerce in the country.

Electronic Transactions Act

The key legislation governing e-commerce in Singapore is the Electronic Transactions Act (ETA). The ETA aims to serve the following purposes, amongst others:[9]

(a) to facilitate e-commerce by removing obstacles to e-commerce arising from uncertainties over writing and signature requirements, and promoting the development of infrastructure necessary for secure e-commerce;

(b) to mitigate the problems of forgery of electronic records[10] and fraud in e-commerce transactions;

(c) to set out uniform rules in relation to the authentication and integrity of electronic records; and

(d) to enhance public confidence in the reliability of electronic records and e-commerce, and to facilitate the development of e-commerce using digital signatures.

The ETA essentially gives legal recognition to information in electronic form, as well as to electronic contracts. Specifically, the ETA provides that information may not be denied its legal effect by virtue of the fact that it is in the form of an electronic record.[11] Further, if any law or regulation requires information to be presented in writing, such requirement may be satisfied using an electronic record which is accessible and usable for subsequent reference.[12] It also recognizes the validity of a contract that is formed by means of electronic communications.

As e-commerce businesses tend to face high volume of transactions each day, it is often the case that their operations are automated so as to maximize efficiency and keep labour costs to a minimum. Hence, consumers may, for example, receive automatic emails confirming their orders for products or services online. The ETA contemplates such situations and provides that "a contract formed by the interaction of an automated message system and a natural person" cannot be denied its validity or enforceability merely because such interaction or the resultant contract was not reviewed by a natural person.[13]

To facilitate e-commerce transactions, Section 19 of the ETA introduces certain presumptions in respect of the authenticity and integrity of secure electronic records and secure electronic signatures, as follows:[14]

(a) the secure electronic record has not been altered since the point in time it was accorded a secure status; and

(b) the secure electronic signature is the signature of the person to whom it relates and was affixed with the intention of signing or approving the electronic record.

An electronic record or signature will be considered secure under the ETA if a specified security procedure or a commercially reasonable security procedure[15] has been applied to it. Under the specified security procedure, a digital signature will be treated as a secure electronic signature if it was created by a holder of a certificate issued by an accredited certification authority during the period of validity of the certificate, and any record signed by such digital signature will consequently be treated as a secure electronic record.[16] In this regard, the use of specified security procedures—essentially obtaining a certificate from an accredited certification authority to issue digital signatures—should be preferred to the use of commercially reasonable security procedures, as the test for whether such procedures are commercially reasonable involves multifarious considerations and may be hard to satisfy.

Personal Data Protection Act 2012[17] (PDPA)

The PDPA prescribes certain rules relating to the collection, retention and transfer of personal data. For data to constitute personal data, two basic requirements should be satisfied (PDPC 2017, para. 5):

(a) the data relates to an individual. This includes information about an individual's health, educational and employment background, and activities such as spending habits; and

(b) the individual concerned can be identified from:
  (i) that data on its own, which includes but is not limited to the full name, identity card number, passport number, personal mobile telephone number, facial image (e.g. photograph or video recording), voice of an individual (e.g. in a voice recording), fingerprint, iris image and DNA profile of an individual; or
  (ii) that data and other information to which the organization has or is likely to have access, such as gender, nationality, age or blood group.

To the extent that an e-commerce business collects, transfers or uses consumer data, it must ensure that the handling of such data complies with the rules set out by the PDPA. Broadly speaking, the PDPA imposes the following obligations on an organization which deals with personal data:

(a) having reasonable purposes for the collection, use or disclosure of personal data;
(b) notifying the purposes for the collection, use or disclosure of personal data and obtaining the consent for the same from the individual concerned;
(c) providing opportunities for individuals to access and correct their personal data;
(d) ensuring the accuracy of personal data in the possession of or under the control of the organization and protecting such personal data from unauthorized use or disclosure;
(e) not retaining personal data if no longer required; and
(f) implementing policies and practices to comply with the PDPA.

Importantly, the PDPA only protects the personal data of natural persons, and not data relating to corporate and other entities. Hence, the PDPA is unlikely to apply to B2B transactions unless the personal data of employees are involved.

Computer Misuse Act[18] (CMA)
The CMA criminalizes various cybercrimes, such as the unauthorized access to and modification of any programme or data stored on a computer and the unauthorized disclosure of the access code to a

computer for any wrongful gain or unlawful purpose. Section 11 of the CMA extends its scope to offences committed outside Singapore, under certain circumstances.

In particular, Section 8A(1), which is a recent addition to the CMA, makes it an offence for any person, knowing or having reason to believe that any personal information about another individual was obtained by an act done in contravention of the CMA, to obtain or retain such personal information, or to supply, transmit or make such information available through any means. However, Section 8A(4) clarifies that the said provision is not meant to catch service providers who merely operate facilities for network access, or provide services relating to or connections for the transmission or routing of data.

While the CMA does not create direct obligations on businesses to take proactive steps to protect against cybersecurity threats and to report cybersecurity incidents, businesses are advised to stay vigilant and prevent their systems from being used to facilitate cybercrimes. This is especially the case with the entry into force of the new Cybersecurity Act 2018.

Cybersecurity Act 2018[19] (CSA 2018)

The CSA 2018 was passed by the Singapore Parliament and took effect earlier in 2018. It aims to enhance the protection over Critical Information Infrastructure (CII), which are computers or computer systems directly involved in the provision of essential services, against cyber-attacks. The CSA 2018 provides the framework for the protection of CII against cyber-attacks and imposes various obligations on CII owners in this connection. The designated CII sectors in Singapore are energy, water, banking and finance, healthcare, transport, info-communications, media, security and emergency services and government sectors.

In addition, the CSA 2018 grants to the Cyber Security Agency of Singapore the powers to investigate cybersecurity threats and incidents and to prevent further harm or cybersecurity incidents from arising out of such cybersecurity threats and incidents. These include directing any person to carry out remedial measures in relation to a computer or computer system that is or was affected by the cybersecurity incident, and requiring the owner of a computer or computer system to take any action to assist with the investigation, such as preserving the state of the computer or computer system and monitoring the computer or computer system for a specified period of time. Such powers are to be exercised in a manner which commensurates with the severity of the cybersecurity threat or incident.

Separately, the CSA 2018 requires the licensing of service providers who conduct penetration testing services and manage security operations centre (SOC) monitoring services, due to the widespread use of such service providers in Singapore and the sensitive nature of the information to which they have access.

Consumer Protection (Fair Trading) Act [20] (CPFTA)

The CPFTA prohibits suppliers resident in Singapore or supplying to consumers resident in Singapore from engaging in unfair practices, such as misleading or taking advantage of consumers. The restrictions against unfair practices under the CPFTA apply where the supplier or consumer is resident in Singapore or, where the offer or acceptance relating to the consumer transaction is made in or is sent from Singapore. As the CPFTA does not differentiate between online and offline consumer transactions, e-commerce retailers are subject to the CPFTA in Singapore like other brick-and-mortar retailers. Moreover, claims that consumers have been misled into purchasing certain goods and services tend to be more prevalent in the e-commerce industry due to the nature of the business. Therefore, e-commerce businesses must abide by consumer protection laws and aim to settle disputes amicably within a reasonable period of time, so as to prevent the risk of consumer complaints or negative feedback which will have an adverse impact on their reputation.

Sale of Goods Act [21] (SOGA)

The SOGA governs the sale of goods to consumers, including the formation and performance of contracts of sale, and provides for remedies in the event of breach of contract, without differentiating between whether such sale is made online or offline. E-commerce retailers should familiarize themselves with the SOGA in order to understand their rights and obligations vis-à-vis consumers in relation to a contract for the sale of goods.

Legislation Concerning Import and Export of Goods

The Regulation of Imports and Exports Act[22] (RIEA) regulates, amongst other things, the import and export of goods to and from Singapore. Pursuant to the RIEA, a permit issued by the Singapore Customs is required before any goods can be imported[23] into, exported[24] out of or transhipped in Singapore, subject to certain exceptions.[25]

Where the goods are not controlled and are imported, exported or transhipped by air, a permit is not required for such import, export or transhipment, as the case may be, if:[26]

(a) in the case of an import, the total value of the goods does not exceed S$400;

(b) in the case of an export, the total value of the goods does not exceed S$1,000; and

(c) in the case of a transhipment, the goods are not transhipped from one free trade zone to another and the total value of the goods does not exceed S$1,000.

Separately, if any of the goods are controlled goods under the purview of certain regulatory authorities in Singapore, then approval from the competent authorities will have to be obtained before such goods can be imported or exported from Singapore. A strategic goods permit issued by the Singapore Customs will also be required to export any goods which are strategic goods within the meaning of the Strategic Goods Control Act.[27]

Hence, foreign e-commerce players who are looking to sell their goods to customers located in Singapore need to be aware of the regulatory requirements in respect of the import of such goods into Singapore. On the other hand, local e-commerce players who wish to expand their sales beyond Singapore should also comply with any export regulations under Singapore law, as well as laws regulating imports in the countries to which they plan to sell.

Tax Law

Goods and services tax (GST) and duties, where applicable, will generally be imposed on goods which are imported into Singapore. Currently, however, GST is not payable for non-controlled and non-dutiable goods which are imported into Singapore by post or air, and which do not exceed S$400 in value.[28] With effect from 1 January 2020,

GST will also be imposed on digital services, including B2B services such as consultancy and marketing services purchased from overseas suppliers, as well as B2C services such as video and music streaming services (IRAS n.d.). This is to level the GST treatment for all services consumed in Singapore, regardless of whether they are procured from local or overseas suppliers.

8. Competition Law and Policy

Competition Act

As e-commerce players compete to expand their reach to consumers in Singapore and beyond, they are subject to local rules against anti-competitive conduct. The primary legislation governing competition in Singapore is the Competition Act (CA) (Chapter 50B) and it is enforced by the Competition and Consumer Commission of Singapore (CCCS).

In recent years, the CCCS has investigated several cases involving online businesses. In 2014, the CCCS assessed the proposed acquisition of JobStreet Singapore by SEEK Asia Investments Pte. Ltd.,[29] which would have led to a merger of the top two online recruitment advertising service providers in Singapore. In that case, the CCCS studied the specific characteristics of online markets, including the fact that an online recruitment advertising service provider functions as a two-sided platform which matches two sets of users: recruiters and employers on one side, and jobseekers on the other. Because of the network effects that characterize two-sided platforms (i.e., the service provider must have a significant jobseeker pool to make it attractive to advertisers, and a significant number of job postings to make it attractive to jobseekers), the CCCS considered that the remaining players in the market may not be able to act as a sufficient competitive constraint to the merged entity in the short term. This could result in the merged entity subsequently raising prices or entering into exclusive contracts, to the detriment of customers. As such, the CCCS conditioned its approval of the transaction on the parties implementing certain behavioural commitments and divestiture commitment to mitigate the competition concerns.

In 2016, the CCCS conducted an investigation into the practice by an online food delivery provider in Singapore of entering into exclusive agreements with certain restaurants which prevented the restaurants from using other providers' services (CCCS 2016). In that case, the CCCS concluded that the exclusive arrangements had not harmed competition and that the market remained competitive. However, the CCCS cautioned that if the online food delivery provider becomes dominant, the entering of such exclusive agreements may affect the competitive state of the market and therefore constitute an infringement of competition law. The CCCS noted that it would continue to closely monitor the market.

More recently, in September 2018, the CCCS issued an infringement decision against ride-hailing companies Grab and Uber in relation to the sale of Uber's regional business to Grab in consideration of Uber holding a 27.5 per cent stake in Grab. The CCCS concluded that the transaction led to a substantial lessening of competition in the market for two-sided platforms matching drivers and riders for the provision of booked chauffeured point-to-point transport services in Singapore. In its assessment, the CCCS considered that the two-sided nature of the ride-hailing platform market means that there are strong indirect network effects—riders value the platform more when there are more drivers, and drivers value the platform more when there are more riders. The indirect network effect strengthens the incumbency of existing players in the market, and increases the amount of time and resources required for a new entrant to establish a network of a similar scale. Under such scenario, exclusivity restrictions imposed by the incumbent platform would reinforce the indirect network effects and significantly raise the barriers to entry and expansion. In accordance with its findings, the CCCS imposed a financial penalty of over S$13 million on the parties and issued directions that required the parties to, amongst others, remove any exclusivity restrictions and arrangements imposed on drivers and partnering taxi fleets.

Findings from the Study on E-commerce in Singapore Commissioned by the CCCS

In 2015, the CCCS commissioned DotEcon Ltd. to conduct a study into the e-commerce industry in Singapore (the DotEcon Study),[30] to better understand the e-commerce landscape in Singapore and assess whether the competition law framework in Singapore can effectively deal with competition issues that might arise in an e-commerce context (DotEcon 2015).

The DotEcon Study highlighted that e-commerce may have many pro-competitive effects, from streamlining supply chains and reducing distribution costs, to facilitating search and information for consumers, to lowering the barriers to entry for retailers, and ultimately increasing the variety of products and services available on the market. However, the study also cautioned that e-commerce businesses may face barriers to expansion as investments are required to establish trust and reputation as well as possibly to set up a logistics system as they seek to gain more customers.

Redefining Market Boundaries

E-commerce may change the definition of product markets, in terms of the substitutability of online and offline channels. Empirical studies show that in the retail sector, online and offline channels are often seen as substitutes by consumers. Yet, for products or services where non-price aspects such as personal experience, product quality and trustworthiness of the seller are valuable to consumers, the extent of substitutability of online and offline channels will be low. E-commerce may also widen the definition of geographical markets as customers can purchase from suppliers located outside of the country, but this may be limited by traditional barriers like selective distribution agreements, legal restrictions and transportation costs.

Impact on Price Competition

E-commerce may stimulate price competition between companies operating in online and offline channels if the cost savings and efficiencies associated with e-commerce are passed on to consumers, causing inefficient firms to be driven out of the market. However, such price competition may be curtailed by companies that engage in practices to inhibit search of price information by consumers, for instance, by setting low headline prices but charging exorbitant shipping costs. Transparency of price information online also increases the risk of collusion, as competitors may monitor and match one another's prices with greater ease.

Network Effects

E-commerce platforms are characterized by network effects where the value of the platform to an individual user depends on the number of other users on the platform. As large platforms continue to expand and improve the quality of customer service provided to users, smaller competitors may not be able to keep up with its pace. This could result in e-commerce markets becoming highly concentrated, with a small number of firms having a large share of the market.

Effects of Online Data Collection and Use

Information about consumers and their purchasing habits collected by existing e-commerce players may act as a source of market power, as such data are hard to replicate. This could result in significant competitive advantages for the incumbent, who would be able to come up with products and services to better meet consumers' needs.

Vertical Restraints

Vertical restraints may be used by manufacturers to restrict the ability of online retailers to compete with physical retailers. For example, manufacturers could quote higher wholesale prices to online retailers or restrict online sales. Although vertical restraints could overcome the problems of free-riding (and incentivize physical retailers to make more investments), they can be injurious to competition as they limit the extent to which firms may reap the economic benefits of e-commerce.

The DotEcon Study concluded that established competition law frameworks such as that in Singapore are generally well suited to address the competition concerns in e-commerce markets. It highlighted that e-commerce does not necessarily call for a more or less interventionist approach by competition authorities. Although network effects could lead to concentrated markets and strong first-mover advantages, the dynamic nature of e-commerce markets suggests that any market power tends to be transitory, and intervention would risk stifling innovation and investment in these markets.

9. Impediments and Opportunities for Growth of E-commerce

Whilst the infrastructure and environmental factors are conducive to the growth of e-commerce in Singapore, impediments do exist—largely in terms of how businesses can adapt quickly enough to the changing shopping habits of consumers.

Shopping Habits of Consumers

According to a study conducted by PayPal, Singaporeans love to shop online, with 73 per cent of adults in Singapore having shopped online and spending an estimated S$3 billion in 2016 (PayPal 2017). The main reason for Singaporeans choosing to shop online is due to its convenience.

When it comes to cross-border online transactions, PayPal observed that Singaporeans are the most confident shoppers in the Asia Pacific, with about 0.5 million Singaporeans spending an estimated S$1.2 billion on such transactions. In this regard, the United States, China and Japan are the top online shopping destinations for Singaporeans. The PayPal study revealed that the primary reasons for shopping online overseas are better prices and purchasing items not available in Singapore. A noteworthy point is that 52 per cent of online shoppers in Singapore indicated that they trust overseas online stores as much as local ones, which is the highest of all the countries surveyed in the region, i.e. India, China, Singapore, Japan and Thailand.

Mobile commerce also appears to be one of the drivers of e-commerce in Singapore, as the average total online spending made using a mobile device was 31 per cent in 2016. This is unsurprising given the high mobile penetration rate in Singapore, as well as the fact that payments can be made easily over mobile applications. The increasing trend of mobile commerce has also led to online retailers such as Zalora and Reebonz launching regular promotions which are only available on their respective mobile applications.

Given the positive trends highlighted above, the e-commerce scene in Singapore is likely to continue to flourish in the coming years.

Barriers in Changing Business Models

While Singaporeans may have taken to shopping online, it may not be as easy for businesses to follow suit, as changing business models tends to require more time than changing personal habits. In particular, businesses may face the following obstacles in adopting e-commerce:

(a) lack of an e-commerce strategy;
(b) insufficient resources;
(c) lack of support from top management;

(d) technical difficulties in integrating the new and old systems; and

(e) concerns over privacy and security in granting access to corporate systems to customers and suppliers.

Despite the said obstacles, in 2016, 56 per cent of companies had a web presence, an increase from 45 per cent in 2015 (IMDA 2017). Another promising trend is that the proportion of businesses which used e-payments increased from 48 per cent in 2015 to 57 per cent in 2016. Amongst businesses that did not use e-payments, the most cited reason was that e-payments were not a good fit for their businesses. This problem can be overcome if e-payment solutions continue to evolve and adapt to changing business needs.

In relation to the proportion of businesses that engaged in e-commerce activities, this remained unchanged at 13 per cent from 2014 to 2016. As with the case of e-payments, most respondents who did not conduct e-commerce activities identified the primary reason as not being a good fit for their businesses. Therefore, to achieve a higher adoption rate of e-commerce, e-commerce solution providers will have to offer a wider range of solutions which cater to the needs of different businesses, so as to help businesses overcome the obstacles of entering the e-commerce market.

Anti-Competitive Conduct of Incumbent E-commerce Players

As noted in the DotEcon Study and the Handbook on E-commerce and Competition in ASEAN (see Appendix 8.1), any market power acquired in e-commerce markets, which are dynamic and constantly evolving, may be transient. Accordingly, to protect their market position, incumbent e-commerce players, especially those with stronger market power, may decide to engage in exclusionary or predatory behaviour to curtail competition.

As noted above, the CCCS had launched an investigation into an alleged abuse of dominance in the online food ordering and delivery market, where the undertaking concerned had entered into exclusive partnerships with restaurants, preventing them from working with its competitors.[31] Although it was found that the exclusive agreement in question did not have adverse effects on competition, should the same conduct be engaged in by an e-commerce player with greater market power, coupled with the network effects, it could well have the effect of preventing actual and potential competitors from competing effectively in the market, stifling the growth of e-commerce.

Indeed, the removal of all exclusivity restrictions was a cornerstone of the CCCS's directions in respect of the Grab-Uber transaction. Amongst others, the CCCS required that Grab did not enter into any exclusive arrangements and/or removed all existing exclusive arrangements with drivers, rental fleet partners as well as taxi fleets in Singapore. These were intended to help increase choices for drivers and riders, and reduce the barriers to entry and expansion into the market so as to increase market contestability post-transaction.

10. Policy Issues and Recommendations

With its well-developed ICT infrastructure and legal framework, Singapore is ready to embrace e-commerce. However, to encourage more consumers to make purchases online, it is important to not only build confidence in the reliability of electronic transactions, but also to educate the public, especially the older generation, on the benefits of e-commerce as well as the potential risks involved. This could be achieved by way of television campaigns, newspaper advertisements, as well as leveraging on social media.

The government should also continue to provide regulatory support to financial institutions and Fintech companies, to allow them to come up with more secure, cost-effective and innovative electronic payment solutions. The government can also make a concerted effort to improve electronic payment systems and further facilitate electronic transactions at a national level. In this regard, the government has been developing a National Digital Identity (NDI) system, which will allow citizens and businesses to conduct online transactions conveniently in a secure environment (Kwang, 21 August 2017). According to the Government Technology Agency of Singapore (GovTech), the NDI system is expected to be operational in 2020. GovTech will also collaborate with the private sector to develop value-added services using the NDI, including signing digital agreements, secure storage of digital documents and building access control.

Although there are various financial assistance schemes and capacity building initiatives put in place by government agencies, none of these initiatives are targeted specifically at e-commerce. While existing businesses or aspiring entrepreneurs may be keen to enter the e-commerce market, some may be constrained by a lack of expertise and resources to operate an e-commerce business. Hence, the government should provide assistance in this area by organizing workshops or training sessions to allow interested parties to acquire the requisite skills and knowledge in e-commerce.

Given that one of the barriers to business e-commerce adoption is the perceived misfit for the nature of their businesses, the government should also put in place incentives for e-commerce solution providers to develop creative solutions to cater to a wider range of businesses and industries. This could be achieved, for instance, by providing funding and creating opportunities for different e-commerce solution providers to combine their resources to come up with improved e-commerce solutions.

APPENDIX 8.1

Handbook on E-commerce and Competition in ASEAN

In 2017, the CCCS commissioned PricewaterhouseCoopers to assist in preparing a Handbook on E-commerce and Competition in ASEAN (hereafter, the Handbook) (CCCS 2017).The Handbook aims to provide insight on the existing development of e-commerce as well as emerging challenges for ASEAN competition authorities. It also seeks to provide guidance to ASEAN competition authorities on how to respond to such challenges while promoting the development of e-commerce for the benefit of consumers and businesses.

Defining Markets, Multi-sided Markets, and Assessing Market Power

The Handbook noted that in multi-sided online markets such as online marketplaces and price comparison websites (PCWs), conventional approaches to market definition may no longer apply due to the relationships and externalities between distinct sides of the market. For instance, due to network effects, a platform may set price below cost on one side of the market to attract users on another side. Therefore, when defining the market, competition authorities should consider the total price charged to all sides of a market, adopt a less technical and more holistic consideration of the competitive constraints that a firm faces on all sides of the market and consider the ability of consumers to switch to alternative providers.

In assessing market power in multi-sided markets, relationships between all sides of the market, network effects and additional feedback effects should all be considered. Competition authorities are also encouraged to modify the approach taken in assessing alleged anti-competitive conduct for multi-sided markets. In assessing harm in such markets, interrelationships between different sides of the market should be considered, although harm on one side need not offset benefits on another.

Vertical Agreements

In e-commerce markets, agreements between firms at different stages of production are likely to generate efficiencies (e.g. overcoming issues of free-riding, reducing price by overcoming double marginalization, and/or resolving potential specific investment hold-up risks). However, they could inhibit intra-brand competition and potentially facilitate collusion where inter-brand competition is limited. The Handbook noted that restrictions which unjustifiably prevent all internet sales or discriminate between online and brick-and-mortar retailers, along with restrictions on cross-border passive sales, are regarded as hardcore restrictions and prohibited in the European Union.

Aside from hardcore restrictions which are harmful to competition, other vertical restraints, such as Most Favoured Nation (MFN) clauses (or best-price guarantees/price parity clauses) and agreements that prevent retailers from selling via online marketplaces or advertising on PCWs, should be assessed on a case-by-case basis.

Horizontal Coordination

Due to price transparency of online markets, coordination can occur between competing firms on the prices charged on platforms, with or without facilitation from the platform itself. Firms operating in e-commerce markets may also implement vertical restraints in a coordinated manner, leading to an increase in prices in a market.

In relation to price algorithms, a key practical concern is the need to investigate the nature of such algorithms and their functions, making it essential to recruit experts in the relevant field. Further concerns are that these technologies may self-learn the optimality of coordination among competitors. The question of where liability would then fall remains unclear.

Unilateral Conduct

While conduct amounting to abuse of dominant position in e-commerce markets are analogous to those in brick-and-mortar markets, some forms of conduct may be more prevalent in the former. For instance, many multi-sided platforms that offer a range of related services have engaged in tying and bundling, and some online platforms have imposed exclusivity agreements. It is important to consider whether a dominant firm is simply more efficient or innovating at a faster pace than its rivals. Although some consider Big Data to be a source of market power and hence a factor in determining whether a firm is dominant, doubts have been raised on it being an essential facility due to its replicable nature.

Mergers and Acquisitions

Competition authorities are encouraged to consider if existing regimes are sufficiently broad in scope so that potential lessening of dynamic competition can be assessed, even with limited or no current overlap in the products and services offered by parties, or when turnover thresholds are not met.

In assessing proposed mergers in multi-sided online markets, the presence and extent of network effects should be considered. Authorities should evaluate when a tipping point is likely to occur, considering the extent to which consumers multi-home, switching costs, interoperability between competing platforms, and the barriers to entry and expansion that smaller firms face. Remedies should also focus on maintaining or improving these market characteristics. Potential issues in mergers between firms at different levels of the supply chain may arise if the merger gives incentive and ability for the merged entity to exclude or marginalize competitors. Whether the merger may give rise to market power from pooling of consumer data held by the merging parties should also be considered, although that may be mitigated if competitors can source equivalent data elsewhere.

Sufficiency of Existing Competition Policy and Law to Protect and Promote Effective Competition in E-commerce Market

The Handbook concluded that legal frameworks provided by existing competition policy and law are largely sufficient to deal with virtually all competition challenges from the emergence and growth of e-commerce. However, the technicality of some alleged anti-competitive behaviour suggests a need for specific resources dealing with potential coordination via pricing algorithms. In addition, different competition authorities have taken contrasting positions in relation to vertical restraints (such as with regards to MFN clauses in the hotel bookings market), posing a challenge for firms operating internationally. Hence, there is a need for harmonization among competition authorities across ASEAN Member States on the approach to investigating alleged anti-competitive conduct in e-commerce markets.

NOTES

1. Based on public information available from various internet service providers' websites, as at December 2017.

2. Latency refers to the responsiveness of the connection between one's home and the servers of the internet service providers.

3. Speedtest data from Q4 2016–Q1 2017 shows that Singapore has an average fixed broadband download speed of 180.61 Mbps and an average mobile download speed of 44.37 Mbps, ranked second in the world for both. In addition, Singapore's fixed broadband and mobile speeds have increased by 18.1 per cent and 16.4 per cent, respectively, over the same period in the previous year. See Speedtest (2017).

4. According to the study, the market will grow to US$10.1 billion (approximately S$14.2 billion) in 2025.

5. It is observed that no online platform accounts for more than 20 per cent of consumers in any country in Southeast Asia.

6. Lazada Singapore Facebook Page, 14 December 2017, https://www.facebook.com/LazadaSingapore/ (accessed 14 December 2017).

7. Williams (2017). See https://www.lazada.sg/capitaland/ for the online mall set up by CapitaLand on Lazada Singapore.

8. SPRING Singapore is an agency under the purview of the Ministry of Trade and Industry, which is responsible for helping Singapore enterprises grow and building trust in Singapore products and services. SPRING provides assistance to enterprises in financing, capability and management development, technology and innovation, and access to markets.

9. Section 3, ETA (Chapter 88).

10. Defined in the ETA as "a record generated, communicated, received or stored by electronic means in an information system or for transmission from one information system to another".

11. Section 6, ETA (Chapter 88).

12. Section 7, ETA (Chapter 88).

13. Section 15, ETA (Chapter 88).

14. Section 18, ETA (Chapter 88). An electronic signature is secure if, through the application of an agreed specified security procedure or a commercially reasonable security procedure, it can be verified that an electronic signature was, at the time it was made:
    (a) unique to the person using it;
    (b) capable of identifying such person;
    (c) created in a manner or using a means under the sole control of the person using it; and

(d) linked to the electronic record to which it relates in a manner such that if the record was changed the electronic signature would be invalidated.

15. Section 17(2), ETA (Chapter 88). Whether a security procedure is commercially reasonable is determined with regards to the purposes of the procedure and the commercial circumstances at the time the procedure was used, including:
    (a) the nature of the transaction;
    (b) the sophistication of the parties;
    (c) the volume of similar transactions engaged in by either or all parties;
    (d) the availability of alternatives offered to but rejected by any party;
    (e) the cost of alternative procedures; and
    (f) the procedures in general use for similar types of transactions.

16. Paragraphs 2 and 3, Third Schedule, ETA (Chapter 88).

17. Chapter 26.

18. Chapter 50A.

19. No. 9 of 2018.

20. Chapter 52A.

21. Chapter 393.

22. Chapter 272A.

23. Section 2(1), RIEA (Chapter 272A). Import means "to bring or cause to be brought into Singapore by land, water or air from any place which is outside Singapore but does not include the bringing into Singapore of goods which are to be taken out of Singapore on the same conveyance on which they were brought into Singapore without any landing or transhipment within Singapore".

24. Section 2(1), RIEA (Chapter 272A). Export means "to take or cause to be taken out of Singapore by land, water or air and includes the placing of any goods in a conveyance for the purpose of the goods being taken out of Singapore but does not include the taking out from Singapore of any goods on the same conveyance on which they were brought into Singapore unless such goods after being brought into Singapore have been landed or transhipped within Singapore".

25. Regulation 3(1), RIER.

26. Regulations 3(2A), 3(3) and 3(4), RIER.

27. Chapter 300.

28. Goods and Services Tax (Imports Relief) Order.

29. "Proposed Acquisition by Seek Asia Investments Pte. Ltd. of the Jobstreet Business", CCS 400/004/14, 13 November 2014.

30. Case Studies section, discussing potential effects of e-commerce on competition.

31. See paragraph 7.6.4 above.

REFERENCES

ADB (Asian Development Bank). "e-Government Procurement Handbook", 2013. https://www.adb.org/sites/default/files/institutional-document/34064/files/e-government-procurement-handbook.pdf (accessed 3 March 2017).

Aravindan, Aradhana. "Alibaba Spending $1 Billion to Raise Stake in Southeast Asia's Lazada". *Thomson Reuters*, 28 June 2017. https://www.reuters.com/article/us-lazada-m-a-alibaba/alibaba-spending-1-billion-to-raise-stake-in-southeast-asias-lazada-idUSKBN19J0XV (accessed 14 December 2017).

AT Kearney and EFMA. "Banking in a Digital World", 2013. https://www.atkearney.com/documents/10192/3054333/Banking+in+a+Digital+World.pdf/91231b20-788e-41a1-a429-3f926834c2b0 (accessed 24 February 2017).

Barquin, Sonia and HV Vinayak. "Digital Banking in Asia: What Do Consumers Really Want?" McKinsey & Company, March 2015. https://www.mckinsey.com/~/media/mckinsey/industries/financial%20services/our%20insights/capitalizing%20on%20asias%20digital%20banking%20boom/digital_banking_in_asia_what_do_consumers_really_want.ashx (accessed 12 December 2017).

Budget 2017. "Budget Speech". https://www.singaporebudget.gov.sg/budget_2017/budgetspeech (accessed 3 March 2017).

CCCS (Competition and Consumer Commission of Singapore). "CCS Investigation Finds Online Food Delivery Industry To Be Currently Competitive But Exclusive Agreements Could Be Problematic In Future", 25 August 2016. https://www.cccs.gov.sg/media-and-consultation/newsroom/media-releases/investigation-of-online-food-delivery-industry (accessed 27 February 2017).

―――. "Handbook on Competition and E-commerce in ASEAN", December 2017. https://www.cccs.gov.sg/resources/publications/other-publications/asean-ecommerce-handbook (accessed 21 December 2017).

Cheok, Jacquelyn. "Food Delivery App War in Singapore on the Boil". *The Straits Times*, 20 November 2017. http://www.straitstimes.com/lifestyle/food/food-delivery-app-war-on-the-boil (accessed 14 December 2017).

Chia Yan Min. "Asean Single Window - A Digital Platform to Simplify Customs Clearance". *The Business Times*, 26 April 2018. https://www.businesstimes.com.sg/asean-business/asean-single-window-a-digital-platform-to-simplify-customs-clearance.

Department of Statistics Singapore. "Latest Data", n.d. http://www.singstat.gov.sg/statistics/latest-data (accessed 12 December 2017).

DotEcon. "E-commerce and its Impact on Competition Policy and Law in Singapore", October 2015. https://www.ccs.gov.sg/~/media/custom/ccs/files/media%20and%20publications/publications/occasional%20paper/e-commerce%20in%20singapore/dotecon%20ecommerce%20final%20report.ashx (accessed 25 February 2017).

Google and Temasek. "e-Economy SEA: Unlocking the $200 Billion Digital Opportunity in Southeast Asia", 24 May 2016. http://www.slideshare.net/economySEA/economy-sea-by-google-and-temasek (accessed 21 February 2017).

Grab. "Grab Delivers a Cashless and Seamless Ride Experience to Everyone with GrabPay Credits", 29 November 2016. https://www.grab.com/sg/press/tech-product/grab-delivers-cashless-seamless-ride-experience-everyone-grabpay-credits.

———. "Grab Launches GrabPay e-Wallet in Hawker Stalls, Restaurants and Shops in Singapore", 2 November 2017. https://www.grab.com/sg/press/others/grab-launches-grabpay-e-wallet-in-hawker-stalls-restaurants-and-shops-in-singapore/ (accessed 18 December 2017).

———. 2019. https://www.grab.com/sg/merchant/pay/.

Hootsuite and We are Social Singapore. "Digital in 2017: Southeast Asia", 26 January 2017. https://www.slideshare.net/wearesocialsg/digital-in-2017-southeast-asia (accessed 14 December 2017).

Hoppe, Florian, Sebastien Lamy and Alessandro Cannarsi. "Can Southeast Asia Live Up to Its E-commerce Potential?" Bain & Company, 2016. http://www.bain.com/Images/BAIN_BRIEF_Can_Southeast_Asia_Live_Up_to_Ecommerce_potential.pdf (accessed 12 December 2017).

IE Singapore (International Enterprise Singapore). "Internationalisation a Key Engine of Growth and Transformation: Companies' Revenues from Overseas Markets Grew 4.2%, Outpacing Total Revenue Growth of 1.3%", 16 February 2017. https://www.gov.sg/~/sgpcmedia/media_releases/ie-singapore/press_release/P-20170216-1/attachment/MR00417_IE%20Singapore%20 2017%20YIR_2017%2002%2016.pdf (accessed 26 February 2017).

———. "IE Singapore Unveils Plan to Help Trading Sector Digitalise for Global Growth and Productivity; Build Industry-ready Talent with Deep Skills", 6 September 2017. https://www.iesingapore.gov.sg/Media-Centre/Media-Releases/2017/9/IE-Singapore-unveils-plan-to-help-trading-sector-digitalise-for-global-growth-and-productivity-build-industry-ready-talent-with-deep-skills (accessed 14 December 2017).

———. "IE Singapore Bands Together SMEs in Logistics, Payments and Platforms to Win E-commerce Projects in Southeast Asia", 9 November 2017. https://www.iesingapore.gov.sg/Media-Centre/Media-Releases/2017/11/

IE-Singapore-bands-together-SMEs-in-logistics-payments-and-platforms-to-win-e-commerce-projects-in-Southeast-Asia (accessed 14 December 2017).

———. "Expand Your Global Presence: Global Company Partnership", n.d.*a*. https://www.iesingapore.gov.sg/-/media/IE-Singapore/Files/Publications/Brochures-Local-Companies/GCP/GCP_Brochure_Insert_19Apr2016.ashx (accessed 26 February 2017).

———. "Take Your First Step Overseas: Market Readiness Assistance", n.d.*b*. https://www.iesingapore.gov.sg/-/media/IE-Singapore/Files/Assistance-for-Local-Companies/IE_MRA_Brochure_Insert_Oct2016.ashx (accessed 26 February 2017).

IMDA (Infocomm Media Development Authority). "Annual Survey on Infocomm Usage by Enterprises for 2016", 2017. https://www.imda.gov.sg/-/media/imda/files/industry-development/fact-and-figures/infocomm-survey-reports/iu2016-public-report.pdf?la=en (accessed 15 December 2017).

———. "iSPRINT Enhanced", 20 February 2017. https://www.imda.gov.sg/infocomm-and-media-news/buzz-central/2012/9/isprint-enhanced (accessed 3 March 2017).

———. "Pre-Approved Digital Solutions for SMEs to Seize New Growth Opportunities", 3 November 2017. https://www.imda.gov.sg/about/newsroom/media-releases/2017/pre-approved-digital-solutions-for-smes-to-seize-new-growth-opportunities (accessed 14 December 2017).

———. "The Future of Drone Delivery", 7 November 2017. https://www.imda.gov.sg/infocomm-and-media-news/viewpoint/2017/3/the-future-of-drone-delivery (accessed 15 January 2018).

———. "Industry Digital Plans", 17 November 2017. https://www.imda.gov.sg/industry-development/programmes-and-grants/small-and-medium-enterprises/smes-go-digital/industry-digital-plans (accessed 14 December 2017).

———. "Infocomm Usage-Households and Individuals", 4 July 2018. https://www.imda.gov.sg/industry-development/facts-and-figures/infocomm-usage-households-and-individuals (accessed 12 December 2017).

———. "Statistic on Telecom Service for 2019 Jan - Jun", 7 August 2019. https://www2.imda.gov.sg/infocomm-media-landscape/research-and-statistics/telecommunications/statistics-on-telecom-services/statistic-on-telecom-service-for-2019-jan.

———. "SME Digital Tech Hub", 31 May 2019. https://www2.imda.gov.sg/programme-listing/smes-go-digital/sme-digital-tech-hub.

Institute of Grocery Distribution. "IGD: Singapore Online Grocery to More than Triple by 2020", 22 February 2017. https://www.igd.com/about-us/

media/press-releases/press-release/t/igd-singapore-online-grocery-to-more-than-triple-by-2020/i/16197 (accessed 26 February 2017).

iPrice. "The Map of E-commerce in Singapore", July 2019. https://iprice.sg/insights/mapofecommerce/.

IRAS. "GST on Imported Services", n.d. https://www.iras.gov.sg/irashome/GST/Consumers/GST-on-Imported-Services/.

Kwang, Kevin. "Amazon Prime Now lands in Singapore App Stores". *Channel NewsAsia*, 26 July 2017. https://www.channelnewsasia.com/news/singapore/amazon-prime-now-lands-in-singapore-app-stores-9066916 (accessed 14 December 2017).

———. "National Digital Identity System to be Cornerstone of Singapore's Smart Nation Vision". *Channel NewsAsia*, 21 August 2017. https://www.channelnewsasia.com/news/singapore/national-digital-identity-system-to-be-cornerstone-of-singapore-9140090 (accessed 15 December 2017).

Lee, Terence. "The Future is Here: Singapore Post Tests Drone Deliveries". *Tech in Asia*, 8 October 2015. https://www.techinasia.com/future-singpost-tests-drone-delivery (accessed 8 March 2017).

———. "DHL is Set to Shake Up eCommerce Logistics in Southeast Asia". *Tech in Asia*, 6 October 2016. https://www.techinasia.com/dhl-ecommerce-logistics-southeast-asia (accessed 26 February 2017).

Lim, Kenneth. "Taxi Companies Get Green Light to Introduce Surge Pricing". *Channel NewsAsia*, 17 March 2017. http://www.channelnewsasia.com/news/singapore/taxi-companies-get-green-light-to-introduce-surge-pricing-8580042 (accessed 14 December 2017).

———. "Airbus Helicopters Partners SingPost for Drone Delivery Trials". *Channel NewsAsia*, 18 April 2017. http://www.channelnewsasia.com/news/singapore/airbus-helicopters-partners-singpost-for-drone-delivery-trials-8735504 (accessed 12 December 2017).

Ministry of Trade and Industry. "Economic Survey of Singapore: Third Quarter of 2017", November 2017. https://www.mti.gov.sg/ResearchRoom/SiteAssets/Pages/Economic-Survey-of-Singapore-Third-Quarter-2017/FullReport_3Q17.pdf (accessed 12 December 2017).

PayPal. "Singaporean's Mobile Commerce Expenditure Expected to Surge", 27 February 2017. https://www.paypal.com/stories/sea/singaporeans-mobile-commerce-expenditure-expected-to-surge (accessed 15 January 2018).

PDPC (Personal Data Protection Commission). "Advisory Guidelines on Key Concepts in the Personal Data Protection Act". Paragraph 5, 27 July 2017. https://www.pdpc.gov.sg/-/media/Files/PDPC/PDF-Files/Advisory-Guidelines/advisory-guidelines-on-key-concepts-in-the-pdpa-(270717).pdf (accessed 15 January 2018).

PWC. "What is FinTech?", 2016. https://www.pwc.com/us/en/financial-services/publications/viewpoints/assets/pwc-fsi-what-is-fintech.pdf (accessed 1 March 2017).

Qoo10. "About Qoo10", n.d. http://blog.qoo10.sg/index.php/about-qoo10/ (accessed 14 December 2017).

sgsme.sg. "Singapore Fintech Investments More than Double to $492m in 2018: Accenture", 1 March 2019. https://www.sgsme.sg/news/singapore-fintech-investments-more-double-492m-2018-accenture.

SingPost. "SingPost to Launch ezyCommerce to Help SMEs Sell Online, Scale and Enhance Productivity", 18 March 2015. http://www.singpost.com/about-us/news-releases/singpost-launch-ezycommerce-help-smes-sell-online-scale-and-enhance-productivity (accessed 26 February 2017).

————. "SingPost Opens its New Regional eCommerce Logistics Hub, a Scalable Facility to Serve the Growth of eCommerce in Asia Pacific", 1 November 2016. http://www.singpost.com/about-us/news-releases/singpost-opens-its-new-regional-ecommerce-logistics-hub-scalable-facility-serve-growth-ecommerce-asia-pacific (accessed 26 February 2017).

————. "Lazada Singapore Moves Entire Warehouse Operations to SingPost's Regional eCommerce Logistics Hub", 17 May 2017. https://www.singpost.com/about-us/news-releases/lazada-singapore-moves-entire-warehouse-operations-singposts-regional-ecommerce-logistics-hub (accessed 12 December 2017).

Speedtest. "Speedtest® Market Report", 24 May 2017. http://www.speedtest.net/reports/singapore/ (accessed 12 December 2017).

SPH. "Giosis Pte Ltd Raises US$82.1 Million in Series A Funding", 22 July 2015. https://www.sph.com.sg/system/assets/2072/SPH%20Announcement%20-%20Qoo10%20Series%20A%20Press%20Release%2020.07.2015.pdf (accessed 25 February 2017).

SPRING Singapore. "Making eCommerce Accessible", 2 December 2015. https://spring.enterprisesg.gov.sg/Inspiring-Success/Enterprise-Stories/Pages/Making-eCommerce-accessible.aspx (accessed 26 February 2017).

Tang See Kit. "Grab Inks Strategic Partnership to Bring Mobile Wallet GrabPay into Thailand". *Channel NewsAsia*, 8 November 2018. https://www.channelnewsasia.com/news/business/grab-grabpay-inks-strategic-partnership-to-bring-mobile-wallet-10908414.

Williams, Ann. "CapitaLand to Manage Alibaba's New Shanghai HQ, Launch Online Mall on Lazada". *The Straits Times*, 23 August 2017. http://www.

straitstimes.com/business/companies-markets/capitaland-to-manage-alibabas-new-shanghai-hq-launch-online-mall-on (accessed 14 December 2017).

World Bank. "Individuals Using the Internet (% of Population)", n.d. https://data.worldbank.org/indicator/IT.NET.USER.ZS (accessed 12 December 2017).

———. "Global Rankings 2018", n.d. https://lpi.worldbank.org/international/global.

9

COMPETITION AND E-COMMERCE IN THE PHILIPPINES

Shanti Aubren T. Prado and Meg L. Regañon

1. Introduction

While the Philippines is home to a large and growing number of internet and mobile phone users, e-commerce in the country is still at a nascent stage. Data from the Better Than Cash Alliance (BTCA) showed that e-commerce makes up less than 1 per cent of total commerce in the Philippines in 2015, compared to 4–5 per cent in other neighbouring countries in Southeast Asia. In terms of the necessary infrastructure to facilitate online transactions, the country ranked 89th out of 137 countries, according to a report by the United Nations Conference on Trade and Development (UNCTAD).[1]

Meanwhile, e-commerce continues to affect an increasing number of traditional businesses and industries. In addition, the last few years saw the emergence of new businesses models such as online platforms like Lazada, Zalora and Shopee, and commercial sharing economy services like GrabTaxi and AirBnB. Considering the increasing role that e-commerce will play in firms, this chapter focuses on how e-commerce affects firm productivity. Further, it seeks to contribute to the debate about e-commerce and its effects on competition. Put together, this poses an interesting question from the competition perspective: how does the interplay of e-commerce use and competition shape firm productivity?

E-commerce directly affects firms' performance by cutting time and costs of production. The resulting savings, in turn, could then be re-allocated to more productive activities. Several studies have shown that selling online results in low distribution costs (Lal and Sarvary 1999; Van Cayseele and Degryse 2000; Wadhwani 2000; DePrince and Ford 1999), as the internet has made it possible for goods and services to move from producers to end-consumers without going through the entire traditional supply chain. Cost efficiency may also be achieved through e-commerce by rationalizing firms' processes in purchasing inputs (Degraeve and Roodhooft 2001; Konings and Roodhoft 2002; Sinha 2000). Purchasing online also lowers administrative and inventory holding costs, reduces maverick buying and saves time (Benjamin and Wigand 1995; Whyte 2000; Aberdeen Group 2001). Examining the impact of the internet on transaction cost, Garicano and Kaplan (2001) find that the internet has resulted in a large drop in coordination costs due to process improvements and marketplace benefits that make it easier and less costly to search for products, compare prices or find buyers.[2] E-commerce can also indirectly affect firm productivity through its impact on the productivity of other inputs and the intensity of competition. Several studies demonstrate that in terms of improving the performance of firms, adoption of e-commerce is complementary to other factors such as research and development (R&D) and labour (Liu et al. 2013; Bertschek et al. 2006; Kraemer et al. 2006).

How does the prospect of competition encourage firms' productivity? There are two streams of literature in this regard. The first one confirms a positive relationship between competition and firm productivity (Blanchflower and Machin 1996; Levinsohn 1993; Nickell 1996; Angelucci et al. 2002). Holding other things constant, having more rivals in the market implies that firms will face the risk of lower profit margins. The threat would encourage them to employ strategies that reduce their costs and increase their production efficiency. The second strand finds that more intense competition through e-commerce does not necessarily result in productivity improvements, under certain assumptions (Bakos and Brynjolfsson 2000; Ulph and Vulkan 2000). While e-commerce allows for more players in the market, it is not certain that the presence of more rivals would drive a firm to be more efficient. It may be the case that e-commerce enables a firm to further differentiate its products from the rest and thus continue to charge at a higher price, without necessarily improving its production process. Moreover, with more choices in the market, decision-making among consumers may become complex and lead consumers to stick to a default choice.

The rest of this chapter is organized as follows. The next section sets the context by surveying the current landscape of e-commerce in the Philippines and the laws, policies and regulations related to e-commerce. The third section examines the impact of e-commerce and competition on the performance of firms in the Philippine context using firm-level data. The fourth section outlines the implications of e-commerce on competition policy and law and briefly discusses the relevant experience of the Philippine Competition Commission (PCC). The last section concludes.

2. Background

State of E-commerce in the Philippines

E-commerce in the Philippines continues to grow and evolve, driven by rising disposable income and a large base of internet and mobile users. In 2015, there are about 40.98 million users in the Philippines (WDI), which is projected to grow to 70 million by 2018 (Euromonitor International 2016). In the same year, mobile cellular subscriptions amount to about 118.26 for every 100 people in the country (WDI).[3] However, while many people have access to phones and the internet, the majority of Filipinos continue to shop in-store and only a few shop online (Google 2018).

E-commerce continues to gain ground in the Philippines, as more retailers go online. Yet it does not threaten the prevalence of brick-and-mortar stores. Figure 9.1 shows sales in retailing in the Philippines from 2011 to 2016 by various channels: store-based, the internet and others (i.e. direct selling, home-shopping and vending). Total retail sales continue to grow, reaching P3.36 trillion in 2016. Of this, about 97 per cent are store-based transactions, while online sales amount to

FIGURE 9.1
Retailing Sales in the Philippines by Channels, 2011–16
(in billion PHP)

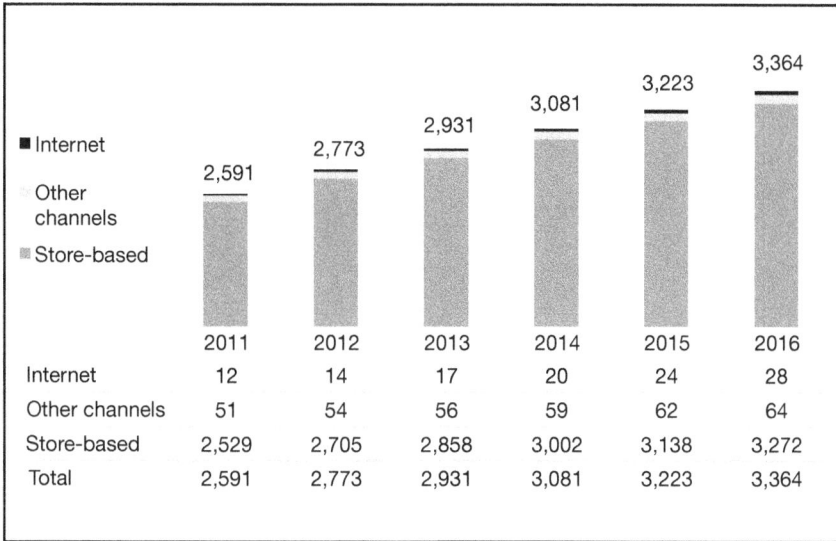

	2011	2012	2013	2014	2015	2016
Internet	12	14	17	20	24	28
Other channels	51	54	56	59	62	64
Store-based	2,529	2,705	2,858	3,002	3,138	3,272
Total	2,591	2,773	2,931	3,081	3,223	3,364

Source: Euromonitor International (2016).

P28.1 billion, which is below 1 per cent of total sales. Internet retailing grew continuously from 2011 to 2016.

While Filipinos still prefer to head to stores for their shopping needs, the growth in internet retailing suggests that a multichannel approach to purchasing is increasingly taken by consumers. That is, they may view physical stores and online counterparts to be complementary. Thus, either they browse in store and then shop online for the least-cost alternative ("showrooming") or research online and buy in stores ("webrooming").

Figure 9.2 shows internet retailing sales in the country per product category. Of the retail products sold online in 2016, media products register the highest sales value at P10.19 billion, followed by consumer electronics (P7.86 billion), and apparel and footwear (P5.78 billion). The least popular categories are home-care products (P2.1 million), traditional toys and games (P22.8 million), and home improvement and gardening (P35.1 million). However, in terms of growth in value,

FIGURE 9.2

Internet Retailing Sales in the Philippines by Category, 2011–16

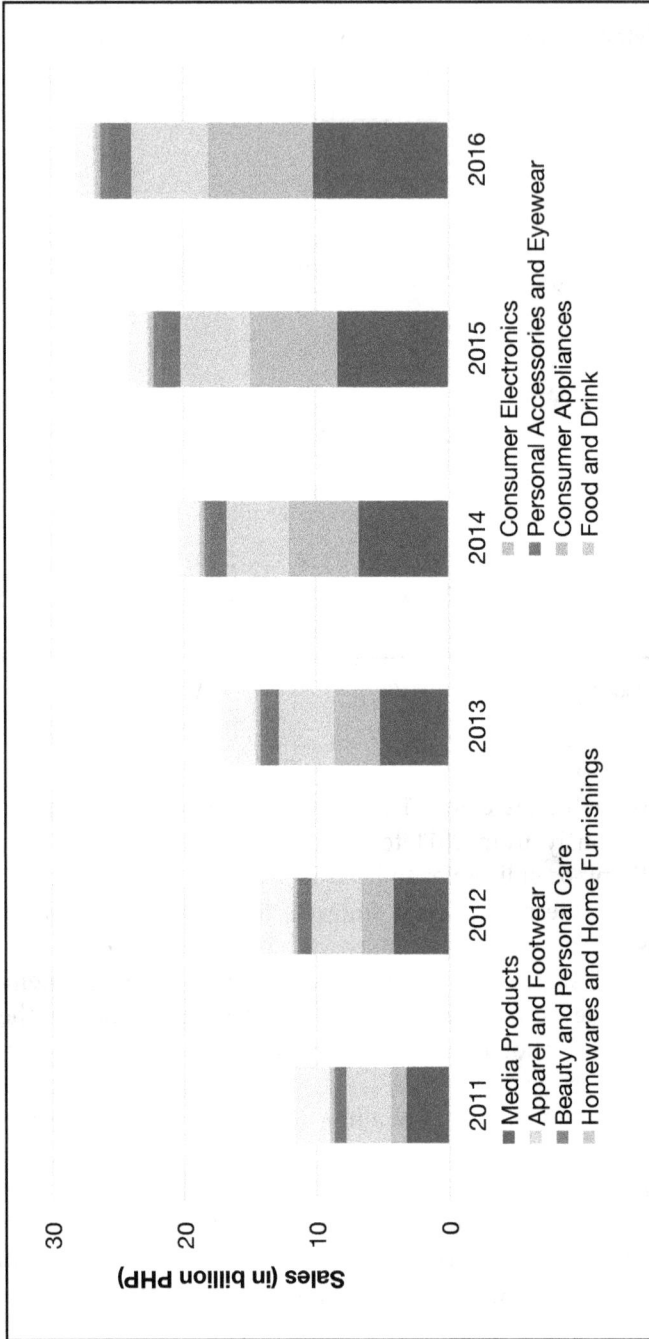

Source: Euromonitor International (2016).

most of the categories exhibit lower growth from the previous year, with consumer health experiencing the slowest increase.

E-commerce has affected how local firms transact with consumers, even for those who have been long time brick-and-mortars. A case in point is the grocery sector, where internet sales with respect to food and drinks alone have been rising over the years at a compound annual growth rate of 5.7 per cent, reaching P102.6 million in 2016 (Euromonitor International 2016). Grocery retailers increasingly recognize the potential of e-commerce as an additional means to tap customers. In 2016, two of the largest supermarket chains in the country namely, Robinsons Supermarket and SM Supermarket, began their partnership with online grocery stores, HappyFresh and MetroMart. While these chains consider the internet as an important retail channel, they maintain their physical stores, seeing the provision of online grocery services merely complementary to their operations. The grocery sector demonstrates the rise of an omnichannel approach in business—operating both online and offline to tailor fit their services to consumers and reach wider markets.

The advent of e-commerce has made it possible for consumers to go beyond borders in searching for sources for their shopping needs. Of the online shoppers surveyed by Nielsen (2016), about 61 per cent have purchased from overseas retailers. Another recent trend is the rise of e-businesses, also known as "pure plays", which are businesses that operate through the internet only. Major players include the online Business to Consumer (B2C) platforms Lazada and Zalora. While Zalora offers fashion merchandise from a wide selection of brands, Lazada offers a wide range of product categories such as electronics, apparel and footwear, health and beauty products, among others. Relative to multichannel retailers, these pure internet retailers exhibited stronger sales growth in 2016, driven by their aggressive marketing, partnership with established brands, and increased consumer awareness of the concept of online shopping.

The travel sector has been changed dramatically by e-commerce. Online travel sales to Philippine residents have grown by 17 per cent in value terms, to reach P298 billion in 2015. Yet, the majority of consumers prefer to make travel arrangements through traditional means, as evidenced by small share of online transactions in certain sectors. For instance, leading airlines such as Philippine Airlines, Cebu

TABLE 9.1
Value and Share of Online Transactions by Sector, 2010–15

in million PHP	2010	2011	2012	2013	2014	2015	Average
Intermediaries	2,176	2,912	3,649	4,422	5,203	6,353	4,119
	11%	13%	14%	16%	17%	19%	15%
Hotels	17,956	20,507	22,912	25,322	28,058	31,045	24,300
	18%	18%	18%	19%	19%	19%	18%
Lodging	18,018	20,582	23,409	26,100	29,435	36,202	25,624
	16%	17%	17%	17%	18%	19%	17%
Airlines	91,800	118,170	145,972	177,766	230,238	267,902	171,975
	26%	30%	32%	36%	44%	48%	36%
Car rental	85	112	132	155	185	212	147
	6%	7%	8%	8%	9%	9%	8%
Other transport	52	58	66	75	87	98	73
	0.15%	0.16%	0.17%	0.18%	0.21%	0.23%	0.19%

Source: Euromonitor International (2016).

Pacific Air and Air Asia have developed online platforms that provide streamlined ticket booking processes, alternative payment options, and occasional online seat sales. Yet, online sales account for about 48.15 per cent of total airlines sales.

Online sales in the accommodation sector have, likewise, improved. Hotels and lodging, both chained and independent, either streamline their direct online booking facilities or partner with major online travel booking sites such as Agoda, Airbnb, AsiaRoom, Booking.com, Expedia, Travelbook and Trivago. In 2015, online sales accounted for 18.8 and 19.5 per cent of total hotel and lodging sales, respectively.

Finally, in the transportation sector, online booking platforms are growing in number. Ridesharing platforms such as Uber and Tripid, as well as taxi booking apps such as GrabTaxi and Easy Taxi, are gaining widespread popularity among commuters especially in the metropolitan areas. Further, domestic leisure travellers are starting to open up to bus booking platforms such as PinoyTravel, IWantSeats, Via Philippines and ClickBus.

Main E-commerce Players in the Philippines

The Philippines is home to several e-commerce players. The main players are Lazada, Zalora, Shopee and local player BeautyMNL in online shopping; Agoda and Airbnb in online booking of accommodations; and GrabTaxi and Uber (prior to its exit) in online booking of car transportation.

Lazada is the most visited online shopping platform in the Philippines in 2017. According to one estimate, Lazada Philippines averages 62.5 million page views each month (Gratela 2018*a*). Lazada is a Singapore-based company offering a range of products from fashion to electronics. The Philippines was one of the five ASEAN countries wherein Lazada soft-launched its website in 2012. Lazada was founded in 2011 by the German firm Rocket Internet and was acquired in 2016 by Alibaba.

Zalora and Shopee are the next largest online shopping platforms used in the country. Zalora specializes in fashion selling apparel, accessories and beauty products. Likewise founded by Rocket Internet, Zalora launched its website in the Philippines and in other Asian countries in 2012. In 2017, local conglomerate Ayala Group acquired a stake in Zalora.

Shopee, on the other hand, is a recent addition and has been tagged as the fastest growing e-commerce player in the Philippines. Having a diverse product offering, Shopee first launched in Singapore in 2015 and has since then expanded into the Philippines. Both Zalora and Shopee are based in Singapore.

BeautyMNL, a local online cosmetics retailer, is the fifth most visited e-commerce website in 2017. It has notably surpassed foreign-owned Sephora, another very popular online cosmetics retailer, in the rankings (Gratela 2018*a*). BeautyMNL is owned by Taste Central, which was founded in 2014. In 2017, large conglomerate Robinsons Group invested in the latter.

Agoda and Airbnb are popular sites among Filipinos for booking travel accommodations. Established in 2005, Agoda is another Singapore-based company with operations in over thirty countries. Airbnb is a US-based company allowing home-owners to rent out their places for short-term lodging. In 2013, Airbnb opened its 12th global sales office in Manila after Singapore. During the same period, almost a thousand rooms and homes were listed in the platform.

GrabTaxi and Uber operate ride booking platforms connecting drivers and riders in Metro Manila. Singapore-based Grab started operations in the Philippines in 2013 first with its GrabTaxi service, while US-based Uber started in 2014. In early 2018, however, Uber stopped operations and decided to exit the entire ASEAN region. With the exit, Uber sold its assets to Grab in the Philippines in exchange for a 27 per cent stake in Grab. The transaction is currently being reviewed by PCC.

Government Initiatives Related to E-commerce

Recognizing the potential of e-commerce contributing to national growth and trade, the Philippine government has embarked on various initiatives to promote and develop e-commerce in the country.

The Philippine E-commerce Act was signed into law in 2000, providing for the recognition and use of electronic forms of transactions, data messages, documents, signatures, and storage of information. The law also sets out penalties for access of data without consent, piracy, hacking, and other violation, and mandates the Department of Trade and Industry (DTI) to directly supervise the promotion and development of e-commerce in the country. However, after almost two decades since the enactment of the E-commerce Law, adoption of e-commerce by consumers and businesses in the Philippines remains sluggish. Reasons often cited are problems of slow internet speed, high costs of broadband connection, weak financial infrastructure, poor logistics, trust and security issues, and lack of necessary technical skills crucial in operationalizing online business platforms (DTI 2016).

That the full potential of e-commerce is not yet tapped by Philippine businesses and consumers may be attributed in part to the slow and expensive internet access in the country. In 2016, the Philippines registered an average connection speed of 4.2 Mbps, ranking 14th out of 15 sampled countries in the Asia-Pacific region whose regional average is 11.4 Mbps (Akamai 2016). In terms of affordability, the cost of fixed broadband in the country is about 7.53 per cent of the country's Gross National Income (GNI), way above the 5 per cent affordability threshold (UNCTAD 2016).

The government undertook various initiatives to improve internet services in the country. More recently, the government rolled out the National Broadband Plan aimed at accelerating the deployment of fiber optic cables and wireless technologies that would primarily cater to underserved areas. While this is a right step toward improving the country's internet structure, a more sustainable solution would be to improve the overall competition in the telecommunications sector, currently dominated by two firms, namely, Philippine Long Distance Telephone Company and Globe Telecommunications Inc.

Another factor contributing to the minimal use of e-commerce in the country is limited access to e-payment services such as internet banking, mobile banking and electronic money. Majority of consumers have no credit or debit card to engage in e-commerce transactions and cash on delivery remains the most commonly used payment method in the Philippines (Nielsen 2016). Of the 2.5 billion payments per month made by consumers in the Philippines, corresponding to a monthly value of over US$74 billion, only 1 per cent of these payments is electronic, with physical cash and checks accounting for the remainder (Hokans 2015). As regards electronic money, while the Philippines is one of the first countries to adopt mobile payments solutions such as Gcash and Smart Money, consumer uptake of these products remains low.

With the objective of promoting e-payments, the Bangko Sentral ng Pilipinas launched in 2015 the National Retail Payments System (NRPS) aimed at raising the share of e-payments to 20 per cent in 2020. The NRPS is envisioned to facilitate the country's transition from a cash-heavy to a cash-lite economy, eventually bringing material benefits for the government and businesses.

Issues related to cybersecurity and data privacy are significant obstacles to greater usage of e-payment and e-commerce systems. Many Filipinos do not trust in giving credit card information online, and have doubts that e-commerce sites will keep their personal information secure and confidential (Nielsen 2016). This lack of trust preventing Filipinos from engaging in online transactions is not without basis. Of the 614 cybercrime incidents reported during the period 2014–15, 22 per cent were internet frauds or scams, and 10 per cent involved violations of the E-Commerce Act and the Access Devices Deregulation Act (Department of Justice 2015). The government has signalled its commitment to addressing such issues through the passage of the Data Privacy Act and the Cybercrime Law in 2012, which are intended to strengthen personal data protection and the penalty provisions under the E-commerce Law.

Another key hurdle is the inability of consumers to examine quality of goods available online. Considering that e-commerce is still in its early stages of development in the Philippines, consumers may have doubts about the accuracy of product characteristics posted online. To ensure consumer protection for e-commerce transactions, the government issued the E-Consumer Protection Guidelines in 2008, which mandates e-commerce sites to comply with minimum requirements such as privacy policy, publishing information about the retailer, seller, distributor, products and services, and consumer transaction, and setting-up of a help desk to internally resolve consumer complaints. Another government initiative in line with consumer protection is the Advisory on Online Shopping Fraud issued by the Department of Justice in 2015. The advisory seeks to inform online shoppers of the risks involved in dealing online, as well as to guide online merchants and platforms in providing a safe and secure online shopping environment. However, the lack of an online dispute settlement process for handling complaints including cross-border disputes remains an obstacle in building consumer and merchant confidence in the use of e-commerce. In this regard, the government intends to revisit its consumer protection policies to address e-commerce-related issues.

Finally, measures have been designed to help local businesses to gain access to online platforms, to enable them to expand their market reach. Recognizing the importance of e-commerce as a platform in facilitating the participation of micro, small and medium enterprises (MSMEs), the DTI launched the Philippine E-commerce Roadmap that targets to engage 100,000 MSMEs by 2020. This involves building capacity, attracting investments in infrastructure, and institute policies to enable MSMEs to leverage the benefits of e-commerce. Despite these initiatives, encouraging entrants into e-commerce remain a challenge, owing to their limited understanding on how e-commerce works. Advocacy efforts must be intensified to promote e-commerce awareness.

While the government has done much to develop the e-commerce infrastructure in the country, several issues and constraints need to be further addressed to close the gaps between the Philippines and its neighbours. To this end, deepened cooperation and coordination with other ASEAN member states would help the country align its laws, policies and programmes with the best practices in the region. In particular, the ASEAN Economic Community Blueprint 2025 outlines the strategic measures necessary towards developing an ASEAN agreement on e-commerce to facilitate cross-border e-commerce transactions in the region, namely: (i) harmonized consumer rights and protection law; (ii) harmonized legal framework for online dispute resolution taking into account available international standards; (iii) inter-operable, mutually recognized, secure, reliable and user-friendly e-identification and authorization (electronic signature) schemes; and, (iv) coherent and comprehensive framework for personal data protection (ASEAN Secretariat 2015).

3. E-commerce Activity of Philippine Businesses

Recognizing the growing importance of e-commerce activities in the country, the Philippine Statistics Authority (PSA) has started to collect data on the e-commerce sales of businesses in 2012 through the Census or Annual Survey of Philippine Business and Industry (CPBI or ASPBI). These surveys provide detailed information on the revenues, expenses, industrial classification and other characteristics of formal businesses across the Philippines. We use the results for the 2012 CPBI and 2013 ASPBI to provide an overview on the e-commerce operations of Philippine businesses.

E-commerce is defined by the PSA as the "selling of products or services over electronic systems such as the internet protocol-based networks and other computer networks, Electronic Data Interchange (EDI) network, or other on-line system", excluding "orders received via telephone, facsimile or emails". In the survey, businesses are asked to report the share of their total revenues that involved e-commerce transactions.

As shown in Table 9.2, e-commerce activities of businesses in the Philippines appear to be limited. Revenues from e-commerce transactions accounted for less than 1 per cent of business revenues in 2012 and 2013. However, the CPBI/ASPBI confines itself to the formal sector of the economy and the estimates likely understate the true extent of e-commerce activities in the country. Single branch-sole proprietorships with less than ten employees, the likely business model for most start-ups, are among those not covered by the survey. Note that the 2013 data have a larger sampling error following the non-inclusion of the informal sector.[4] Nonetheless, it is evident that

TABLE 9.2
Share of E-commerce Industry to the Philippine Economy, 2012–13

in billion PHP	2012			2013		
	Total Revenue	E-commerce Revenue	Share of E-commerce to Revenue (%)	Total Revenue	E-commerce Revenue	Share of E-commerce to Revenue (%)
Agriculture	138	–	–	148	–	–
Industry	5,908	19	0.32	5,872	7	0.12
Services	7,905	60	0.76	7,702	39	0.51
TOTAL	**13,951**	**79**	**0.57**	**13,723**	**47**	**0.34**

Source: 2013 ASPBI and 2012 CPBI, Philippine Statistics Authority.

e-commerce only comprised a small share of the Philippine economy in 2012 and 2013.

By sector, e-commerce activities are highest in the services sector. Agriculture did not register any e-commerce revenues for both 2012 and 2013. This is not surprising since agricultural goods, being non-durables, are not conveniently sold over electronic channels. Nielsen (2014) reports that the most popular product category type sold online are durable goods.

The preference to buy online or in-store also depends in part on whether the product is an experience or a search good. These two types differ in how easy their features and characteristics can be ascertained before purchase. For a search good, product characteristics such as price and quality can be observed in advance. Whereas, for an experience good such as agricultural produce, product characteristics can only be determined upon consumption.[5] Thus, relative to an experience good, a search good is more likely to be bought online than in-store (Santarelli and D'Altri 2003).

Table 9.3 shows selected subsectors under services that posted e-commerce revenue. In 2012 and 2013, transportation and storage contributed the largest share of e-commerce revenue. In contrast to most subsectors where e-commerce accounts for less than 1 per cent of revenue, e-commerce comprised as much as 14 per cent of the revenue in transportation and storage. A closer look at the data reveals that this is driven by the sales of international and domestic airline tickets. Similar to the experience of other jurisdictions, airline companies were the first pioneers of e-commerce in the country when Philippine Airlines (PAL) launched E-ticketing in May 2004 allowing passengers to book and pay for their tickets through the internet.

Other subsectors that reported e-commerce activities in 2012 and 2013 are financial and insurance; accommodation and food service; administrative and support services; information and communication; and wholesale and retail trade. We note that most of these subsectors have seen an increase in e-commerce revenue nominally and as a share of the subsector's total revenue from 2012 to 2013. A full breakdown of e-commerce activities in other sectors can be found in Annex 9.1.

TABLE 9.3
Share of E-commerce Industry to the Services Sector, 2012–13

in billion PHP	2012			2013		
	Total Revenue	E-commerce Revenue	Share of E-commerce to Revenue (%)	Total Revenue	E-commerce Revenue	Share of E-commerce to Revenue (%)
SERVICES	**7,905**	**60**	**0.76**	**7,702**	**39**	**0.51**
Transportation and Storage	373	53	14.32	411	17	4.2
Financial and Insurance	1,127	2	0.15	1,218	9	0.75
Accommodation and Food Service	361	0.11	0.03	405	4	1.04
Administrative and Support Services	386	3	0.68	383	3	0.83
Information and Communication	465	0.29	0.06	542	3	0.57
Wholesale and Retail Trade; Repair of Motor Vehicles and Motorcycles	3,771	2	0.05	3,666	2	0.05

Source: 2013 ASPBI and 2012 CPBI, Philippine Statistics Authority.

Overall, the extent of e-commerce activities by Philippine businesses has been rather limited despite the high mobile and internet penetration rates among Filipinos. However, the emergence of prominent e-commerce players such as Lazada, GrabTaxi and Uber in recent years holds significant promise on the future expansion of e-commerce in the Philippines.

4. E-commerce, Competition and Productivity: Philippine Data

We also explore the empirical link between e-commerce, competition and productivity at the firm-level using the 2012 CPBI establishment-level data.[6] The dataset covered 46,302 establishments, weighted subsequently to represent 219,201 establishments. We use the 2012 CPBI firm-level dataset over the 2013 ASPBI for its larger sample size.[7]

Out of the more than 200,000 establishments in the 2012 CPBI, very few reported having e-commerce transactions (only 277 out of 219,201 establishments). Most of them are found in manufacturing, financial and insurance, and wholesale and retail trade. As shown in Table 9.4, 258 out of the 277 establishments (93 per cent) are micro, small and medium enterprises (MSMEs). Note that the number of MSMEs is likely underestimated since many start-ups turn to the internet to launch their businesses and these are not captured by the dataset.

Table 9.4 also shows that large establishments contributed 95 per cent of the reported e-commerce revenue in 2012 while small establishments contributed (4 per cent) more than medium establishments. Also, e-commerce appears to account for a higher share of revenue as establishment size increases. The average revenue share of e-commerce for micro establishments is 14 per cent, 29 per cent for small and medium establishments, and 54 per cent for large establishments.

In Table 9.5, the majority of establishments with e-commerce activities (85 per cent) are found in unconcentrated subclasses. Interestingly, there are more establishments engaged in e-commerce in subclasses that are highly concentrated than those that are moderately concentrated. Highly concentrated subclasses contributed 73 per cent of the total e-commerce revenue while the remaining is accounted for by the unconcentrated subclasses.

TABLE 9.4
Establishments with E-commerce Activities by Size

Size	Number of Establishments	Total E-commerce Revenue (in billion PHP)	Average Share of E-commerce to the Establishment's Revenue (%)
Micro	84	0.04	14
Small	155	3.1	29
Medium	19	0.6	28
Large	19	71.3	54
Total	**277**	**75**	**26**

Notes: (1) Establishments with 0–9 employees are classified as micro; 10–99 employees are small; 100–199 are medium; and those with over 200 employees are classified as large.

(2) We note that our estimate of total e-commerce revenues of P75 billion is slightly lower than the P79 billion official estimate found in the published reports of the 2012 CPBI.

Source: Authors' own computations using the 2012 CPBI firm-level dataset.

TABLE 9.5
Establishments with E-commerce Activities Across Concentration Level

Concentration Level	Number of Establishments	Total E-commerce Revenue (in billion PHP)
Unconcentrated	235	20
Moderately Concentrated	9	0.6
Highly Concentrated	33	55
Total	**277**	**75**

Note: Based on US thresholds, industries with an HHI of above 2,500 are considered highly concentrated; industries with an HHI between 1,500 and 2,500 are moderately concentrated, while industries with an HHI below 1,500 are unconcentrated.

Source: Authors' own computations using the 2012 CPBI firm-level dataset.

Following Konings and Roodhooft (2002) and Liu et. al. (2013), we estimate a standard model explaining firm productivity using ordinary least square (OLS) regression. The innovation introduced is the inclusion of a competition variable, along with an e-commerce variable in the model:

$$Y = f(K, L, E, C, \mathbf{X})$$

Y is a measure of firm productivity (i.e. value added, labour productivity, and total factor productivity), K is capital, L is labour, E is a measure of e-commerce activity, C is a measure of competition, and $\mathbf{X}$ is a vector of control variables on firms such as their age, size, investments, research and development (R&D) expenses, as well as industry dummies. We interact our measures of competition and e-commerce activity to account for possible non-linear effects on firm productivity.

To determine if e-commerce adoption does affect firm productivity, we confine the analysis among establishments found in subclasses wherein e-commerce has proven viable. Out of 1,006 subclasses, 82 had e-commerce operations. Enclosed in Appendix 9.2 is a further discussion on the methodology and data.

Table 9.6 presents the results of the OLS regressions using value added. We found that e-commerce adoption does not significantly explain variations in firm productivity in the Philippines. In Model 1, one per cent increase in e-commerce revenue predicted a .081 per cent increase in value-added ($p < 0.01$), but the gradual addition of other variables in Models 3 to 5 diminished its significance.

This is inconsistent with the findings of Liu et. al. (2013) and Konings and Roodhoft (2002), wherein e-commerce is strongly linked with firm productivity. One reason for this inconsistency is that e-commerce has yet to completely transform the production processes of firms in the Philippines, given its limited adoption. For instance, the cost efficiency resulting from Business to Business (B2B) e-commerce (Degraeve and Roodhoft 2001) requires that the majority of the firm's suppliers have also adopted e-commerce channels. Even among Taiwanese firms, wherein e-commerce adoption is high, Liu et al. (2013) estimated that one per cent increase in e-commerce sales and procurement via the internet only induces a 0.002 per cent increase in value-added. This

TABLE 9.6
Regression Results Dependent Variable: Log Value Added

	Model 1	Model 2	Model 3	Model 4	Model 5
Log E-commerce Revenues	0.081	0.028	0.012	0.047	0.030
	(0.023)****	(0.007)****	(0.007)**	(0.034)	(0.040)
Log Labour Compensation		0.655	0.630	0.630	0.684
		(0.038)****	(0.040)****	(0.040)****	(0.071)****
Log Assets		0.060	0.053	0.053	0.036
		(0.007)****	(0.007)****	(0.007)****	(0.008)****
Market Share			0.832	0.856	0.490
			(0.115)****	(0.102)****	(0.074)****
Log HHI			0.116	0.118	0.027
			(0.022)****	(0.023)****	(0.034)
Market Share* Log HHI			−0.096	−0.100	−0.057
			(0.014)****	(0.013)****	(0.009)****
Log E-commerce Revenues* Market Share				0.001	0.001
				(0.001)	(0.001)
Log E-commerce Revenues* Log HHI				−0.006	−0.004
				(0.006)	(0.006)
Log R&D Expenditures					0.017
					(0.006)****
Log Investments					0.007
					(0.004)**
Age					0.001
					(0.001)
With Firm Size Dummies?					Yes
With Industry Dummies?					Yes
Constant	14.376	4.668	4.414	4.406	3.963
R2	0.004	0.731	0.752	0.752	0.832
N	7,946	7,946	7,946	7,946	7,694
Population Size	23,588	23,588	23,588	23,588	22,996

Note: * $p < 0.15$; ** $p < 0.1$; *** $p < 0.05$; **** $p < 0.01$; the numbers in parentheses are standard errors.

suggests that apart from the limited extent of e-commerce activities in the Philippines, other factors may also be limiting firms from realizing the productivity gains of e-commerce adoption.

As for our measures of competition, we found that both market share and its interaction with HHI are statistically significant in Model 5 ($p < 0.01$). An increase in market share is associated with an increase in firm productivity, but only below a certain level of HHI. This critical level of HHI is estimated to be about 5,136, which is considered highly concentrated based on US thresholds.[8] For industries beyond this level of HHI, an increase in market share predicts a decrease in firm productivity. These results indicate that given fierce competition, substantial improvements in a firm's production processes will likely result as a firm increases its market share; in contrast, this may not necessarily be the case for a firm increasing its share in a less competitive market. Dudu et. al. (2009) report similar findings for a panel of Turkish manufacturing firms from 1993–2003. With respect to industrial concentration, an increase in HHI is related to lower firm productivity. In general, while our findings are consistent with Blanchflower and Machin (1996), Levinsohn (1993), Nickell (1996), and Angelucci et al. (2002) in confirming a positive link between competition and firm productivity, our results also suggest a complex relationship underlying the two.

Finally, the interactions between our measures of e-commerce activity and competition are statistically insignificant. R&D expenditures and investments are significant, while age is insignificant in explaining firm productivity.[9]

Other cross-sectional studies have linked market competition and firm productivity (Caves and Barton 1990; Green and Mayes 1991; Caves 1992; Tang and Wang 2002), but more recent studies have utilized panel datasets (Haskel 1991; Nickell 1996; Disney, Haskel and Heden 2003; Ospina and Schiffbauer 2010). The advantage of a panel dataset is that actual changes in competition and actual changes in firm productivity are observed. As additional firm-level data from the ASPBI/CPBI becomes available, future research is encouraged in this area for a fuller understanding of how competition impacts firm productivity in the Philippines.[10]

5. Potential Competition Issues and the Experience of the Philippine Competition Commission

E-commerce has changed the competition dynamics of most markets. While its adoption may intensify competition, it could also allow some players to achieve significant market power, which they can use to stifle competition. Therefore, assessing competition issues in the presence of e-commerce is not as straightforward as those in conventional markets. It is worth noting some potential issues that are prevalent in e-commerce:

1. Competition concerns may arise when players engage in B2B transactions, particularly when these firms belong in the same production chain and hold significant market shares in the upstream or downstream markets. In this regard, there is a possibility that the players will engage in strategic acts such as input and customer foreclosure to preserve or maintain their market power.

2. Widespread use of e-commerce increases the likelihood of tacit collusion among competing players. Increased market transparency in e-commerce sites makes it easier for competitors to coordinate their actions even without any form of explicit agreement, and to observe deviations more readily.

3. In relation to online platforms, defining the relevant market in which to confine the competitive assessment is a challenge. Online platforms, also known as multisided platforms, act as intermediaries between different users. For instance, B2C marketplaces such Zalora, Lazada, Ebay and Amazon connect retailers and end-consumers. Other examples include online news portals, booking apps, and aggregators. Understanding the characteristics of the platform, its different users and how they interact will inform analysis of competition issues.

4. Online consumer data that firms engaging in e-commerce collect may encourage anti-competitive conduct. Online data enables companies to tailor-fit their products and services to targeted consumers. Sometimes, however, such information is essential for players who want to enter the market or undergo

expansion. Thus, it is important to consider how online data possessed by incumbents can create a barrier to entry and expansion.

5. Vertical agreements between online platforms and suppliers may restrict competition. For instance, suppliers and an online platform could enter into contracts with Most Favoured Nation (MFN) clauses. An MFN clause obligates the supplier to offer the platform a price no higher than the lowest offered to other sales channels. Such clause may have pro-competitive benefits to consumers by protecting them against price increases; to sellers in the form of brand protection; and to the platform by enhancing its value (CCS). However, the MFN clause restricts competition in various ways: (1) it prevents sellers from offering the product at a lower price to other sales channels; (2) it raises barriers to entry by preventing new platforms from offering the product at a lower price; (3) it promotes collusive behaviour by effectively aligning prices and terms across platforms; and (4) it reinforces position and facilitates abuse of dominance in the market. The Philippine Competition Act prohibits anti-competitive agreements like this.

6. Given that competition issues relating to e-commerce markets involve multinational companies and span borders, effective competition enforcement and advocacy efforts necessitate stronger coordination among competition authorities.

The PCC has encountered some of the issues and challenges outlined above in reviewing mergers and acquisitions involving e-commerce players. So far the PCC has reviewed three e-commerce transactions, namely: (1) Ayala and Zalora, (2) Alipay and Gcash, and (3) Uber and Grab. The first two have been cleared by the PCC, while the last one is an ongoing case.

In 2016, conglomerate giant Ayala Group acquired stakes in online fashion retailer, Zalora. One of the overlaps identified stems from Ayala Group's control over another online fashion retailer, Ava. Defining the relevant market involved considering whether brick-and-mortar stores constrain online platforms. Most pressing were the vertical overlaps posed by the transaction. Ayala Group has wide-ranging interests and holds substantial market power in banking

(Bank of the Philippine Islands or BPI), electronic payments (Gcash), retail space (Ayala Malls), and telecommunications (Globe). Concerns were raised whether the conglomerate can effectively leverage its market power from these sectors to foreclose access to Zalora or to foreclose Zalora's online competitors. For instance, Zalora may only list BPI credit cards or Gcash as payment options, limiting the ability of other payment systems to service Zalora. Vertical restraints may also be imposed requiring fashion retailers renting in Ayala Malls to sell online exclusively on Zalora. These concerns underscore the complexity of analysing e-commerce transactions. The Commission did not issue a decision after the lapse of the thirty-day Phase I review period resulting in the transaction being deemed approved.

In 2017, Alibaba-owned payment system Alipay indirectly acquired stakes in the country's leading electronic payment system, Gcash. Understanding the nascent market for electronic money, as well as the complex corporate structure of the conglomerate giants involved, were considerable challenges in reviewing the transaction. As in the previous case, the assessment considered how Alibaba can leverage its market power in online retailing platform through Lazada. Similarly, Lazada may favour payments made through Gcash at the expense of other electronic money providers. Unique to this case is the extensive consideration placed on how the merged entity will utilize the data it collects from its users. This transaction emphasizes that data is increasingly becoming an important asset for e-commerce players. The case proceeded to Phase II review, and the Commission eventually cleared the transaction.

In March 2018, Uber exited the ASEAN region in exchange for a stake in its rival Grab. The transaction has raised a host of challenges for the PCC. The first is the inability of merger thresholds to capture potentially problematic transactions in the asset-light e-commerce space. In the same month, the PCC has revised its thresholds upwards, but even under the old thresholds, the transaction would not have been notifiable. For the first time, the PCC used its powers to open a motu proprio review given that the parties were unlikely to notify and were taking steps to consummate the transaction. Defining the relevant market involved careful analysis which takes into account the perspective of both riders and drivers. In contrast to traditional markets, Grab and Uber has pioneered the use of dynamic pricing to balance supply and demand in real time, adding another layer of complexity in the assessment. As e-commerce markets mature and acquire public importance, they come to be covered by sector regulations. In the Philippines, Grab and Uber are classified as Transportation Network Companies (TNCs) and are regulated by the Land Transport Franchising Regulatory Board (LTFRB). The assessment had to be mindful of the new regulations issued by the LTFRB during the review period. Finally, the transaction allowed for increased coordination with other competition authorities in the ASEAN region.

6. Conclusion

The take-up of e-commerce in the Philippines is low even though the country is home to a large and growing number of internet and mobile phone users. Meanwhile, e-commerce continues to affect an increasing number of traditional businesses and industries. In addition, the last few years saw the emergence of new business models by online platforms like Lazada and Zalora, and commercial sharing-economy services like GrabTaxi and Airbnb.

This study examines the empirical link between e-commerce use and competition, on one hand, and firm productivity, on the other. Using the 2012 CPBI establishment-level data, we consider the e-commerce activities in Philippine businesses. Only 277 of the 219,201 establishments surveyed had e-commerce transactions. Of which 93 per cent are MSMEs and 84 per cent are found in unconcentrated subclasses. Our findings indicate that e-commerce is not yet significant in explaining variations in firm productivity among Philippine businesses. Further, we found that while competition significantly impacts firm productivity, the interactions between e-commerce activities and competition are statistically insignificant. Finally, we note that e-commerce has changed the competition dynamics of most markets which could have implications on how competition issues are assessed.

APPENDIX 9.1

TABLE 9.1A

Share of E-commerce Industry Across Sectors, 2012–13

in billion PHP	2012			2013		
	Total Revenue	E-commerce Revenue	Share of E-commerce to Revenue (%)	Total Revenue	E-commerce Revenue	Share of E-commerce to Revenue (%)
PHILIPPINES	**13,951**	**79**	**0.57**	**13,723**	**47**	**0.34**
AGRICULTURE	138	–	–	148	–	–
A Agriculture, Forestry and Fishing	138	–	–	148	–	–
INDUSTRY	5,908	19	0.32	5,872	7	0.12
B Mining and Quarrying	187	–	–	179	–	0.00
C Manufacturing	4,569	19	0.41	4,465	7	0.16
D Electricity, Gas, Steam and Air Conditioning	778	–	–	799	–	–
E Water Supply; Sewerage, Waste Management and Remediation Activities	72	–	–	78	–	–
F Construction	301	–	–	351	–	–
SERVICES	7,905	60	0.76	7,702	39	0.51
G Wholesale and Retail Trade; Repair of Motor Vehicles and Motorcycles	3,771	2	0.05	3,666	2	0.05
H Transportation and Storage	373	53	14.32	411	17	4.20
I Accommodation and Food Service Activities	361	0.11	0.03	405	4	1.04
J Information and Communication	465	0.29	0.06	542	3	0.57

APPENDIX 9.1 (*continued*)

in billion PHP

	2012			2013		
	Total Revenue	E-commerce Revenue	Share of E-commerce to Revenue (%)	Total Revenue	E-commerce Revenue	Share of E-commerce to Revenue (%)
K Financial and Insurance Activities	1,127	2	0.15	1,218	9	0.75
L Real Estate Activities	803	–	–	423	–	–
M Professional, Scientific and Technical Activities	170	–	–	272	–	–
N Administrative and Support Service Activities	386	3	0.68	383	3	0.83
P Education	161	0.07	0.04	174	0.4	0.23
Q Human Health and Social Work Activities	107	–	–	130	–	–
R Arts, Entertainment and Recreation	132	0.003	0.002	54	0.2	0.31
S Other Service Activities	47	0.0002	0.0003	25	0.3	1.06

Source: 2013 ASPBI and 2012 CPBI, Philippine Statistics Authority.

APPENDIX 9.2

Methodology and Data

We constructed three measures of firm productivity: value added, labour productivity, and total factor productivity (TFP). Value added is estimated through the factor-income approach, particularly as the sum of labour compensation, depreciation expenses and profit.[12] Labour productivity is calculated as firm value added over the number of employees. TFP is measured as the residual plus the constant of the regression, wherein value added is regressed on labour (compensation) and capital (all variables were in log form).

Capital K is proxied by the book value of tangible fixed assets while labour L is proxied by the compensation received by employees. For the measures of competition, we computed for the revenue market share of each establishment at the subclass level using the five-digit 2009 Philippine Standard Industrial Classification (PSIC) Code. We also estimate the Herfindahl-Hirschman Index (HHI) at the subclass level.[13]

E-commerce activity is taken to be the establishment's revenue arising from e-commerce transactions. For the dummy variables, investments pertain to expenditures on new tangible and intangible assets and the alpha character of the 2009 PSIC is used to determine the eighteen industry dummies.

Lastly, we utilize OLS regressions and the svy command option of Stata to account for the weights associated with each observation in the dataset. To facilitate the interpretation, we take the logarithmic transformation for most of the variables. Furthermore, we interact our measures of competition and e-commerce activity to account for possible non-linear effects on firm productivity.

TABLE 9.2A

Summary Statistics of Regression Variables

Variable	Obs.	Population Obs.	Mean	Std. Dev.	Min	Max
Value Added	7,946	23,588	35,800,000	1,350,000,000	0	202,000,000,000
Labour Productivity	7,945	23,546	309,221	893,777	0	68,400,000
TFP	7,946	23,588	10,745	623,416	0	85,500,000
E-commerce Revenues	7,946	23,588	3,182,187	349,000,000	0	52,700,000,000
Labour Compensation	7,946	23,588	13,800,000	141,000,000	0	12,800,000,000
Assets	7,946	23,588	27,000,000	485,000,000	0	49,800,000,000
Market Share	7,946	23,588	0	2	0	100
HHI	7,946	23,588	443	677	31	10,000
R&D Expenditures	7,946	23,588	82,726	4,154,664	0	537,000,000
Investments	7,946	23,588	2,584,304	71,000,000	0	6,500,000,000
Age	7,694	22,996	19	15	5	292

Note: Variables corresponding to monetary terms are in PHP.

APPENDIX 9.3

Regression Results Using Labour Productivity, Total Factor Productivity and Sectoral Regressions

TABLE 9.3A

Regression Results Dependent Variable:
Log Labour Productivity

	Model 1	Model 2	Model 3	Model 4	Model 5
Log E-commerce Revenues	0.034	0.015	0.010	0.107	0.085
	(0.01)****	(0.017)	(0.018)	(0.078)	(0.082)
Log Labour Compensation		0.254	0.242	0.242	0.431
		(0.015)****	(0.015)****	(0.015)****	(0.04)****
Log Assets		0.014	0.011	0.011	0.027
		(0.009)*	(0.009)	(0.009)	(0.009)****
Market Share			0.368	0.383	0.474
			(0.061)****	(0.06)****	(0.061)****
Log HHI			0.018	0.022	0.028
			(0.026)	(0.026)	(0.040)
Market Share * Log HHI			-0.043	-0.045	-0.055
			(0.008)****	(0.007)****	(0.008)****
Log E-commerce Revenues * Market Share				0.001	0.001
				(0.001)**	(0.001)
Log Ecommerce Revenues * Log HHI				-0.017	-0.013
				(0.011)*	(0.012)
Log R&D Expenditures					0.013
					(0.005)****

APPENDIX 9.3A *(continued)*

	Model 1	Model 2	Model 3	Model 4	Model 5
Log Investments					0.009 (0.004)***
Age					0.0001 (0.002)
With Firm Size Dummies?					Yes
With Industry Dummies?					Yes
Constant	11.920	8.266	8.334	8.313	5.770
R2	0.002	0.306	0.315	0.316	0.490
N	7,939	7,939	7,939	7,939	7,687
Population Size	23,507	23,507	23,507	23,507	22,915

Table 9.3B
Regression Results Dependent Variable:
Log TFP

	Model 1	Model 2	Model 3	Model 4
Log E-commerce Revenues	0.032	0.013	0.031	0.014
	(0.008)****	(0.007)**	(0.031)	(0.041)
Market Share		0.949	0.976	0.557
		(0.103)****	(0.083)****	(0.068)****
Log HHI		0.100	0.101	0.051
		(0.024)****	(0.025)****	(0.036)
Market Share * Log HHI		-0.110	-0.114	-0.065
		(0.014)****	(0.011)****	(0.009)****
Log E-commerce Revenues * Market Share			0.001	0.001
			(0.002)	(0.001)
Log E-commerce Revenues * Log HHI			-0.004	-0.002
			(0.005)	(0.006)
Log R&D Expenditures				0.020
				(0.006)****
Log Investments				0.005
				(0.003)
Age				0.002
				(0.002)
With Firm Size Dummies?				Yes
With Industry Dummies?				Yes
Constant	6.082	5.480	5.474	5.188
R2	0.002	0.093	0.093	0.329
N	7,946	7,946	7,946	7,694
Population Size	23,588	23,588	23,588	22,996

TABLE 9.3C
Sectoral Regression Results

	Dependent Variable: Log Value Added			Dependent Variable: Log Labour Productivity			Dependent Variable: Log TFP		
	Manufacturing	Wholesale and Retail	Financial and Insurance	Manufacturing	Wholesale and Retail	Financial and Insurance	Manufacturing	Wholesale and Retail	Financial and Insurance
Log E-commerce Revenues	-0.071 (0.051)	0.044 (0.024)**	0.015 (0.183)	-0.071 (0.063)	-0.007 (0.031)	0.303 (0.247)	-0.121 (0.060)***	0.052 (0.023)***	-0.092 (0.226)
Log Labour Compensation	0.732 (0.064)****	0.757 (0.102)****	0.529 (0.124)****	0.517 (0.047)****	0.415 (0.092)****	0.334 (0.062)****			
Log Assets	0.054 (0.009)****	0.047 (0.015)****	-0.012 (0.024)	0.048 (0.01)****	0.050 (0.019)****	-0.009 (0.025)			
Market Share	0.319 (0.058)****	0.861 (0.297)****	1.127 (0.678)**	0.241 (0.05)****	0.770 (0.302)***	1.268 (0.696)**	0.398 (0.057)****	1.018 (0.326)****	1.241 (0.760)*
Log HHI	-0.033 (0.039)	0.113 (0.051)***	-0.127 (0.118)	-0.119 (0.054)***	0.084 (0.057)*	-0.016 (0.155)	-0.031 (0.044)	0.128 (0.051)***	-0.030 (0.158)
Market Share * Log HHI	-0.037 (0.007)****	-0.105 (0.038)****	-0.135 (0.088)****	-0.028 (0.006)****	-0.095 (0.038)****	-0.154 (0.092)**	-0.046 (0.007)****	-0.124 (0.041)****	-0.154 (0.101)*
Log E-commerce Revenues * Market Share	-0.001 (0.001)	-0.003 (0.003)	0.009 (0.006)*	-0.0002 (0.001)	0.001 (0.007)	0.013 (0.008)*	-0.001 (0.001)*	-0.005 (0.004)	0.004 (0.006)
Log E-commerce Revenues * Log HHI	0.011 (0.007)*	-0.007 (0.005)	-0.007 (0.033)	0.009 (0.009)	-0.001 (0.007)	-0.050 (0.045)	0.019 (0.009)***	-0.006 (0.006)	0.014 (0.039)
Log R&D Expenditures	0.025 (0.008)****	Omitted	-0.031 (0.022)	0.018 (0.007)****	Omitted	-0.009 (0.019)	0.034 (0.008)****	Omitted	-0.031 (0.021)*

Log Investments	0.008 (0.005)**	-0.015 (0.013)	0.031 (0.017)**	0.006 (0.004)	-0.010 (0.012)	0.027 (0.024)	0.015 (0.005)****	-0.012 (0.013)	-0.001 (0.017)
Age	0.001 (0.002)	-0.005 (0.0080)	0.010 (0.007)*	-0.0004 (0.002)	0.0010 (0.011)	0.009 (0.008)	0.003 (0.003)	-0.006 (0.009)	0.004 (0.008)
With Firm Size Dummies?	Yes	Yes	Yes	Yes	Yes	Yes	Yes	Yes	Yes
Constant	3.805	2.642	7.122	5.635	5.528	7.642	5.944	5.045	5.858
R2	0.885	0.794	0.690	0.650	0.386	0.484	0.356	0.308	0.138
N	1,533	796	481	1,533	796	480	1,533	796	481
Population Size	4,033	4,603	3,903	4,033	4,603	3,873	4,033	4,603	3,903

NOTES

1. UNCTAD's B2C E-commerce Index 2016 comprises four indicators: internet-use penetration, secure servers per one million inhabitants, credit-card penetration and a postal reliability score.

2. However, with respect to costs due to asymmetry of information and imperfect commitment between buyers and sellers, the authors do not find e-commerce better than the physical marketplace. For goods that consumers need to evaluate physically, informational asymmetry may even be worse in e-commerce transactions. As for commitment, online transactions usually follow standardized process and leave electronic trail. While this mechanism encourages commitment, consumers usually use the internet to examine the product, but buys from physical stores.

3. Based on a survey of adult online consumers by Google (2018), smartphone is a crucial access point for coming online for Filipinos across age groups. The results of the survey also point to the relevance of the internet as a convenient source for product information, as respondents use the internet for online research before buying. Nielsen (2016) deduces that the importance of online research is likely driven by wide variation in product quality, prevalence of social networks and importance of keeping up with the latest trends.

4. The larger sampling error stems from the fact that the 2013 ASPBI sampled fewer establishments than the 2012 CPBI. To the extent that fewer e-commerce businesses were sampled in 2013, this would explain the decrease in reported e-commerce revenue. Moreover, formal businesses with e-commerce operations in 2012 may have reorganized to be classified as informal in 2013, further contributing to the observed decline.

5. In the Philippines, it is common that buyers scrutinize agricultural produce such as fruits, vegetables and meat especially in wet markets. In fact, sellers sometimes offer a free sample of their produce, especially for fruits, to assure buyers of their product's quality.

6. The use of the 2012 CPBI establishment-level data is highly restricted due to the confidentiality provisions under the Commonwealth Act No. 591. Establishment-level data can only be accessed and handled within the premises of PSA under the supervision of a designated staff. Moreover, as of this writing, establishment-level data for the 2013 ASPBI was not yet accessible to the authors.

7. As of writing, the 2014 ASPBI firm-level dataset has been made available but also suffers from a smaller sample size. In addition, the total e-commerce revenue has appeared to decrease at P39 billion. This is unlikely to materially affect our regression results.

8. This did not consider the coefficient of the interaction term between Log E-commerce Revenues and Market Share.

9. The results obtained above are similar with the results obtained using other measures of firm productivity, namely labour productivity and total factor productivity (TFP). These are found in Appendix 9.3. We also ran sectoral regressions for manufacturing, wholesale and retail trade, and financial and insurance. These sectors contain the most number of establishments with e-commerce activities.

10. One challenge that is expected to arise from constructing a panel data from the CPBI/ASPBI is the accuracy of measuring changes in HHI (or other measure of market competition) due to the establishment-level nature of the dataset. An increase in establishments from the previous period will be interpreted as an increase in competition, when it may actually be a decrease in competition—the new establishments may just be additional branches of an existing player in the market. Nonetheless, future research topics should include using other measures of firm productivity and other measures of competition.

12. Calculating value added in this manner avoids the problem of identifying what constitutes intermediate costs for each sector, which is inherent in the production approach of calculating for value-added (gross output minus intermediate costs). We note that our estimate of total value-added (P3.6 trillion) closely approximates the official value-added figure (P3.9 trillion) published in the 2012 CPBI report.

13. Due to data limitations, our estimates of market competition are taken with a grain of salt. Competition may be understated when foreign and informal businesses, unaccounted for by the dataset, are major players in certain markets. On the other hand, competition can also be overstated due to the establishment-level nature of the dataset. Multiple establishments in a subclass will be estimated as very competitive, when in reality these establishments may all be part of a single enterprise.

REFERENCES

Aberdeen Group. *Best Practices in e-Procurement: The Abridged Report.* Boston, Massachusetts, 2001.

Akamai. *Akamai's [State of the Internet] Q3 2016 Report.* 2016. https://www.akamai.com/us/en/multimedia/documents/state-of-the-internet/q3-2016-state-of-the-internet-connectivity-report.pdf.

Angelucci, Manuela, Saul Estrin, Jozef Konings and Zbigniew Zolkiewski. "The Effect of Ownership and Competitive Pressure on Firm Performance in Transition Countries: Micro Evidence from Bulgaria, Romania and Poland". William Davidson Working Paper no. 434 (2002).

ASEAN Secretariat. *ASEAN Economic Community Blueprint 2025*. Jakarta: ASEAN Secretariat, 2015. http://www.asean.org/storage/2016/03/AECBP_2025r_FINAL.pdf.

Bakos, Yannis and Erik Brynjolfsson. "Bundling and Competition on the Internet". *Marketing Science* 19, no. 1 (2000): 63–82.

Benjamin, Robert I. and Rolf T. Wigand. "Electronic Markets and Virtual Value Chains on the Information Superhighway: New Links in the Value Chain". *MIT Sloan Management Review* 36, no. 2 (1995).

Bertschek, Irene, Helmut Fryges and Ulrich Kaiser. "B2B or Not To Be: Does B2B E-commerce Increase Labour Productivity?" *International Journal of the Economics of Business* 13, no. 3 (2006): 387–405.

Blanchflower, David and Stephen Machin. "Product Market Competition Wages and Productivity: International Evidence from Establishment-Level Data". *The Microeconometrics of Human-Resource Management: Multinational Studies of Firm Practices* 41/42 (1996): 219–53.

Caves, Richard E. *Industrial Efficiency in Six Nations*. Cambridge, Mass.: MIT Press, 1992.

Caves, Richard E. and David Barton. *Efficiency in U.S. Manufacturing Industries*. Cambridge, Mass.: MIT Press, 1990.

Degraeve, Zeger and Filip Roodhooft. "A Smarter Way to Buy". *Harvard Business Review*, 2001.

Department of Justice, Office of Cybercrime. "Philippines 2014–2015 Cybercrime Report: The Rule of Law in Cyberspace". Manila, 15 March 2015.

Department of Trade and Industry. "Philippine E-commerce Roadmap 2016–2020". Manila, January 2016.

DePrince, Albert E. and William F. Ford. "A Primer on Internet Economics: Macro and Micro Impact of the Internet on the Economy". *Business Economics* 34, no. 4 (1999): 42–50.

Disney, Richard, Jonathan Haskel and Ylva Heden. "Restructuring and Productivity Growth in UK Manufacturing". *The Economic Journal* 113, no. 489 (2003): 666–94.

DotEcon. "E-commerce and Its Impact on Competition Policy and Law in Singapore". A DotEcon Study for the Competition Commission of Singapore, October 2015.

Dudu, H. and Y. Kılıçaslan. "Concentration, Profitability and (In)Efficiency in Large Scale Firms". In *Productivity, Efficiency, and Economic Growth in the Asia-Pacific Region*, edited by Jeong-Dong Lee and Almas Heshmati. Heidelberg, Germany: Springer-Verlag Berlin and Heidelberg GmbH & Co. KG, 2009.

Euromonitor International. *Passport–Various Sector Reports for the Philippines*. 2016.

Garicano, Luis and Steven N. Kaplan. "The Effects of Business-to-Business E-commerce on Transaction Costs". *The Journal of Industrial Economics* 49, no. 4 (2001): 463–85.

Google. "The Online and Multiscreen World (PH)". Google Consumer Barometer Report, 2018. https://www.consumerbarometer.com/en/insights/?countryCode=PH.

Gratela, Angela. "A Look Back at the Highlights of the Philippine eCommerce 2017". iPrice Group, 8 January 2018. https://iprice.ph/trends/insights/a-look-back-at-the-highlights-of-the-philippine-ecommerce-2017/.

———. "A Year-end Tally of the Philippine Ecommerce Scene". *TechinAsia*, 12 January 2018. https://www.techinasia.com/talk/philippine-ecommerce-2017-tally.

Green, Alison and David Mayes. "Technical Inefficiency in Manufacturing Industries". *The Economic Journal* 101, no. 406 (1991): 523–38.

Haskel, Jonathan. "Imperfect Competition, Work Practices and Productivity Growth". *Oxford Bulletin of Economics and Statistics* 53, no. 3 (1991): 265–79.

Hokans, James. "Country Diagnostic: Philippines". Better Than Cash Alliance, July 2015.

Konings, Jozef and Filip Roodhooft. "The Effect of E-Business on Corporate Performance: Firm Level Evidence for Belgium". *De Economist* 150, no. 5 (2002): 569–81.

Kraemer, Kenneth L., Jennifer Gibbs and Jason Dedrick. "Impacts of Globalization on E-Commerce Use and Firm Performance: A Cross-Country Investigation". *The Information Society* 21, no. 5 (2006): 323–40.

Lal, Rajiv and Miklos Sarvary. "When and How is the Internet Likely to Decrease Price Competition?" *Marketing Science* 18, no. 4 (1999): 485–503.

Levinsohn, James. "Testing the Imports-as-Market-Discipline Hypothesis". *Journal of International Economics* 35 (1993): 1–22.

Liu, Ting-Kun, Jong-Rong Chen, Cliff C.J. Huang and Chih-Hai Yang. "E-commerce, R&D, and Productivity: Firm-level Evidence from Taiwan". *Information Economics and Policy* 25 (2013): 272–83.

Montecillo, Paolo G. "Airbnb.com Launches 'Unhotels' in PH". *Philippine Daily Inquirer*, 2 January 2013. http://business.inquirer.net/100945/airbnb-com-launches-unhotels-in-ph.

Nickell, Stephen J. "Competition and Corporate Performance". *The Journal of Political Economy* 104, no. 4 (1996): 724–46.

Nielsen. "E-commerce: Evolution or Revolution in the Fast-Moving Consumer Goods World?", 26 August 2014.

———. "Global Connected Commerce: Is E-tail Therapy the New Retail Therapy?", January 2016.

Ospina, Sandra and Marc Schiffbauer. "Competition and Firm Productivity: Evidence from Firm-Level Data". IMF Working Papers, 2010.

Philippine Statistics Authority. "2012 Census of Philippine Business and Industry". 2015.

———. "2013 Annual Survey of Philippine Business and Industry". 2016.

Santarelli, Enrico and Samuele D'Altri. "The Diffusion of E-commerce Among SMEs: Theoretical Implications and Empirical Evidence". *Small Business Economics* 21, no. 3 (2003): 273–83.

Sinha, Indrajit. "Cost Transparency: The Net's Threat to Prices and Brands". *Harvard Business Review* (2000).

Subido, Lorenzo Kyle. "Who are the Leading Foreign and Local Players in PH E-commerce?" *Entrepreneur Philippines*, 24 October 2017. https://www.entrepreneur.com.ph/news-and-events/who-are-the-leading-foreign-and-local-players-in-ph-e-commerce-a00200-20171024.

Tang, Jianmin and Weimin Wang. "Competition and Productivity: Evidence from Canadian Manufacturing Firms". Micro Economic Policy Analysis Branch, Industry Canada, 2002.

Ulph, David and Nir Vulkan. "Electronic Commerce and Competitive First-Degree Price Discrimination". University of College London Discussion Papers, 2000.

United Nations Conference on Trade and Development (UNCTAD). "UNCTAD B2C E-commerce Index 2016". 2016._

United Nations International Telecommunications Union. *Measuring the Information Society Report 2016*. Geneva, Switzerland: International Telecommunications Union, 2016.

Van Cayseele, Patrick and Hans Degryse. "The New Economy and Banking Market Structures". *Leuvense Economische Standpunten* (2000).

Wadhwani, Sushil. "The Impact of the Internet on UK Inflation". *Bank of England Quarterly Bulletin*, 2000.

Whyte, C.K. "E-procurement: The New Competitive Weapon". *Purchasing Today*, April 2000.

World Bank. "World Development Indicators – Philippines", 2017. http://databank.worldbank.org/data/reports.aspx?source=2&country=PHL.

10

VIETNAM
E-commerce Market Overview
and Trends

Nguyen Van Thoan and Nguyen Thi Hong Van

1. Introduction

After thirty years of "Doi Moi",[1] Vietnam has emerged from a backward country to an emerging economy through an industrialization and modernization process. The country's socio-economic infrastructure has improved greatly during the reform period. Vietnam's per capita income has increased sharply from US$471 in 2001 to US$2,300 in 2015 (VietnamPlus 2018). As a result of six years of implementing the E-commerce Development Master Plan from 2011 to 2016, Vietnam has successfully developed infrastructure for sustainable growth in its e-commerce market. E-commerce has become more common in Vietnam and has contributed significantly in strengthening the competitiveness of enterprises. This chapter summarizes the achievements of Vietnam's e-commerce market from 2011 to 2016, and discusses the key trends in the coming years.

2. Vietnam's Socio-economic Structure and Performance

Vietnam is a Southeast Asian country and is a member of the Association of Southeast Asian Nations (ASEAN) since 1995 and the World Trade Organization (WTO) since 2007. It has a population size of more than 92 billion. Its total gross domestic product (GDP) growth rate in 2016 was 6.21 per cent. As a result of thirty years of "Doi Moi", Vietnam has demonstrated great achievements in its socio-economic development. Even in the context of the global economic slowdown in recent years, Vietnam has been considered as one of the emerging economies in Asia with high economic growth rate. Its average GDP growth rate from 2011 to 2015 was about 5.88 per cent.

Vietnam has shown great efforts and determination for reforms in the Socio-Economic Development Strategy (SEDS) for the period of 2011–20. Its economic growth is supported by the growth of industrial production, including processing and manufacturing growth. In 2016–20, the government will show strong determination in promoting the market economy's operation to speed up the economy.

With regard to the structure of Vietnam's economy in 2016, the service sector's 40.92 per cent represented the largest proportion. This is followed by the industry and construction sector (32.72 per cent); the agriculture, forestry and fishery sector (16.32 per cent); and product taxes less subsidies on production sector (10.04 per cent). Export turnovers of Vietnam in 2016 reached an estimated US$175.9 billion. This represents a rise of 8.6 per cent over the same period in 2015. Import turnovers of goods in 2016 was estimated at US$173.3 billion, which represents an increase of approximately 4.6 per cent compared to 2015. Estimated service export turnovers in 2016 reached US$12.3 billion, up by 8.9 per cent from last year, while service import turnovers in 2016 were estimated to attain US$17.7 billion, up by 7 per cent over 2015. In 2016, the average CPI climbed by 2.66 per cent, compared to that in 2015 (General Statistics Office of Vietnam 2017). These figures demonstrate that sector restructuring in Vietnam is in the right direction but is progressing slowly. Moreover, sector development is not stable, as it relies on cheap labour, natural resources exploitation, and raw materials exporting (Chu Ngoc Anh 2016).

Vietnam's labour force within working age was about 47.7 million persons in 2016, of which trained labour accounted for about 21.9 per cent. Moreover, Vietnam has a young population, with more than half of its population aged 34 years or younger. The young labour would be advantageous for e-commerce development in Vietnam, as the younger generation would be more open to engaging in e-commerce. The unemployment rate in Vietnam was estimated at 2.3 per cent (General Statistics Office of Vietnam 2017). Social labour productivity in 2016 was estimated at US$3,853 per employee. This has improved significantly over the years, but is still low in comparison with other countries in the ASEAN region.

With regard to the science and technology adoption in Vietnam, it is assessed that Vietnam lags behind in this area compared to other countries in the world. This presents great challenges to the country in terms of international integration under the fourth industrial revolution. In 2016–20, Vietnam will focus on three strategic breakthroughs as follows:

1. finalizing the mechanism of socialist-oriented market economy;
2. construction of a synchronous system of infrastructure; and
3. improvement in human resource quality which is closely linked to science and technology.

These are key strategic goals to restructure the economy and renew the growth model in Vietnam. In order to bridge the gap with other countries in the region, Vietnam will concentrate on improving the quality of growth, competitiveness of the economy and labour productivity in 2022 (Le Dinh An 2016).

3. Infrastructure Services for E-commerce

In 2016, with the recovery of the economy, Vietnam's e-commerce market has grown tremendously. The current market size of Vietnam's e-commerce market is estimated at about US$4 billion at the end of 2016, which is up by about 35 per cent compared to that in 2015. In the period of 2018–20, it is estimated that the e-commerce market will continue to grow at 20–30 per cent per year (Vecom 2019). This growth of Vietnam's e-commerce market is the result of the improvement of the ICT services infrastructure, such as the internet, mobile, logistics, online banking and payment which have been modernized and expanded to support e-commerce transactions.

Firstly, with regard to the internet infrastructure in Vietnam, its telecommunication system has improved tremendously in respect of the internet stability and speed during the 2011–15 period. ICT services in Vietnam can now satisfy customers' needs for e-commerce transaction anytime and anywhere at a low charge. Fiber optic cable has been widely used and the cost of having an internet connection has decreased steadily. The number of internet users in Vietnam is over 49 million as of June 2016, which accounts for 51.5 per cent of the population (Vecom 2017). Among that, the time spent online by a typical Vietnam internet user is 25 hours per week, which is high in comparison with other countries in ASEAN (Vecom 2017).

Mobile internet has also developed strongly in 2016 and it continues to improve in 2017 with the launch of 4G services by leading telecommunication providers in Vietnam, including VNPT and Viettel. These improvements show clear evidences that Vietnam is adopting the latest technological inventions for its internet service and this, in turn, supports e-commerce development in Vietnam.

According to Vietnam E-commerce Report 2015, accessing the internet via mobile phones is the first choice for internet users in Vietnam. It is predicted that, with the launch of 4G services, mobile internet will continue to be the preferred choice for internet users in Vietnam. Moreover, with more than 130 million mobile subscribers, mobile commerce will continue to be the key driver for Vietnam's e-commerce market in the next few years. In the Vietnam Online Business Forum organized in Hanoi on 24 February 2017, it is indicated that the trend of Mobile Connect is considered as the next development of Vietnam mobile technology which replaces Mobile First in the market.

The popularity of smartphones is also generating better opportunities for businesses to reach internet customers via mobile websites as well as mobile applications. The large number of smartphone users has also supported the growth of mobile banking and mobile payment. Shopping online via mobile has gained popularity. This is good news for online businesses in Vietnam. From the consumer side, statistics show that 20 per cent of mobile users in Vietnam are using smartphones, and half of them have shopped online via their smartphones (Vecom 2017). In the next few years, it is certain that the mobile platform will continue to be the first choice for businesses to introduce their products, services, information, and deals to consumers.

Secondly, with respect to the logistics services in Vietnam, outsourcing fulfillment services are being adopted more often by online businesses, next to self-service fulfillment. The two largest state-owned post and delivery providers include VNPost and Viettel Post. These post and delivery providers provide local delivery and fulfillment services, which cover almost all districts in Vietnam. Additionally, in large cities such as Hanoi, Haiphong, Ho Chi Minh, and Danang, Giaohangnhanh (https://giaohangnhanh.vn), Nhanh (https://nhanh.vn), Giaohangtietkiem (https://giaohangtietkiem.vn), and Proship (http://proship.vn) are emerging as the first choice in cash on delivery (COD) and quick delivery services for both businesses and individuals selling on the online platform. However, delivery and fulfillment services have not developed sufficiently to support the rapid growth of e-commerce. In this regard, the connection and collaboration between e-commerce businesses and logistics services companies needs to be strengthened in order to enhance the order fulfillment in Vietnam. There have been efforts to sharpen the collaboration between e-commerce businesses and logistics services companies. In 2016, Vietnam E-commerce Association (VECOM) and Vietnam Logistics Business Association (VLA) had a mutual agreement in the following areas: (1) putting e-logistics and e-commerce in strategic cooperation; (2) connecting members of the two associations to increase cooperation services; and (3) collaborating in supporting activities, policy and law consulting (Vecom 2017). It is expected that the closer cooperation between logistics and e-commerce enterprises will boost e-commerce transactions by up to 20–30 per cent in the next few years. Furthermore, the omni-channel, which is considered as the leading trend in Business to Consumer (B2C) e-commerce in Vietnam, would offer larger opportunities for both e-commerce and logistics companies to tighten their collaboration.

Thirdly, the online banking and payment services are expected to support the growth of the e-commerce market in Vietnam in the next five years. However, while consumers are educated on the online and mobile payment methods, they do not use e-payment methods due to concerns on data security for online payments. This is the greatest challenge to the adoption of e-payment methods in the country, and is the reason why COD is still the most popular method for online shopping in Vietnam. According to the survey by VECITA in 2015,

91 per cent of online shoppers preferred the COD method; nearly half of those chose bank transfer, while only 20 per cent people used the e-payment and mobile payment methods (VECITA 2015). It is noted that bank account ownership in Vietnam has increased dramatically from about 30 per cent of the adult population in 2016 to 59 per cent in 2017. However, due to concerns on data security for online payments, more people prefer cash than other payment method.

In order to educate customers and diversify the online payment methods to facilitate e-commerce, Vietnamese e-commerce enterprises are constantly improving both quantity and quality of online payment services. Modern technologies in online payment are currently applied in most of the e-commerce websites.

As shown in Figure 10.1, most of the online customers chose COD and bank transfer as their preferred payment method. The survey findings of VECITA in 2015 also shows that 77 per cent of e-commerce websites allow bank transfer, and 25 per cent allow online payments such as credit card, debit card, e-wallets, and mobile payment (VECITA

FIGURE 10.1
Major Payment Methods of Online Shopping

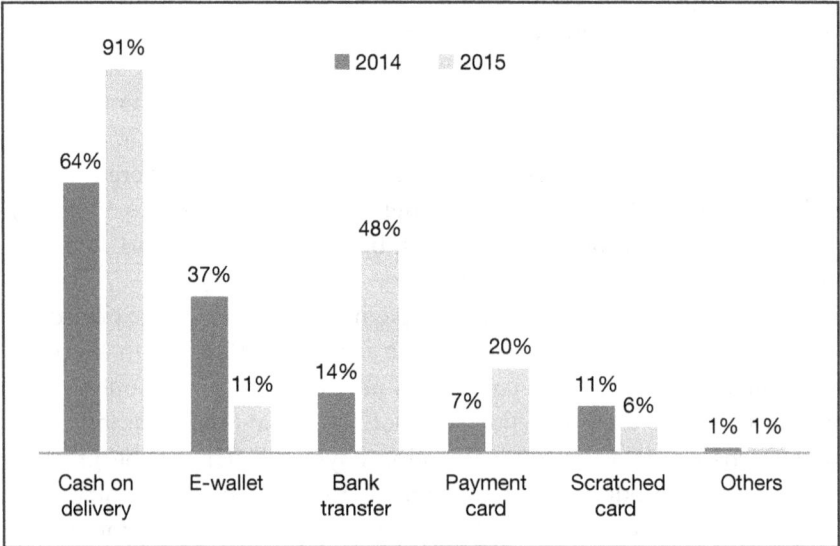

Source: VECITA (2016).

2015).[2] The major providers of online payment services include Bao Kim, Ngan luong, One Pay, Banknetvn (which is now Napas), and Paypal with a market share of 40 per cent, 20 per cent, 10 per cent, 5 per cent, and 4 per cent respectively (see Figure 10.2).

FIGURE 10.2
Top Five Online Payment Service Providers in Vietnam

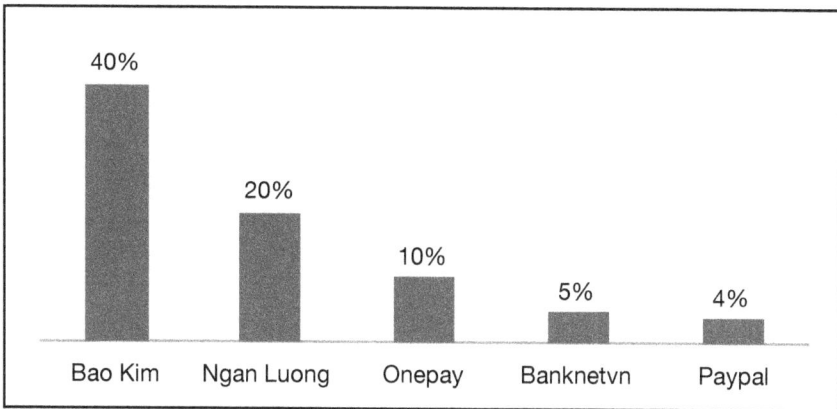

Source: VECITA (2016).

The largest electronic payment service provider in Vietnam is National Payment Corporation of Vietnam (NAPAS). The entity is the result of the merger between Banknetvn and Smartlink.[3] It also manages and operates an inter-bank connection system throughout the country, which provides switching and electronic clearing and settlement services with total transaction value of US$320 trillion in 2016. This inter-bank connection system connects about 17,000 ATM, 245,000 POS and 97 million domestic cards of 44 commercial banks, including domestic and foreign banks in Vietnam (Digital Journal 2017).

To sum up, the infrastructure for e-commerce in Vietnam has been modernized and has made tremendous progress in recent years. However, one of the challenges to growing the e-commerce market is the huge gap in development among provinces in Vietnam. Hanoi and Ho Chi Minh city still lead the market with the EBI (Electronic Business Index[4]) tripling to ten times as compared to other provinces.

This will likely remain the case for the coming years and present an obstacle to businesses in their expansion to other provinces in Vietnam.

4. E-commerce Market Key Statistics

The e-commerce market in Vietnam has become one of the most exciting market in the region with an annual growth rate of about 20–30 per cent in recent years. Most enterprises use e-commerce and information technology in their businesses in different areas such as information commerce, transaction commerce, and collaboration business. All different modern e-commerce models are practised in the Vietnam market with the dynamic and active role of market leaders such as Adayroi, Vatgia, Chodientu in B2C e-commerce; Vinamilk, Petrolimex, Viettel in Business to Business (B2B) e-commerce; as well as Google, Facebook, and other global technology "titans" in e-commerce services. Vietnam's e-commerce market also follows the latest trends of the global e-commerce including social, local, and mobile e-commerce. However, the transaction value of e-commerce in Vietnam is still very low in comparison with other countries in the region. This current status of Vietnam e-commerce suggests that there are tremendous opportunities for the local as well as foreign investors. The paragraphs below describe the status of Vietnam's e-commerce market.

B2C E-commerce

The total B2C e-commerce sales in Vietnam are estimated to be about US$4 billion in 2015 (Vecom 2019). This accounts for 0.28 per cent of total retail sales in Vietnam. Online purchase value per person was just about US$160 in 2015. Sixty-two per cent of internet users in Vietnam made purchases online. The number of internet users in Vietnam who make purchases online is expected to grow in the next few years. As shown in Figure 10.3, 64 per cent of online customers purchased clothing, footwear, and cosmetics; 56 per cent and 49 per cent of online customers bought technology and home appliance products respectively. Books, stationery, and tickets were also popular products and services purchased online.

According to a survey conducted by VECITA in 2015, the e-commerce website is the most popular choice for online customers to make purchases, with 76 per cent of the survey respondents indicating this

FIGURE 10.3
Popular Goods/Services on E-commerce Websites

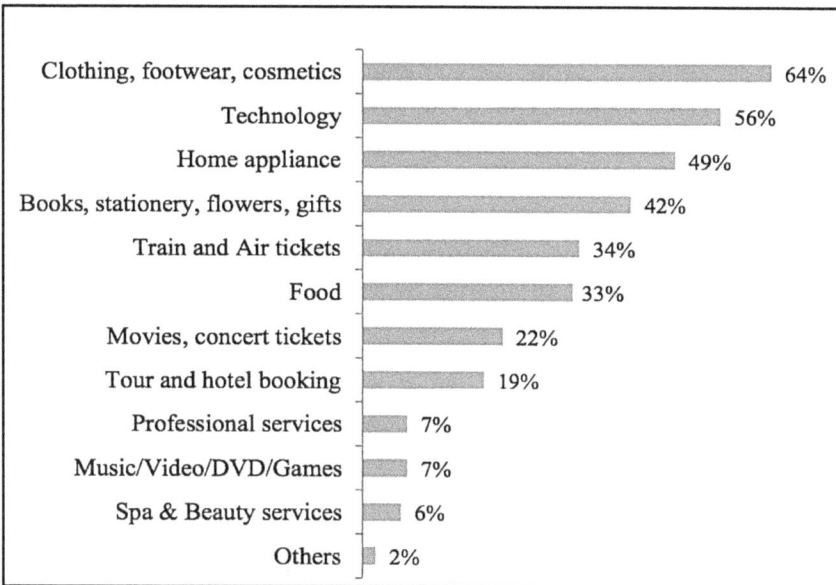

Clothing, footwear, cosmetics	64%
Technology	56%
Home appliance	49%
Books, stationery, flowers, gifts	42%
Train and Air tickets	34%
Food	33%
Movies, concert tickets	22%
Tour and hotel booking	19%
Professional services	7%
Music/Video/DVD/Games	7%
Spa & Beauty services	6%
Others	2%

Source: VECITA (2016).

as their preferred mode to purchase. The second most popular mode to purchase of online customers is the social network, with 68 per cent of the survey respondents indicating this as their preferred mode to purchase. According to another statistics released by eMarketer in November 2015, one third of the Vietnamese population used the social network to make online purchases frequently. As such, social networks are one of the favourite platforms for online retailers to advertise and sell their products and services. In 2015, 28 per cent of enterprises in Vietnam chose to advertise and sell their products and services via social networks such as Facebook, Zing, and Instagram. The percentage of enterprises in Vietnam choosing to sell their products and services via the social network is predicted to steadily increase in the coming years. Online forums, blogs, and online shops in e-marketplaces such as Chodientu, Vatgia, Lazada, Adayroi are expected to play an increasing role in helping retailers expand their businesses online. In addition, mobile commerce is also becoming more popular in the B2C market, due to the increasing number of smartphone users in Vietnam. Messaging apps such as Zalo, Viber, WhatsApp, Skype, Facebook Messenger are getting more and more popular and this will accelerate the growth of mobile commerce. To sum up, social networks and mobile commerce are emerging developments in Vietnam's B2C market, which will contribute to the growth of omni-channel retailing in Vietnam.

B2B E-commerce

In 2013, B2B e-commerce in Vietnam amounted to US$700 million and is estimated to grow by more than 30 per cent per year (EVBN 2016). Since the early 2000s, Vietnam enterprises involved in exporting and/or importing goods and services had used email to reach out to international customers and partners. Businesses involved in the traditional sectors of goods and services have used e-commerce to expand their markets, reduce business costs, and improve their customer service for years and have generally succeeded. Vinamilk JSC, Petrolimex Group, and Kinh Do Corporation are some examples of enterprises that have successfully implemented the Enterprise Resource Planning (ERP) and the enterprises information systems (Nguyen Van Thoan et al. 2012). These enterprises started by setting up online websites, and subsequently introduced product information and online services on their websites. They then collaborated with suppliers and partners, and succeeded in expanding their businesses via the online platform. They have also become more efficient and have reduced costs through the adoption of online public services, such as e-customs and electronic certificates of origin. Many businesses have found new customers and entered new markets as a result of e-commerce. They were able to export many new products to foreign markets and are also linked up with foreign customers via websites and state support channels.

B2B e-marketplaces such as Alibaba.com, Taiwantrade.com, and Europages.com are popular platforms for Vietnam enterprises involved in exporting and/or importing goods and services to seek information on foreign markets and partners on the internet. In the coming years, emails and B2B e-marketplaces will continue to be effective tools for contract negotiation and signing for Vietnam enterprises. Moreover, the increasing adoption of online public service systems such as online tax declaration, e-customs, and e-C/O will contribute to the e-commerce development in Vietnam.

To sum up, these statistics demonstrate the same picture as the B2C market. Despite the high projected growth rate, the current size of B2B and B2C e-commerce in Vietnam is very small. There is still a long way for Vietnam's B2B e-commerce to reach the targeted proportion of 30 per cent of total export turnover by 2020 as noted in the Vietnam E-commerce Master Plan in 2016–20. According to the master plan, B2B e-commerce in Vietnam is also expected to boost cross-nation transactions in the coming years, and contribute to the integration of Vietnam into global markets and value chains.

5. E-commerce Major Players

As a result of the improvement in infrastructure including internet connection, online payment system, and logistics, the Vietnam's e-commerce market has witnessed double-digit growth rate in recent years. The leading players on the e-commerce market will continue to contribute to the increase in online transactions in Vietnam. The following paragraphs provide a description of the key e-commerce major players in the country.

In 2014, according to the survey by VECITA, the top e-marketplace for retail commerce in Vietnam were Lazada.vn (with a 21 per cent market share of total sales in e-marketplaces), Sendo.vn (with a 10 per cent market share), 123mua.vn, Zalora.vn, Tiki.vn, Chodientu.vn, and eBay.vn (see Figure 10.4).

Among them, Lazada.vn has grown rapidly and has attracted online shoppers with a wide range of products from electronics, fashion, to household goods. Customers have preferred Lazada.vn for their good product quality, low shipping cost, and fast delivery. Another emerging e-marketplace is Adayroi.com, which is owned by VinEcom. Positioning itself as an "all in one" e-marketplace, Adayroi offers a wide range of products from diverse sectors including food, fashion, tourism, electronics, and even real estate. With the presence of Vinmart and Vinpro stores in Adayroi, VinGroup offers a multi-channel experience to customers. Other famous e-marketplaces in Vietnam include Chodientu and Vatgia which are established more than ten years ago and had received billions of dollars of funding from IDG Ventures. Nguyen Hoa Binh, CEO of Chodientu.vn, and Nguyen Ngoc Diep, CEO of Vatgia, are the most famous people involved in the e-commerce market in Vietnam. Nguyen Ngoc Diep has launched a series of projects such

FIGURE 10.4
Share of Sales in B2C E-marketplaces

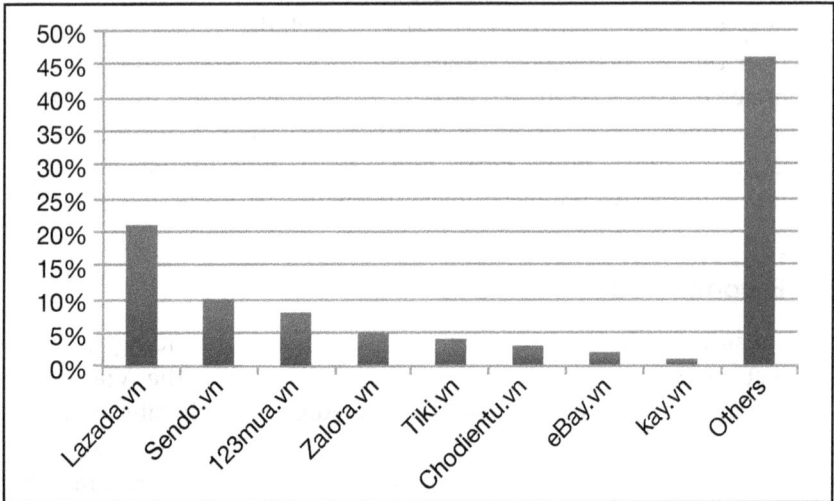

Source: VECITA (2015).

as Vatgia.vn (an online marketplace), Baokim.vn (an online payment portal), and Nhanh.vn (an e-marketing sales management services provider). Another successful e-commerce platform is Tiki.vn, which started as an online bookstore and subsequently expanded to sell fashion and electronics.

As for click-and-mortar retailers, Mobile World, Nguyen Kim Trading JSC, FPT Digital Retail JSC, Pico JSC are prominent electronic retailers in both online and offline markets in Vietnam. These giant click-and-mortar retailers have set up their own supply chain and logistics arm in Hanoi, Ho Chi Minh City, and other provinces in Vietnam. For example, Mobile World, which is the owner of retail chains such as Thegioididong.com.vn and Dienmayxanh.com, has expanded into sixty-three provinces with hundreds of outlets. These electronic retailers have also participated in e-marketplaces such as Lazada.vn and Adayroi.vn to broaden their channels and to offer an integrated shopping experience for Vietnam customers.

Despite the successful expansion of Lazada.vn, Adayroi.vn, Tiki.vn, and Shopee.vn, the Vietnam's e-commerce market has also experienced the failures and disappears of many e-commerce platforms such as

Cucre.vn (Vatgia Group), Deca.vn (24h Group), Beyeu.com (Project LANA), and Lingo.vn (VMG Group) in 2015 and 2016. The exit of these e-commerce players demonstrates the harsh reality of Vietnam's e-commerce market, which is a "race of money spenders". The farewell message of Beyeu.com provides a wake-up call for all e-commerce startups that "online business is not cheap at all" (EVBN 2016):

> E-commerce requires lots of money. Many companies will decide to stop burning. Good luck to the rest who are still trying.

The cases of Deca.vn and Beyeu.com in the baby and mom online stores provide a lesson that the discount strategy to acquire customers adopted by e-commerce players should not be long lasting. Instead, e-commerce players should focus on providing high quality products and services with suitable prices for customers. These learning points are successfully applied in famous click-and-mortar kids and moms chains like Kidsplaza.vn, Bibomart.com.vn, Tuticare.com, and Shoptretho.com.vn.

Figure 10.5 provides a description of the top e-commerce websites in Vietnam in 2017 by the type of business model. These major players are predicted to continue to be dominant in the coming years and contribute to the growth of Vietnam's e-commerce market. Other online business activities such as online tourism, e-tickets, e-marketing services, and e-learning have also recorded impressive development. However, e-commerce websites that have adopted the group buying

FIGURE 10.5
Top E-commerce Websites by Business Model in Vietnam, 2017

Top Five E-marketplaces	Top Five B2C Websites	Top Five C2C Websites	Top Five Social Networks
Lazada.vn	Thegioididong.com.vn	Vatgia.com	Facebook.com
Adayroi.vn	Nguyenkim.com	Chotot.com	Zing.vn
Tiki.vn	Fptshop.com.vn	5giay.vn	Youtube.com
Sendo.vn	Dienmayxanh.com	Chodientu.vn	LinkedIn
Shopee.vn	VienthongA.vn	Webmuaban.vn	Twitter

Source: Authors.

business model such as Hotdeal.vn, Muachung.vn, and Cungmua.com are becoming less attractive to customers.

With regards to mobile commerce, the increasing mobile subscribers and smartphone users in Vietnam have enabled the growth of messaging apps and conversational commerce. Figure 10.6 demonstrates the top messaging apps in Vietnam with the most popular apps being Zalo, Facebook Messenger, and Viber.

FIGURE 10.6
Top Messaging Apps in Vietnam

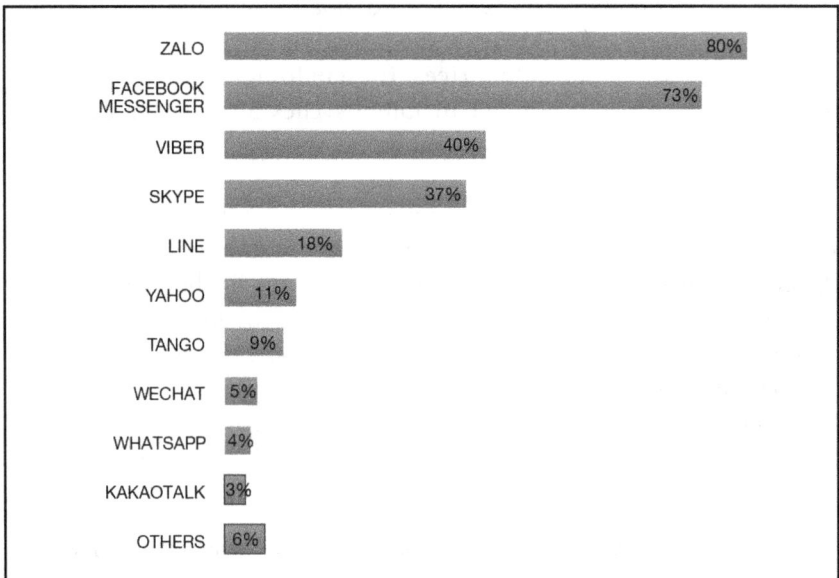

Source: Appota (2016).

To sum up, the development of e-commerce market in Vietnam is contributed by both foreign and domestic businesses. The market will continue to attract international investors in different online businesses, which a focus on the trends of social, local, and mobile commerce. The impressive growth rate of about 30 per cent per year is expected to generate enormous opportunities for enterprises in all business models in the coming years.

6. E-commerce Government Agencies/Departments

Vietnam E-commerce and Information Technology Agency (VECITA), under the Ministry of Industry and Trade, is the top-level public government agency in Vietnam, which fulfills the State management and legal enforcement in e-commerce and information technology application. The main tasks and powers of VECITA include the following:

1. Build up strategies, plans, programmes, projects, regulations on management of e-commerce and information technology applications within the Agency's management scope and submit them to the Minister for approval or for the Minister's submission to the competent State management authorities for approval.
2. Formulate legal documents, mechanisms, policies, technical standards of e-commerce and information technology applications and submit them to the Minister for promulgation or for the Minister's submission to the competent state agencies for promulgation.
3. Formulate particular and internal documents in terms of the Agency's field.
4. Conduct, instruct, and inspect the implementation of legal documents, strategies, plans, programmes, projects, standards, processes, technical-economic norms of e-commerce and information technology applications in the industry and trade sector.[5]

The VECITA conducts surveys on e-commerce applications and development throughout the country and publishes the annual Vietnam E-commerce Report.[6] Its official website is http://www.vecita.gov.vn/ and the annual reports can be downloaded at http://www.vecita.gov.vn/anphamvner. The reports cover all aspects of e-commerce market development in Vietnam. After more than ten years of development, VECITA has accomplished its tasks in e-commerce management and strongly contributed to the development of e-commerce in Vietnam.

The second largest organization supporting the growth of e-commerce in Vietnam is the Vietnam E-commerce Association (Vecom). Founded in 2007, Vecom is a non-governmental organization which has hundreds of members conducting businesses in e-commerce and information technology. The key members of Vecom included VNPT, Lazada, Google Asia, DKT, Chodientu, Vatgia, Tiki, Netnam, and so on. Its official website is http://www.vecom.vn. Since its establishment ten years ago, Vecom has successfully fulfilled its goals of cooperating and supporting e-commerce businesses in Vietnam as well as boosting international cooperation activities in e-commerce.

7. E-commerce Policy and Law

The e-commerce legal framework in Vietnam has been developed and basically completed to date, and provides a direction of defining obligations of enterprises in e-commerce activities. Next to the Penal Code and Civil Code, and other related laws and regulations, Figure 10.7 provides a summary of basic regulations and laws on e-commerce in Vietnam.

The regulations and laws on e-commerce also include circulars that guide the implementation of decrees which helps enterprises and organizations in clarifying terms and conditions. To sum up, the e-commerce policy and laws of Vietnam was developed and strengthened over recent years. The greatest contribution of the above legal framework is generating an equal and competitive e-commerce environment, and provides guidance for the development of the market towards the latest trends of global e-commerce and the fourth industrial revolution.

Specifically, the regulations related to the handling of violations in the field of e-commerce are the following: Decree No. 158/2013/ND-CP dated 12 November 2013 regulating sanctions against administrative violations in the fields of culture, sports, tourism and advertising; Decree No. 174/2013/ND-CP dated 13 November 2013 regulating the sanctioning of administrative violations in the fields of posts, telecommunications, information technology and radio frequency; Decree No. 25/2014/ND-CP dated 7 April 2014 regulating the prevention and combat of crimes and other violations of law using hi-technologies. Consumer protection regulations are stipulated in the following decrees: Decree No. 185/2013/ND-CP dated 15 November 2013 regulating sanctions against administrative violations in commercial activities, production, trading of counterfeit or prohibited goods and protection of consumers' rights; Decree No. 124/2015/ND-CP dated 19 November 2015, amending and supplementing some articles of Decree No. 185/2013/ND-CP dated 15 November 2013 on sanctioning

FIGURE 10.7
Basic Direct Regulations and Laws on E-commerce in Vietnam

No.	Year	Law
1	2005	Commercial Law
2	2005	Law on Electronic Transactions
3	2006	Law on Information Technology
4	2009	Law on Telecommunication
5	2015	Law on Network Information Safety (w.e.f 1 July 2016)
6	2007	Decree No. 26/2007/ND-CP guiding the implementation of the E-transaction Law on digital signature and C/A services
7	2007	Decree No. 27/2007/ND-CP on electronic transactions in financial activities
8	2007	Decree No. 27/2007/ND-CP on electronic transactions in financial activities
9	2008	Decree No. 90/2008/ND-CP on anti-spam
10	2013	Decree No. 52/2013/ND-CP on e-commerce
11	2013	Decree No. 72/2013/ND-CP on management, provision and use of internet services and online information
12	2013	Decree No. 158/2013/ND-CP on sanctioning administrative violations in the fields of culture, sports, tourism and advertising
13	2013	Decree No. 174/2013/ND-CP on sanctioning administrative violations in the fields of posts, telecommunications, information technology and radio frequency
14	2013	Decree No. 185/2013/ND-CP on sanctioning administrative violations in commercial activities, production, trading of counterfeit or prohibited goods and protection of consumer rights
15	2014	Decree No. 25/2014/ND-CP on the prevention and combat of crimes and other violations of law using high technologies
16	2015	Decree No. 124/2015/ND-CP amending and supplementing some articles of Decree No. 185/2013/ND-CP on sanctioning of administrative violations in commercial activities, production, trading of counterfeit or prohibited goods and protection of consumer rights

Source: VECITA (2016).

of administrative violations in commercial activities, production, trading of counterfeit or prohibited goods and protection of consumers' rights. Decree No. 185/2013/ND-CP and Decree No. 124/2015/ND-CP added administrative sanctions for e-commerce activities on websites and mobile applications.

Vietnam has a regulatory framework in the field of e-commerce, consistent with the four major goals of the AEC Blueprint for E-commerce. However, the IT technology and e-commerce models are constantly changing. Therefore, it is difficult for the legal framework of e-commerce to fully reflect and cover the impact of online businesses on social and economic life. Therefore, in order to facilitate the development of e-commerce and to have a favourable mechanism for resolving disputes in e-commerce, legal regulations should add provisions for social network management, mobile platform business, electronic data collection, and e-commerce opportunities and threats.

The fourth industrial revolution generates enormous opportunities and threats on Vietnam's e-commerce market. Additionally, the pressure from the structure reinvention of the entire economy and the presence of foreign players forces enterprises in Vietnam to innovate and change accordingly. The following paragraphs summarize the opportunities and threats of Vietnam's e-commerce markets in the coming years:

Opportunities: as a result of a stable, high speed, and cheap internet connection, online transactions will experience a double-digit growth rate. The huge internet users and rising number of mobile users will lend support to the growth of online retail in Vietnam especially in social, local, and mobile commerce. Moreover, deeper international economic integration is expected to promote the growth of cross-nation transactions in e-commerce. The expansion of overseas e-commerce players such as Lazada and Shoppe will provide greater choices for customers, but will also put higher pressure on the competitive environment of Vietnam.

Threats and obstacles: although the growth rate of e-commerce in Vietnam is quite high, the revenue of online businesses is still very low. The main challenges to e-commerce adoption are internet security, customers' trust and behaviour, consumer culture, the fragmentation of the market, and the differences in development among provinces in the country. According to a survey by VECITA, low customers' trust

FIGURE 10.8
Reasons for Not Shopping Online

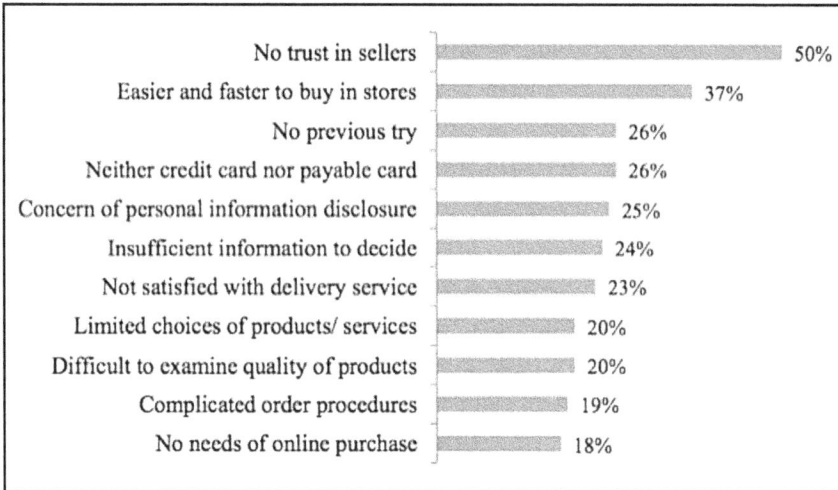

Reason	Percentage
No trust in sellers	50%
Easier and faster to buy in stores	37%
No previous try	26%
Neither credit card nor payable card	26%
Concern of personal information disclosure	25%
Insufficient information to decide	24%
Not satisfied with delivery service	23%
Limited choices of products/ services	20%
Difficult to examine quality of products	20%
Complicated order procedures	19%
No needs of online purchase	18%

Source: VECITA (2016).

in online shopping is the first and foremost reason for not making purchases online (see Figure 10.8). Most of the consumers in Vietnam raised concerns on the quality of online products and services, as they may be worse than what was published on online advertisements.

The second reason raised by survey respondents for not making purchases online is the customers' preference for face-to-face and direct shopping. Cash on delivery is still the most popular payment method. Moreover, the fragmented online retail market and differences in development among provinces hinder the development of logistics and fulfillment activities and restrict the expansion of e-commerce, especially in the rural areas.

As previously noted in Section 5, "E-commerce requires lots of money". To survive in Vietnam's e-commerce market, both foreign and domestic players need long-term investment strategies. The dominance of Lazada, Adayroi, and Tiki in the e-commerce market creates a high level of entry barrier for newcomers in the market. Moreover, the expansion of both online and offline channels by VinRetail with Adayroi.vn, and Vinmart retail chains also pose great challenges for those want to enter the market. Other large click-and-mortar players such as Mobile World Group and Nguyen Kim Group have set up their own retail chain and fulfillment systems throughout the country, which will strengthen their market position and set up high barriers for entrants.

8. Policy Issues and Recommendations

In the context of the fourth industrial revolution and international integration (especially economic integration amongst ASEAN countries) through the e-commerce sector, the Vietnam government and businesses should seize the opportunities from e-commerce and overcome the challenges and obstacles. The following paragraphs put forth some suggestions and recommendations for policymakers and businesses to enhance the growth of e-commerce in Vietnam.

Recommendations for policymakers: continued efforts to improve information technology infrastructure throughout the country is the first and foremost essential supporting programme from the government. This solution will help in the socio-economic development as well as e-commerce development in other areas outside of Hanoi and Ho Chi Minh City. It also helps to close the gap in development among provinces and allow Vietnam to take advantages of the large internet population. The second most important policy should focus on improving and developing the quality of human resources. The third most important policy should focus on the cooperation with ASEAN competition authorities as this can help Vietnamese e-commerce entrepreneurs compete by removing anti-competitive obstacles in ASEAN markets. And finally, implementing policies to support administrative reforms and online public services would be vital to expanding e-commerce activities in Vietnam.

Recommendations for businesses: Vietnam is considered as a land of hope for businesses seeking to enter the online market. However, businesses would need to understand the market and find the right channel to reach customers in order to ensure success. The lessons from the failures of Deca, Lingo, Beyeu demonstrate that businesses need to adopt long-term investments and strategies in the market. We suggest three key solutions for business to improve e-commerce activities in Vietnam as follows.

Firstly, businesses should adopt new e-commerce toolkits to promote online sales such as e-commerce websites, web shops, forums, blogs, YouTube, Facebook and other social network channels to reach customers. In particular, businesses should take advantage of omni-channel, e-commerce toolkits, and online advertising, as these are crucial for businesses in all industries such as online retail, tourism, and other services sectors.

Secondly, building customer trust plays a pivotal role in market development and expansion strategies of all e-businesses. While Vietnam is considered as a price-sensitive market, the quality of products and services is the most important factor to keep customers in both online and offline channels. Furthermore, businesses would need to provide excellent customer service in order to maintain customer loyalty.

Finally, applying modern technology in business management such as customer relationship management (CRM), supply chain management (SCM), and ERP are vital for businesses to save cost, increase sales, expand market, and improve customer service. This is fundamental for businesses to enhance e-commerce applications in business and management as well as to accelerate e-commerce transactions growth in Vietnam (Nguyen Van Thoan et al. 2012).

9. Conclusion

Vietnam's e-commerce market has overcome the first stage of e-commerce development with infrastructure development in internet connection, e-payment system, and logistics. The e-commerce businesses in Vietnam could be categorized into three main groups: (1) traditional businesses that have adopted websites and management information systems to expand their markets, reduce business costs, and improve customer service; (2) businesses involved in the importation or exportation of goods and services that have taken advantages of e-commerce and online public services to improve efficiency, save time and money, seek new foreign customers and partners, enter new markets, and export new products and services; (3) providers of e-commerce services such as e-commerce marketplaces, online marketing or online travel (Lazada, Tiki, Vatgia, Chodientu, Gotadi, etc.), and new businesses whose successes have been built mainly on e-commerce. While the performance of the first two groups have been stable, the third group has been facing some difficulties and challenges as they do not take the initiative to source for goods and services, penetrate new markets, and attract customers. This is, however, a small group whose activity is only in e-commerce. Businesses in dozens of other industries have adopted e-commerce successfully, such as travel, movie entertainment, online learning, hotels, factories, and others. Businesses in these industries have a traditional commerce background and now participate in e-commerce to grow and expand their businesses. Thus, e-commerce must be accompanied by modernization of production, services, management, and business.

In the next few years, adoption of information technology and e-commerce will continue to be the key enablers of economic growth and international integration of Vietnam into ASEAN and the global market. The period of 2016–20 can be considered as a new stage of IT application in management and business, and in particular, e-commerce. Businesses in Vietnam will have many opportunities to enter the international market, but they will also face the risk of lagging behind competitors and losing market share. It is therefore necessary to invest, cooperate and coordinate with all stakeholders to overcome the risks and challenges during the integration period.

From the perspective of ASEAN integration, the implementation of the ASEAN ICT Master Plan 2020 and the Master Plan on ASEAN Connectivity 2025 which focus on promoting sustainable infrastructure, digital innovation, regulatory excellence, and human capital development will boost integration amongst the ASEAN countries. This will enable the dynamic development of the information technology and e-commerce sector as a pioneering integration field to connect the economy, and contribute to the overall prosperity and progress of the ASEAN Community. It is therefore necessary to develop country policies and strategies aligned with the above master plans of ASEAN to ensure the realization and efficiency of those plans.

Appendix 10.1
Key Findings of E-commerce Study

The key research on e-commerce in Vietnam is conducted by the Vietnam E-commerce and Information Technology Agency and recorded in the Vietnam E-commerce Report. The main topics of the reports over the five years from 2011 to 2016 are summarized below.

Vietnam E-commerce Report 2011 records the development of e-payment, which includes e-payment infrastructure, services, and models. The Vietnam E-commerce Report 2011 shows that the e-payment market in Vietnam is becoming more competitive, as the service providers are not limited to banks. Instead, the service providers include other organizations such as payment solution providers. By 2011, online businesses were offered the basic e-payment models such as electronic payment gateway services, electronic wallet services, and integration of e-payment services.

Vietnam E-commerce Report 2012 records key figures and statistics concerning the development of e-commerce infrastructure, applications, and online businesses in Vietnam. It describes the e-commerce market in Vietnam in 2012 with tables, charts, and numbers.

Vietnam E-commerce Report 2013 provides a summary of the legal framework, infrastructure, and applications of e-commerce in Vietnam. The highlight of this report is the e-commerce applications in the communities and it includes information on the number of internet users, types of online shopping and online payment, sociological analytics of customer behaviour and obstacles when shopping online. In 2013, e-commerce and IT service websites were booming with diversified services being provided such as social network marketing, SMS marketing, and online customer services. Search engine optimization and pay per click advertisements also increased the attractiveness and attention of businesses to customers.

Vietnam E-commerce Report 2014 provides a summary and analysis of policies and guidelines for e-commerce applications and development in Vietnam. The report also summarizes the surveys and analysis of the performance of e-commerce businesses. The key topic of this report is mobile commerce and trends in the market. In 2014, Online Friday was launched. This had illustrated the efforts of state organizations to boost e-commerce transactions in the country.

Vietnam E-commerce Report 2015 provides a progress update of the first five years of the implementation of the Master Plan on E-commerce Development for the 2011–20 period. This is the most comprehensive report on the legal framework of e-commerce in Vietnam. It also presents a summary of public services in e-commerce such as customs declaration, online tax declaration (iHTKK), bar codes declaration, and dependent codes.

Vietnam E-commerce Report 2016 is not published. Instead, there are two big reports in 2017, including **Vietnam E-commerce Report 2017** and Vietnam E-commerce Business Index (EBI) 2017. E-commerce activities in Vietnam have experienced remarkable progress in both quantity and quality, given the rise of new trends and applications of latest technology. The main topic of the 2017 report is startups in e-commerce and information technology applications. In the report, it is anticipated that social, local, and mobile commerce will continue to dominate the market in the coming years. The Vietnam EBI 2018 was published in April 2018 with updated data of Vietnam's e-commerce market.

To sum up, the Vietnam e-commerce annual reports by the Vietnam E-commerce and Information Technology Agency are the most comprehensive and sophisticated reports on this field in the country. Other organizations and market research companies have also conducted other surveys and reports regarding e-businesses such as the E-commerce Report 2016 published by the EU–Vietnam Business Network (EVBN), Global E-commerce and the New Retail Report and country results for Vietnam published by Nielsen, and Vietnam Mobile Report by Appota. These publications summarize different aspects of the status and development of the e-commerce market in Vietnam.

NOTES

1. "Doi Moi" refers to the economic reforms initiated in Vietnam in 1986 with the goal of creating a "socialist-oriented market economy".
2. VECITA and VECOM undertake annual surveys and release official reports about e-commerce in Vietnam. The surveys cover all types of businesses.
3. Smartlink is a network developed by Vietcombank to connect e-payment gateway between banks in Vietnam which is similar to Banknetvn. But the two systems were merged in 2016.
4. The Electronic Business Index (EBI) measures the percentage of enterprises that have access to the website of the state agencies to collect business information and percentage of enterprises using online public services.

5. *Source*: Decision No. 669/QD-BCT dated 29 January 2013, Ministry of Industry and Trade.
6. A summary of the annual e-commerce reports in Vietnam is provided in Appendix 10.1.

REFERENCES

Appota Group. "Vietnam Mobile Report Q3: An Overview of Trends and Insights". 2016.

Chu Ngoc Anh. "Comprehensive Renovation of Management, Investment and Financial Mechanism in Science and Technologies". *Communist Review*, 26 December 2016. http://english.tapchicongsan.org.vn/Home/Economy/2016/1012/Comprehensive-renovation-of-management-investment-and-financial-mechanism-in-science-and-technologies.aspx (accessed 20 February 2017).

Digital Journal. "ACI Powers eCommerce for Vietnam's National Payment Switch, Accelerating Country's Online and Mobile Shopping Explosion", 27 February 2017. http://www.digitaljournal.com/pr/3250219.

EVBN. "E-Commerce Report 2016", 2016. https://evbn.org/evbn-e-commerce-report-edition-2016/.

General Statistics Office of Vietnam. "Socio-economic Situation in 2016", 2017. <https://www.gso.gov.vn/default_en.aspx?tabid=622&ItemID=16194 (accessed 20 February 2017).

Le Dinh An. "Comprehensive Renovation of Management, Investment and Financial Mechanism in Science and Technologies". *The Communist Review* 879 (January 2016).

Ministry of Industry and Trade. Decision No. 669/QD-BCT dated 29 January 2013.

Nguyen Van Thoan et al. *Ecommerce Principle*. Hong Duc Publishing, 2012.

Nguyen Van Thoan and Nguyen Thi Hong Van. "Application of Enterprise Resource Planning (ERP) System in Some Vietnamese Enterprises and Lessons Learned". *Journal of External Economics* 57 (2013).

VECITA (Vietnam E-commerce and Information Technology Agency). *Vietnam E-commerce Report 2011*, 2011.

———. *Vietnam E-commerce Report 2012*, 2012.

———. *Vietnam E-commerce Report 2013*, 2013.

———. *Vietnam E-commerce Report 2014*, 2014.

———. *Vietnam E-commerce Report 2015*, 2015.

Vecom. "Vietnam E-business Index 2017", 2017. http://vecom.vn/wp-content/uploads/2017/02/Bao-cao-EBI-2017-Final.pdfVecom.

————. "Vietnam Business Index Report 2019", 2019. https://drive.google.com/file/d/1i-KZhYgwSb4WIadjwj4hvpj8V-jYrTrU/view (accessed 22 July 2019).

Vietnam Government. "Vietnam's Socio-economic Development Strategy for the Period of 2011–2020", 2010.

VietnamPlus. "Vietnam's GDP Growth Rate in 2018 Highest in 11 Years", 2018. https://en.vietnamplus.vn/vietnams-gdp-growth-rate-in-2018-highest-in-11-years/144259.vnp (accessed 27 December 2018).

INDEX

Note: Page numbers followed by "n" refer to endnotes.